Aesthetic Pleasure in
Twentieth-Century Women's Food Writing

Routledge Studies in Twentieth-Century Literature

Aesthetic Pleasure in Twentieth-Century Women's Food Writing

The Innovative Appetites of M. F. K. Fisher, Alice B. Toklas, and Elizabeth David

Alice L. McLean

Routledge
Taylor & Francis Group
NEW YORK   LONDON

First published 2012
by Routledge
711 Third Avenue, New York, NY 10017

Simultaneously published in the UK
by Routledge
2 Park Square, Milton Park, Abingdon, Oxon OX14 4RN

*Routledge is an imprint of the Taylor & Francis Group,
an informa business*

© 2012 Taylor & Francis

Typeset in Sabon by IBT Global.
Printed and bound in the United States of America on acid-free paper by
IBT Global.

Library of Congress Cataloging-in-Publication Data
McLean, Alice L.
  Aesthetic pleasure in twentieth-century women's food writing : the
innovative appetites of M. F. K. Fisher, Alice B. Toklas, and Elizabeth
David / by Alice L. McLean.
     p. cm. — (Routledge studies in twentieth-century literature ; 18)
  Includes bibliographical references and index.
  1. Food writing—History.   2. Women food writers.   3. Fisher, M. F. K.
(Mary Frances Kennedy), 1908–1992.   4. Toklas, Alice B.   5. David,
Elizabeth, 1913–1992.   I. Title.   II. Title: Aesthetic pleasure in 20th century
women's food writing.
  TX644.M386 2011
  808'.066641—dc22
  2010050301

ISBN13: 978-0-415-87138-9 (hbk)
ISBN13: 978-0-203-81439-0 (ebk)

Dedicated to H. D. M. & G. F. J.
and
For my Mother

Contents

x *Contents*

Acknowledgments

Among those people and associations who have contributed to the completion of this project, I would like to thank the Association for the Study of Food and Society and the College English Association for inviting me to contribute portions of my research in article form to their respective journals: *Food, Culture, and Society* and the *CEA Critic*. "Tasting Language: The Aesthetic Pleasures of Elizabeth David," which first appeared in the ASFS journal *Food, Culture and Society*, appears in this volume in sections of Chapter 4. "Food, Sex, Language: The Lost Lovers and Later Words of M. F. K. Fisher and Elizabeth David," which first appeared in the *CEA Critic*, is included in portions of Chapters 2 and 3. Among those individuals without whom this book would not have been possible, I owe special thanks to Kate Beach and Palmer McLean for their tireless editorial assistance and advice. For her faith in my initial research, Patricia Moran also deserves my heartfelt thanks.

Introduction

As English and American food writing flourished during the nineteenth-century, it developed along rigid gender lines, with women authoring domestic cookbooks and men authoring professional cookbooks and gastronomic literature. By the close of the century, however, select women had begun to transgress the bounds of domesticity in order claim the aesthetic pleasures of gastronomy and to construct a place for physical and intellectual appetite within the woman's food writing tradition. *Aesthetic Pleasure* traces the development of gastronomy within women's food writing in England and the United States, focusing primarily on M. F. K. Fisher, Alice B. Toklas, and Elizabeth David.

Through the practice of gastronomy, Fisher, Toklas, and David learned how to nourish physical and intellectual pleasures. The sustenance these women gained from such self-nourishment enabled them to forge lives that journeyed well beyond the domestic constraints within which they were raised and expected to perform. For each author, food encouraged a sensory engagement with her environment and a physical receptivity toward pleasure that engendered her creative aesthetic. This openness to pleasure was enhanced by each author's international travels and by her extended exposure to cultures that honor food along with the well-being, conviviality, and creative expression it nourishes. Creating a language that configures female desire, Fisher, Toklas, and David expanded women's food writing beyond the domestic realm to establish a tradition of English and American literature that celebrates female appetite for pleasure and for gastronomic adventure.

Such gusto for pleasure and adventure stood in ideological opposition to the goal of traditional women's food writing, which took shape in the domestic cookbook. From the late eighteen to the early twentieth centuries, the domestic cookbook concerned itself with the construction and maintenance of the private sphere, thereby determining the boundaries within which the housewife was expected to perform. Domestic cookbooks were written for and by women. Duty, practical instruction, self-effacement, and economy of style characterized nineteenth-century women's food writing. Domestic cookbooks eschewed pleasure and defined the proper housewife as dutifully bound to the home and economically minded. Concerned with practical instruction, they also adhered to a rigid format and often downplayed the author's creativity and sense of humor, presenting in their stead a didactic, matronly persona.

While such proscriptive women's food writing proliferated in England and the United States, a whole new genre of food writing began to develop in France, which, like the professional cookbook, was authored exclusively by men. In particular, the early nineteenth century saw the rise of gastronomic literature, a genre primarily concerned with honing the sensual and intellectual pleasure of gastronomy. Gastronomic literature worked to define gastronomy as an art and the gourmand as an artist in his own right. Such literature, written for and by men, arose as a genre in France, but soon spread to England and to the United States. This male-authored genre concerned itself with the aesthetics of taste and the pursuit of pleasure. It also enjoyed an unbounded form, incorporating an array of genres, styles, and formats. Although nineteenth-century gastronomic literature and domestic cookbooks stood in direct ideological opposition to one another, both coded eating as a masculine endeavor.

By the end of the century, however, a select number of women had chosen to move beyond the domestic realm in order to nurture their own gustatory pleasures and to express such pleasures in writing. In order to do so, they needed to find a form more conducive to the celebration of female appetite than the domestic cookbook. The drive to incorporate pleasure into their own writing led female authors toward the practice of gastronomy. These pleasure-oriented women drew on the male form of gastronomic literature in order to move beyond the restrictive bounds of nineteenth-century women's food writing.

One of the first women food writers to claim gustatory pleasures as a female right, Elizabeth Robins Pennell eschewed the cookbook genre altogether, choosing instead to adopt the masculine form of gastronomic literature. In the introduction to her collected gastronomic essays, *Feasts of Autolycus* (1896), Pennell acknowledges the radical nature of her endeavor, noting that "the great interest of the following papers lies in the fact that they are written by a woman—a greedy woman" (8). Whereas Pennell adopted the masculine genre wholeheartedly, most innovative women food writers drew from both the women's and the men's traditions to fashion a form that suited their particular goals. M. F. K. Fisher moved the culinary autobiography out of the home kitchen and into the world at large. Her most innovative book, *The Gastronomical Me* (1943), likewise transforms women's traditional emphasis on cookery into a philosophical reflection on the art of eating and a celebration of female desire. In so doing, Fisher pioneered a form of gastronomic memoir in which food serves as a structural metaphor for female identity and informs an aesthetic engagement with the surrounding world. Alice B. Toklas dissolved the boundaries that separated gastronomic literature from the domestic cookbook by merging these categories in one book, simultaneously challenging and reconfiguring the rigidly gendered bounds of both genres. In particular, *The Alice B. Toklas Cook Book* (1954) inserts recipes into a gastronomic travelogue to fashion a text that moves freely between the private and the public realms.

Elizabeth David shared with male gastronomes a heavy reliance on food scholarship, travel writing, elegance of self-expression, and the aesthetic pleasures of gastronomy in order to capture and convey the way of life that flavored the recipes housed in her books. In particular, David's writing conveys an aesthetic firmly grounded in the body and its pleasure, an aesthetic redolent with sensual imagery that captures the gastronomic rhythms, aromas, and flavors of a given land and showcases food's capacity to nourish language. By articulating a gusto for pleasure and adventure that draws on the male tradition of food writing, David, like Pennell, Fisher, and Toklas, claimed the rewards of gastronomy.

This project's closing focus lies on three contemporary works that extend the pathbreaking tradition in provocative and innovative ways. Just as Fisher, Toklas, and David blended the men's and women's food writing traditions in order to make room for female appetite and its self-expression, myriad contemporary authors continue to "play" with the form of food writing in order to effect social change. Three such authors include Vertamae Smart Grosvenor, Patience Gray, and Monique Truong. Grosvenor's *Vibration Cooking* (1970) politically mobilizes the culinary autobiography and parodies the cookbook in order to challenge culinary racism. In so doing, *Vibration Cooking* not only celebrates African American appetite but also enables Grosvenor to openly claim the rewards of gastronomic reflection. Patience Gray's autobiographical cookbook, *Honey from a Weed* (1986), figures an appetite surfeited by commercialism and excess. Such surfeit leads Gray toward an aesthetic that elegantly coheres a case for culinary minimalism—a reverence for local ingredients allowed to speak for themselves, prepared and eaten in their place of origin. Monique Truong's novel *The Book of Salt* (2003), which features a Vietnamese exile who works for Toklas and Gertrude Stein, simultaneously investigates the dynamics of culinary colonialism by giving voice to the colonized Other and playfully engages with *The Alice B. Toklas Cook Book*, imaginatively filling in the textual gaps in Toklas' memoir and crafting a transnational culinary aesthetic.

NINETEENTH-CENTURY FOOD WRITING AND THE GENDERING OF PLEASURE

Since its invention in 1801, the word gastronomy has been tightly linked to masculinity—a well-educated, cosmopolitan, witty, and articulate masculinity to be precise. The term gourmand was used in French and often in English to designate one who practices gastronomy. Some English and American authors preferred the term epicure, however, given that the term gourmand was often linked in the popular imagination with gluttony. [1] Yet another term developed to designate the gourmand, or epicure, who authored gastronomic literature—the gastronome. In his seminal work *All Manners of Food: Eating and Taste in England and France from the Middle Ages to the Present*, Stephen Mennell defines the gastronome as:

> a person who not only cultivates his own 'refined taste for the pleasures of the table' but also, by *writing* about it, helps to cultivate other people's too. The gastronome is more than a gourmet—he is also a theorist and a propagandist about culinary taste. (267)

Nineteenth-century gastronomic literature, as it developed in France, England, and the United States, sought to create a readership of cultivated palates and to define a code of etiquette to differentiate the true gourmand from the mere pretender. It also showcased the link between gastronomy and creativity. According to the gastronome, the practice of gastronomy nourishes aesthetic pleasures that, in turn, give rise to poetic self-expression. In depicting the pleasures of eating as nourishment for literary inspiration, gastronomes sought, as one scholar elegantly describes it, "the poetic transformation of food into discourse" (Abramson 153).[2]

In addition to a shared belief that gastronomy nourishes poetic expression, French, English, and American gastronomic literature demonstrates a set of common characteristics, including (1) a reverence for the pleasures of the table and for cookery as an art form (2) an unconventional form that incorporates and crisscrosses between several styles of writing, including personal anecdote, historical reference, witty commentary, and literary allusion (3) a cosmopolitan flair and a transnational frame of reference (4) an emphasis on eating, public eateries, and on dining as a social event (5) a

---

1. As Stephen Mennell explains: "'Epicure' had by the beginning of the nineteenth century, particularly in English, acquired a more favourable sense of 'one who cultivates a refined taste for the pleasures of the table; one who is choice and dainty in eating and drinking'. In France, the word gourmand had acquired the same favourable sense" (267). In early nineteenth-century England, Mennell explains, gourmand likewise carried positive connotations.

2. In her essay on "Grimod's Debt," Abramson defines *écriture gourmande* as "poeticized metadiscourse on food" as well as "the poetic transformation of food into discourse" (142, 153). In doing so, she draws on the previous work of Beatrice Fink who, in "Enlightened Eating in Non-Fictional Context and the First Stirrings of *Écriture Gourmande*," argues that Grimod's *Almanach* "creates a link between the world and word of food, thus inscribing cuisine and savoir-manger in *écriture* and poeticizing the gastronomic act" (17).

penchant toward self-indulgence, or outright egotism, and (6) a decidedly undomesticated approach toward pleasure.

In her introduction to the anthology *Gusto: Essential Writings in Nineteenth-Century Gastronomy*, Denise Gigante draws a direct connection between the undomesticated and aesthetically oriented spirit of the flâneur, or dandy, and the gourmand. As Gigante explains:

> Whereas bourgeois morality mandated that we eat to gather our energies for work (no matter what kind), gourmands reversed this traditional formula to assert, in the spirit of dandies, that we must work for our own pleasure. Unlike earlier eighteenth-century forms of eating that were coded feminine..., nineteenth-century gastronomy was a male-gendered aesthetic and the culinary dandy a distinctly male (if not masculine) figure: a gastronomically revamped Man of Taste. Their writings worked in many ways against the feminized aesthetic of the novel, founded on ideals of bourgeois domesticity. . . . At a time when the vital energies of society were becoming more explicitly economic in nature, gastronomers (like dandies) insisted on the continuing value of remaining alive to sensation. (xxxv)

The nineteenth-century gourmand and, by extension, authors of gastronomic literature concerned themselves with raising "gourmandism to the status of the fine arts and establishing its legitimate link to aesthetic taste" (*Taste* 166).[3]

If, as Gigante convincingly argues, male-authored gastronomic literature articulated a cultural resistance to the rise of bourgeois domestication, female-authored cookbooks worked to articulate and to configure the domesticated bounds within which the nineteenth-century woman was expected to perform. Whereas gastronomic literature showcases the art of eating as a means of nourishing self-expression, cookbooks bear witness to the domestication of female appetite. In particular, nineteenth century women food writers in the United States and England participated in an ideology that defined a woman's role as obtaining and keeping a husband, bearing his children, and nourishing the nation's moral values. Such cookbooks helped to codify the boundaries and guidelines of middle class domesticity.

THE LITERARY GENRES OF FOOD WRITING

Scholars have carefully documented the development of gastronomic literature as well as the domestic cookbook, often detailing the gendered

---

3. For more on the literary and philosophical development of the aesthetics of taste, see Gigante's introduction to *Gusto* and her book-length exploration *Taste: A Literary History* as well as Carolyn Korsmeyer's *Making Sense of Taste*.

ideology they promote. Only rarely, however, have scholars provided a sustained comparison of these two genres. This study develops the existing scholarship on food writing, focusing in particular on the gendered divide between gastronomy and domesticity. Juxtaposing the key elements of gastronomic literature with domestic cookbooks illuminates the role of food writing in the construction and maintenance of gendered ideologies, especially those that work to differentiate feminine from masculine appetites. Such comparison also elucidates gastronomy as a practice that enabled twentieth-century English and American women to hone and articulate an aesthetics of pleasure previously reserved for men.

In 1985, Stephen Mennell first drew attention to the gendered history of food writing within England, pointing out that men authored gastronomic literature, which concerns itself with public appetite. Women, on the other hand, authored domestic cookbooks, which focus on the private realm. Although Mennell drew this conclusion about English food writing, an examination of American food writing illustrates that the same gendered divisions were carried across the Atlantic to take hold in the nineteenth-century United States.

Mennell devotes a portion of his *All Manners of Food* to "Gastronomy as a Literary Genre." Like any study of gastronomic literature, Mennell's analysis begins with the founding French works of the genre by Alexandre Balthazar Laurent Grimod de la Reynière and Jean Anthelme Brillat-Savarin. Unlike most studies, however, which focus specifically on the development of the genre in France, Mennell follows gastronomic literature to England, concluding that "[i]n England, gastronomic writing has mainly consisted of close imitations of French models" (269). More recently Denise Gigante has revisited the sociological study of gastronomic literature begun by Mennell from a literary angle, finding that nineteenth-century British gastronomic literature should be understood as "an expansion of the eighteenth-century discourse of aesthetic taste, a cultural field opening onto the material pleasures of appetite" (*Gusto* xvii). A logical development in the literary and philosophical history of aesthetic taste, gastronomy sought to raise dining to an artform and to configure gustatory pleasure as an essential component of aesthetic appreciation.

The present study extends Mennell's and Gigante's examinations of English gastronomic literature to the United States. It also situates the genre alongside and within women's food writing to show how gastronomy enabled women to hone aesthetic pleasures largely absent from the nineteenth-century domestic cookbook. In so doing, this project extends the two existing studies that compare gastronomic literature with the women's food writing tradition. The first appeared as an article in 1974, in which Paul Schmidt examines the literature of Alice B. Toklas and M. F. K. Fisher to argue that it belongs to a tradition of writing about food that can be traced back to Brillat-Savarin's *Physiology of Taste*. Schmidt argues that Toklas and Fisher "are Savarinists" and, as such, amateurs of the table whose literary aesthetic arises from "anecdote stimulated by food, the memory of taste awakened by anecdote" (180–181). The second comparison was conducted by Steve Jones and Ben Taylor who, while reading through Mennell's *All Manners of Food*, were especially struck by the following passage:

> [T]here is an ill-defined margin at which the gastronomic essay gradually shades into the cookery book. The more learned sort of cookery book, such as those of Dumas and Ali-Bab, or more recently of Elizabeth David or Jane Grigson might be considered gastronomic literature as much as cookery books. In either case, they seem intended to be read as literature. (271)

In an article published in 2001, Jones and Taylor examine the work of Elizabeth David and Jane Grigson in order to uncover precisely how their writing overcomes the gendered divide between domestic cookbook and gastronomic literature to articulate pleasure, or what they term "culinary *joie de vivre*," lacking in nineteenth-century women's food writing (175). Jones and Taylor conclude that it was their "appetite to explore the culture of food beyond the confines of domesticity, which enabled David and Grigson so successfully to occupy the 'ill-defined margin' between gastronomic literature and the cookery book, and to gesture toward the myths, histories and memorable meals which lay beyond the home" (178). Such thinking lies at the core of *Aesthetic Pleasure*, which investigates how innovative women authors transformed a tradition based on domesticity into one that openly celebrates female pleasure.

In addition to the above studies of gastronomic literature, three analyses of women's food writing especially inform *Aesthetic Pleasure*. These include Jessamyn Neuhaus' *Manly Meals and Mom's Home Cooking*, which traces the gendering of the American domestic cookbook from 1796 up through the 1960s to demonstrate that the genre "helped to reinforce the notion that women had inherently domestic natures" (2); Nicola Humble's *Culinary Pleasures* provides an invaluable study of the development of the English cookbook since the mid-nineteenth century. As Humble's and Neuhaus' findings show, aesthetics played a more prominent role in early twentieth-century English women's food writing than it did in the United States. This fact can likely be attributed to the considerably greater influence of gastronomic literature in England than in the United States; England authored far more books on gastronomy and by more prominent authors than did the United States.

The third study of mention here, Traci Marie Kelly's "'If I Were a Voodoo Priestess,' examines the twentieth-century genre of women's culinary autobiography. Defining the genre as a literary extension of the stories that generations of women have told while "sitting around a table or standing around a kitchen counter," Kelly concludes that culinary autobiographies fit loosely into three subcategories: culinary memoir, autobiographical cookbook, and auto-ethnographic cookbook (252). The first two subcategories are of particular interest here, as Fisher's work is often categorized as culinary memoir, while Toklas' work can be labeled as autobiographical cookbook. According to Kelly, the primary goal in culinary memoir "is to set forth the personal memories of the author. Food is a recurring theme, but it is not the controlling mechanism. . . . [I]f recipes are included in the book, they are not indexed" (256). In comparison, the autobiographical cookbook is one in which the recipes are an inseparable part of the life story. As such, "the recipes are not removed from the prose flow. As well, the recipes are indexed, conveying the notion that the author wants the book and its reader to move readily between the reading room and the kitchen" (258).[4] These two definitions arise from an understanding of the culinary autobiography as a genre that merges the domestic cookbook with kitchen storytelling, a task accomplished by countless authors, beginning with such American classics as Della Lutes' *Country Kitchen* (1936) and Marjorie Kinnan Rawlings' *Cross Creek Cookery* (1942). Kelly's definition proves invaluable in that it pinpoints how twentieth-century women learned to express their lives as well as their appetites and desires while housed within the domestic realm.

Those authors examined here, however, suggest the need to create yet another set of subcategories to take into account the role of gastronomy within women's food writing. These categories would denominate texts that venture beyond the domestic realm to explore traditionally male territory. Like their turn-of-the-century predecessor Elizabeth Robins Pennell, Fisher, Toklas, and David incorporate key tenets of gastronomic literature into their own writing. These include (1) a focus on dining as an art form and on the aesthetic pleasures of eating, (2) an unconventional form that incorporates personal anecdote, historical reference, and literary allusion, (3) a cosmopolitan sensibility, (4) an emphasis on dining as a social event, (5) a concern with elegance of expression and with writing as an artistic medium nourished by the pleasures of gastronomy, and (6) an undomesticated appetite. In other words, the authors examined here are gastronomes as well as cooks. Their work does not take the form of the domestic cookbook, in large part, because the authors lay claim to an undomesticated task. They each craft gastronomically grounded works.

---

4. Kelly describes the third category of auto-ethnographic cookbook as one similar to the autobiographical cookbook in that the life story and the recipes share equal weight. However, the auto-ethnographic cookbook is not concerned with "one person's life story." Rather, it "details both the food methods and foodways of a particular culture. . . . [T]he text reveals and decodes traditions and rituals for people who are not familiar with them" (262).

M. F. K. Fisher's *The Gastronomical Me* can be defined as gastronomic memoir, a term that takes into account the book's focus on the art of eating. Fisher links gastronomy with wisdom and eloquent self-expression, pioneering a form of gastronomic memoir that celebrates women's pleasure. Beginning with her first book, *Serve It Forth* (1937), Fisher liberates women's food writing from the home kitchen, depicting herself as a female gastronome at home in the world at large. She also showcases how the pleasures of eating, whether embodied or expressed in language, nourish moments of communion and integrity. In Toklas' case, the term gastronomy might be appended to the designation autobiographical cookbook as defined by Kelly, thereby taking into account Toklas' immersion in both the culinary and the gastronomic arts.[5] Applied to Toklas' *Cook Book*, "gastronomy" would specifically indicate the author's keen attention the art of eating and to what she describes as "the aesthetic emotion" of a dish, an emotion imparted by the cook and incorporated by the appreciative diner. It also captures Toklas as a gastronomic tour guide who describes the restaurants, chefs, and dishes that she and Stein encountered on their myriad journeys throughout France, Spain, and the United States.

Understood to designate a debt to the literature of gastronomy, the term "gastronomic" appended to "cookbook" would aptly describe Elizabeth David's oeuvre. In keeping with gastronomic literature, Elizabeth David's writing is heavily informed by the literary, historical, and cultural contexts that surround a given dish or a way of cookery. Like the most eloquent gastronomes, David illuminates the evocative powers of language by fashioning a written aesthetic redolent with sensual pleasure. Toklas and David each authored texts meant to be engaged with as cookbooks. However, their emphasis on gastronomy, or the aesthetics of eating and gustatory pleasures, marks their cookbooks as gastronomical in nature.

CHAPTER OVERVIEW

The first chapter of *Aesthetic Pleasure* explores the gendering of appetite in nineteenth-century food writing. Because this chapter examines the key traits of gastronomic literature, it begins with the genre's French founding fathers, Grimod de la Reynière and Brillat-Savarin, before tracing the development of gastronomic literature and the role of the gastronome within England

---

5. Given the disinviting length and ring of the term gastroautobiographical, however, a shortened term might be coined. Rosalia Baena has proposed the term gastrography, but since this term also designates a common medical procedure (stomach radiography) perhaps appending the term "gusto" in lieu of "gastro" would do the trick. Thus the shortened term gustographic cookbook might suffice for Toklas' project. Or perhaps an elegant term might be coined to denominate the gastronomically grounded autobiographical cookbook, one that would echo the genre's emphasis on elegance of expression.

and the United States. After surveying selected works of gastronomic literature from England (including works by Launcelot Sturgeon, Charles Lamb,
Thomas Walker, A. V. Kirwan, John Cordy Jeaffreson, and Eneas Sweetland
Dallas) and the United States (including works by Theodore Child, John Barber, and George Ellwanger), Chapter 1 examines the ideology of domesticity
espoused by seven of the most popular female cookbook authors of the nineteenth century (including Maria Eliza Rundell, Eliza Acton, Isabella Beeton,
Mary Randolph, Lydia Maria Child, Eliza Leslie, and Marion Harland). The
chapter closes with an exploration of three nineteenth-century works that
question or transgress the restrictive bounds of domestic ideology, including
two gastronomically grounded cookbooks—Catherine Owen's *Culture and
Cooking; or, Art in the Kitchen* and Julia C. Andrews' *Breakfast, Dinner,
and Tea*. The final text under consideration is the first work of gastronomic
literature written by a woman in the English language—Elizabeth Robins
Pennell's *Feasts of Autolycus*, which openly challenges the gendered divide of
food writing to celebrate the undomesticated hungers of "a greedy woman."
Pennell's wholesale adoption of gastronomic literature is fraught with noticeable tensions that bear witness to the difficulties she encountered celebrating
her own appetite within a culture that denigrated appetitive women. Nonetheless, *Feasts* remains a radical work in its defiant assertion of woman's
right to gastronomic knowledge. It also elegantly showcases the link between
an educated palate and creative expression.

Chapters 2, 3, and 4 examine the forms of food writing developed by
Fisher, Toklas, and David. Chapters 2 and 4 also trace the loosening constraints on women's domestic cookbooks during the 1920s and 1930s within
the United States and England respectively, a trend that, in part, paved the
way for Fisher's and David's own innovative works. With few notable excep-
tions, authors of the more aesthetically oriented and unconventional of these
works hailed from England. Written in the 1920s, Alice Jekyll's *Kitchen
Essays* (1922) and Dorothy Allhusen's *Book of Scents and Dishes* (1926) celebrate food as an aesthetic object; Hilda Leyel's *Gentle Art of Cookery* (1925)
includes such imaginative recipes that her work would help inspire Elizabeth
David's career. Published in the 1930s, Ruth Lowinsky's *Lovely Food* offers
menus selected for a variety of occasions ranging from the need "to create
a favourable impression on a father-in-law, who comes prepared to judge
you as either the laziest housekeeper in Europe, or the most extravagant"
to "the first of a series of little dinners with a chosen friend" to be enjoyed
when "your husband has gone to America on business" (8, 32). From across
the Atlantic came Countess Morphy, whose *Recipes of All Nations* (1935)
includes dishes from such locales as Sub-Saharan Africa with the expressed
goal of helping housewives to overcome their fear of foreign cookery. So
too came *The National Cookbook* by Sheila Hibben (1932) and *Through
the Kitchen Door* (1938) by Grace and Beverly Smith, both of which gather
regional recipes from around the United States in order to capture "the grace
of American cooking" (*American* iii).

The loosening constraints on female-authored cookbooks during the interwar years paralleled a relaxation in the strict alignment of women with domesticity that took place on a broader social level. As women became less rigidly bound to the domestic realm, American men, in particular, began to enter the home kitchen in order to author domestic cookbooks. Whereas their English counterparts had long authored cookbooks geared to the housewife, American men began to enter the home kitchen in the 1930s. Chapter 3 provides a brief overview of male-authored cookbooks in the early twentieth-century United States in order to underscore the comparative ease with which Toklas managed to maneuver between the public and the private realms. Unlike Toklas who freely moved between the role of a gourmand and that of a home cook, male authors who entered the feminized space of the home kitchen felt the need to protect their masculinity. In order to do so, many authors clearly defined themselves as gastronomes. Like their nineteenth-century predecessors, these authors depicted themselves as artists at the table and as amateurs in the kitchen. They also hierarchized male creativity and male taste as innately greater in men than in women.

While male authors who entered the home kitchen called on the nineteenth-century gastronome and professional chef to gird their masculinity, Fisher relied heavily on Brillat-Savarin's *Physiology of Taste* to expand the range of women's food writing from the home kitchen into the world at large. In particular, Fisher's focus on the aesthetics of eating in France and on the attainment of wisdom and self-knowledge through gastronomy is both inspired and informed by Brillat-Savarin. Fisher fashioned the gastronomic reflection, social commentary, and philosophical musing so pervasive in *The Physiology of Taste* into a genre that celebrates female appetite and critiques the social rules and regulations that limit its expression. In so doing, Fisher became the first female author to successfully establish herself as a much revered professional gastronome by adopting a focus on desire and on the act of eating traditionally reserved for male food writers. Chapter 2 charts Fisher's development as a writer and the role of gastronomy in her oeuvre to argue that her most gastronomically grounded memoirs figure eating as an act of self-construction and as a means of attaining social communion. For Fisher, food not only functioned as a medium through which she communed with others, but also as a metaphor through which she shaped this psychological union into an aesthetic form.

Whereas Fisher fashioned a form of gastronomic literature that openly celebrates female appetite, Toklas merged the gastronomic travelogue with the domestic cookbook, thereby figuring the home cook as gastronome. Chapter 3 examines *The Alice B. Toklas Cook Book* as a text that uses considerable wit and self-assurance to blend the men's and women's food writing traditions. Moving freely between home and restaurant kitchens, the United States and France, the war front and the home front, Toklas' *Cook Book* gathers its mobility from the gastronomic tour guide, a relative newcomer to the genre of food writing and one Toklas consulted on her travels around the French provinces in search of delectable meals. Refusing to be neatly contained within men's or women's food writing traditions, the *Cook Book* blends the first-person narrative, dry wit, attunement to aesthetic pleasure, and emphasis on eating, on public eateries, and on dining as a social event that characterizes gastronomic literature with the practical instruction and domestic detail of a traditional cookbook, thereby effectively reconfiguring the gendered boundaries of both genres.

Chapter 4 explores the written aesthetic of David's gastronomic cookbooks, an aesthetic that David developed during six years living in the Mediterranean, where she learned to honor food as a source of pleasure and as a medium for artistic expression. Upon her return to a war-rationed England in 1946, she learned to fashion these former pleasures into language. David replaced the emphasis on duty and practicality of the domestic cookbook with the emphasis on intellectual stimulation, poetic self-expression, and aesthetic reflection characteristic of gastronomic literature. By creating a body of writing that articulates a sensual engagement with foreign foodways and showcases the intellectual pleasures gastronomy, David helped to aesthetisize the English women's food writing tradition, replacing its domestic ideology with a reverence for sensual pleasure and for the embodied knowledge it nourishes.

Chapter 5 examines Patience Gray's *Honey from a Weed*, Vertamae Smart Grosvenor's *Vibration Cooking*, and Monique Truong's *Book of Salt*, three works that extend and reconfigure the innovative forms of food writing pioneered by their predecessors. Published in 1986, Gray's gastroautobiographical cookbook, *Honey from a Weed*, marries the lyricism of David's *Mediterranean Food* with the self-expression of Fisher's *Gastronomical Me* to capture her rugged and well-fed life on the shores of the Mediterranean. *Honey from a Weed* showcases a minimalist aesthetic firmly grounded in the wild environs of the southern Mediterranean, an aesthetic that vigorously and uncompromisingly rejects excess and commercialism to embrace the local, the regional, and the provincial.

Whereas Gray, like Fisher, Toklas, and David before her, undertook a privileged voyage of rebellion, leaving England to set up permanent residence in the Mediterranean, the final two authors explore journeys of dislocation. Inspired by the geographic and cultural fluidity of Toklas' cookbook, which presages the hybridity of the postmodern palate, Vertamae Smart Grosvenor's *Vibration Cooking* (1970) and Monique Truong's *The Book of Salt* (2003) each articulate a postcolonial culinary aesthetic, one that illuminates cookery as a means of mediating cultural dissonance. Grosvenor politicizes the autobiographical cookbook in order to openly confront racism and to celebrate the culturally rich foods of the African diaspora. She also parodies and reconfigures the cookbook, a genre that typically elided the African American voice and the African American contribution to American cookery. Inspired by *The Alice B. Toklas Cook Book* and its description of the servants who worked for Toklas and Gertrude

Stein, Monique Truong wrote *The Book of Salt*, a novel narrated by a Vietnamese exile who cooks for the famous couple. *The Book of Salt* deftly interweaves cultures and cultural values into a poignant tale about cookery as a form of communication with the power to assuage the cultural dissonance of colonization, immigration, and exile. It also engages imaginatively with *The Alice B. Toklas Cook Book*, filling cultural and textual gaps in Toklas' memoir. Such intertextuality enables Truong to offer a postcolonial critique of Western appetite and its impact on Vietnam.

1 The Gendering of Appetite in Nineteenth-Century Food Writing

Cooking is an art, but the artistry lies as much in the eating as in the preparing of food.

—Alin Laubreaux, *The Happy Glutton*

Over the course of the nineteenth century, a rigid gender gap solidified between men's and women's food writing. Men sought to determine public taste and to refine the aesthetic pleasures of eating. Professional chefs authored cookbooks that codified the culinary arts and gastronomes wrote literature that worked to establish gastronomy as an art form and the gourmand as an artist in his own right. Women provided instruction on managing the household and worked to define and promote domestic ideology. They wrote domestic manuals and cookbooks, which included practical instruction for daily home cooking and promoted the principles of duty, economy, and practicality. Beginning at the close of the nineteenth century, however, the occasional woman had begun to articulate an aesthetics of pleasure in keeping with the male-authored tradition, effectively expanding women's food writing beyond the home kitchen. These women did so by blending elements of male-authored gastronomic literature into the women's tradition. A comparison of men's and women's food writing traditions not only illustrates why women who chose to celebrate an undomesticated appetite found elements of gastronomy essential to the task, but also reveals striking details about the construction of gender in nineteenth-century food writing and its strong distaste of female pleasure.

Taken as a whole, nineteenth-century gastronomic literature worked to define gastronomy and to codify gourmand etiquette, articulating an aesthetics of eating that strives to maximize pleasure and conviviality. According to gastronomic literature, the gourmand not only nourishes sensual and social pleasures through the act of eating, but also hones his capacity to appreciate and to exhibit good taste. The educated palate and conviviality of the gourmand was rewarded with social currency; a repository of wit, a fluent conversationalist, and an aesthete attuned to the nuances of the flavors, composition, and progression of the meal, the gourmand was in high demand as a dining companion.

In its emphasis on poetic self-expression and pleasure, gastronomic literature stood in ideological opposition to the nineteenth-century women's food writing tradition that developed in England and the United States. Beginning in the eighteenth century, women's food writing in these two countries largely consisted of domestic cookbooks. Such cookbooks focused on economy, order, and practicality, not only promoting these traits in the home kitchen, but also embodying them stylistically. These traits epitomize one of the most popular cookbooks on both sides of the Atlantic, Hannah Glasse's *Art of Cookery Made Plain and Easy*. First published in 1747 in London, where it was to remain a best seller for close to a hundred years, Glasse's *Art of Cookery* was adopted wholeheartedly by Americans at the turn of the century; George Washington and Thomas Jefferson owned copies (Hess, *Art of Cookery* v). Although Glasse's personality slips through every now and again, much of her prose epitomizes the no-nonsense streak that coursed throughout domestic cookbooks. To wit, she offers the following instruction on roasting a hare:

> Take your hare when it is cased; truss it in this manner, bring the two hind legs up to its sides, pull the fore legs back, your skewer first into the hind-leg, then into the fore leg, and thrust it though the body; put the fore-leg on, and then the hind-leg, and a skewer through the top of the shoulders and back part of the head, which will hold the head up. (21)

Glasse's pragmatic and frugal style would reverberate throughout nineteenth-century domestic cookbooks.

Whereas female cookbook authors helped to define middle-class domesticity, promoting familial duty, practicality, and economy of self-expression, male authors of gastronomic literature promoted playful self-indulgence, wit, pleasure-seeking, elegant self-expression, and a cosmopolitan sensibility. Certainly, not all authors exhibited such neatly gendered characteristics. For example, numerous authors of gastronomic literature fell far short in their attempts to extend Grimod's and Brillat-Savarin's literary inheritance; at its worst, the gastronomic essay substitutes what M. F. K. Fisher describes as "whimsy" for "wit," "dull reminiscences" for "delightful anecdotes," and "blunt statistics" for "piercing observations" (*Serve It Forth* v).

As for the domesticated genre, some female cookbook authors rivaled or outstripped many of their male counterparts in luxuriousness of expression, sense of humor, and *savoir vivre*. For example, Eliza Acton's *Modern Cookery for Private Families* from England and Eliza Leslie's *Directions for Cookery* from the United States remain two of the most elegantly written cookbooks to date, while the anonymous author of *Domestic Economy and Cookery for Rich and Poor* (1827), by "A Lady," includes recipes gathered first-hand from Europe as well as "mulakatannes and curries of India," "cold soups and mixed meats of Russia," and "cuscussou and honeyed paste of Africa" (iv). Taken as a whole, however, nineteenth-century cookbooks focused tightly on the domestic realm and on its economic management, remaining markedly devoid of pleasure, while nineteenth-century male "gastronomers stressed the value of appetite, the importance of maintaining and pampering, rather than denying it" (Gigante, *Gusto* xxxviii). As Priscilla Parkhurst Ferguson summarizes the distinction: gastronomes, invariably men, concerned themselves with "the public pursuit of sensual pleasures," whereas women dealt with "the private satisfaction of physiological need" (*Accounting for Taste* 93).

The absence of physical pleasure in women's food writing reflects the cultural constraints on female appetite that rigidified over the course of the nineteenth century. By the mid-nineteenth century, middle- and upper-class American and English convention had coded the appetites for food, for sex, and for power as masculine. Unlike their male counterparts, who were understood to have inherently large appetites, middle- and upper-class Victorian women were encouraged to suppress and to regulate their own hungers—for food, for sex, and for public acclaim.[1] Toward that end, cookbooks modeled and reproduced heteronormative domesticity, an ideological dynamic that defined a woman's role as obtaining and keeping a husband, bearing his children, and nourishing the nation's moral values. This ideology permeates seven of the most popular and influential domestic cookbooks of the century, including Maria Eliza Rundell's *A New System of Domestic Cookery*, Eliza Acton's *Modern Cookery for Private Families*, Isabella Beeton's *Book of Household Management*, Mary Randolph's *Virginia Housewife*, Lydia Maria Child's *The Frugal Housewife*, Eliza Leslie's *Directions for Cookery*, and Marion Harland's *Common Sense in the Household*.

Although domestic ideology dominated nineteenth-century women's food writing, the rare author would pen a gastronomically grounded work. In particular, three American authors stand out for their focus on gastronomy—Julia C. Andrews, Catherine Owen, and Elizabeth Robins Pennell.[2] Andrews and Owen each penned cookbooks that showcase the author's deep familiarity with gastronomic literature. Andrews authored *Breakfast, Dinner, and Tea: Viewed Classically, Poetically, and Practically* (1859), which draws on gastronomic literature as well as a variety of widely-flung travelogues and cookbooks to craft what well might be the first gastronomic cookbook authored by a woman. Catherine Owen, the pen name of Helen Alice Matthews Nitsch, wrote *Culture and Cooking; or, Art in the Kitchen* (1881), which clearly aligns cookery with the arts, enlisting gastronomic literature and literary gourmands in order to do so. In the 1890s, Elizabeth Robins Pennell turned her back on the cookbook format altogether, penning instead a series of gastronomic essays that flout the domesticated genre in order to celebrate female appetite. Originally written for London's *Pall Mall Gazette*, Pennell's essays were collected as the *Feasts of Autolycus* (1896), a collection that simultaneously showcases Pennell's

---

1. The first chapter of Helena Michie's *Flesh Made Word*, "Ladylike Anorexia: Hunger, Sexuality, and Etiquette" directly addresses the cultural suppression of female appetite. See also Susan Bordo's *Unbearable Weight*, Joan Jacobs Brumberg's "The Appetite as Voice," and Anna Krugovoy Silver's *Victorian Literature and the Anorexic Body*.

2. Whereas American women tended to be avant-garde in their emphasis on cookery as an art in the nineteenth century, by the 1920s English women had begun to craft a noticeably larger number of gastronomically grounded cookbooks than American women.

defiance of domestic ideology and illustrates the difficulty she encountered voicing female pleasure at the turn of the century.

GASTRONOMIC LITERATURE: A MALE TRADITION

Gastronomic literature, which first developed in France after the Revolution, included books and essays focused on the palate's education as an essential component of self-knowledge.[3] Food criticism dates back to Alexandre Balthazar Laurent Grimod de la Reynière's eight volume *Almanach des Gourmands* (1803–1812), the first Parisian food guide to review restaurants, caterers, and their goods. Within the *Almanach*, Grimod worked to promote an aesthetic sensibility, to define good taste, and to create a standard of etiquette for the gourmand. Jean Anthelme Brillat-Savarin fathered a form of gastronomic memoir in his *Physiology of Taste* (1826), which blends personal anecdote with abstract reflection to assert: "Gastronomical knowledge is necessary to every man, because it tends to add to the sum of his predestined pleasure" (53). The influence of Grimod and Brillat-Savarin would permeate gastronomic literature as it developed over the nineteenth and early twentieth centuries. As sociologist Stephen Mennell explains, "Virtually everything of the sort written since quotes or harks back to these two authors one way or another" (267). Grimod's *Almanach des Gourmands* and *Manuel des Amphitryons* along with Brillat-Savarin's *Physiology of Taste* exemplify gastronomic literature at its best, illustrating the wit, intelligence, and elegant self-expression expected of a true gourmand.

While France gave birth to and skillfully nourished the genre, it was soon adopted by England, where writers altered it to suit English sensibilities. Authors such as the pseudonymous Launcelot Sturgeon as well as Charles Lamb penned partially tongue-in-cheek essays, simultaneously creating a tradition of gastronomic literature in England and playfully underscoring the egotism and self-indulgence of Grimod's *Almanach*. Other English authors modeled their writings after the French tradition, encouraging their compatriots to introduce key aspects of French gastronomy to the English table. Among such writings can be found Thomas Walker's *Aristology, or the Art of Dining* (first published as *The Original* in 1835), A. V. Kirwan's *Host*

---

3. In "A Cultural Field in the Making," Priscilla Parkhurst Ferguson argues that gastronomic literature was a driving force behind the formation of a gastronomic field in nineteenth-century France. In particular, she states that "[t]he 'professional' genres that contributed most obviously and directly to the formation of the gastronomic field were: the gastronomic journalism of Alexandre Balthazar Laurent Grimod de la Reynière (1758–1838); the culinary treatises of Antonin Carême (1784–1833); and the cultural commentary and protosociology of Anthelm Brillat-Savarin (1755–1826). . . . Each aimed to systematize culinary knowledge; each contributed to the formalization and, hence, the very definition of modern French cuisine" (611).

and Guest (1864), John Cordy Jeaffreson's *A Book About the Table* (1875), and Eneas Sweetland Dallas' *Kettner's Book of the Table* (1877). Americans were slower to take up the genre and contributed to it less prolifically than their English counterparts. Three American gastronomic works stand out, however, as exemplars of the aesthetically oriented genre, Joseph Barber's *Crumbs From the Round Table* (1866), Theodore Child's *Delicate Feasting* (1890), and George Ellwanger's *The Pleasures of the Table* (1902).[4]

Grimod de la Reynière

A man poised between the *ancien regime* and post-revolutionary France, Grimod fathered food criticism as we know it today. Along with the other members of a "Tasting Jury," Grimod critiqued Parisian food purveyors and their products. The results were published annually in the *Almanach des Gourmands* (1803–1812), the first book-length series devoted to "the critical appraisal of the food then available to [its] readers" (Davidson 355). In addition to such critiques, the *Almanach* included restaurant reviews; recipes; seasonal charts; essays and poetry on serving, cooking, hosting, and dining; and commentary on recent trends in the culinary sciences.[5] With the *Almanach*, Grimod developed a literature of gastronomy characterized by linguistic playfulness, eccentric wit, mercurial form, and an authoritative command over public taste.

According to Grimod, the *Almanach* was driven by the Revolution and the resulting redistribution of wealth, which

> has transferred old riches into new hands. As the mentality of the majority of these overnight millionaires revolves around purely animal pleasures, it is believed that a service might be rendered them by offering them a reliable guide to the most solid part of their affections. (MacDonogh 196)

In other words, Grimod educated the post-Revolutionary consumer in matters of taste. The democratization of taste, however, was only the most explicit of Grimod's goals.[6] Grimod received repeated censorship for his theater and literary criticism, which often contained jabs directed at the oppressive French state. In 1798 the administration went as far as to shut down Grimod's theater magazine, *Censeur Dramatique*. Soon

4. Theodore Child actually hailed from England. His *Delicate Feasting*, however, has been categorized as an American work because it was first published in the United States and is expressly addressed to an American audience.

5. As Beatrice Fink explains in her essay "Enlightened Eating," the list can be considerably extended to include "gourmand letters to the gourmand editor, reports on the latest gourmand scandals, articles on aphrodisiacs, patent medicines, the latest latrines, and updates on food and kitchen technology" (17).

6. For more on Grimod's democratization of taste, see Stephen Mennell and Denise Gigante.

after, Grimod began the *Almanach*. Inspired, in part, by state censorship, Grimod's *Almanach* harnessed gastronomic discourse as a means
of delivering strong political and cultural commentary.[7] As Alice Arndt
succinctly explains: "Through the lens of food, Grimod scrutinized literature, history, and the contemporary world. Through the metaphor of
gastronomy, he critiqued commercialism at home in France as well as
Napoleon's policy of military expansionism across Europe" (191).

Despite the irony, satire, and hyperbole that characterizes Grimod's
writing, the *Almanach* worked seriously and effectively to raise dining and,
by extension, the practice of gourmandise to an art form and to dissociate
the gourmand from the glutton in order to define him as a man of taste.[8]
Toward that end, Grimod posits that the gourmand, like the Enlightenment
man of taste, is not born, but cultivated. The finely tuned senses of the
gourmand are honed through experience and reflection; the body and its
pleasures nourish the mind, engaging it in philosophical exploration. Not
everyone, however, who studies gourmandise can achieve the status of a
gourmand, who must come equipped with an innate sensibility to comple-
ment his proper training.

Above all, the accomplished gourmand must possess a finely tuned palate,
a keen aesthetic sensibility, and an eloquent, witty mode of self-expression.
He must know how to function as an impeccable host and how to behave
as the ideal guest—to orchestrate dinners and to participate in them. When
a gourmand plays host, his finely tuned aesthetic becomes materialized in
the décor of the dining room, the shape and setting of the table, and the
appearance, progression, and flavor of the dishes served. Such attention to
the dinner table nourishes the ultimate goal of gourmandise—to maximize
aesthetic pleasure and social well-being. As Grimod explains:

> Fine food and wine are the very wellspring of wit, pleasure, and good
> cheer. . . . [T]he Gourmand . . . is congenial by nature, indeed his first
> priority is to ingratiate himself, and he has all that it takes to accom-
> plish this: his playfulness, his sparkling wit, and his infectious cheer-
> fulness make him the life of the party, its very heart and soul. (24)

Despite his congenial, ingratiating nature, however, the gourmand must,
according to Grimod, place his own pleasure above all other concerns.
Toward that end, he must "know how to carve and serve well. This offers a
quite natural opportunity to get one's hands on the dish, in which case one

---

7. In addition to censorship, Grimod faced the incarceration of his own mother
and sister as well as the beheading of numerous friends and relatives, experiences that
add layers of political and social meaning to Grimod's gastronomic commentary.

8. Fink describes Grimod's tone as varying from "that of painstaking demon-
strator and teacher of etiquette to that of narrator of risqué or comic anecdotes,
composer of bawdy verse (for instance, on the sad fate of truncated beef), solemn
judge presiding over a 'jury de dégustateurs'. . . ." (16–17).

would have to be most unskillful not to set aside the best pieces for oneself" (29). In other words, the gourmand must be self-indulgent and place his own palate's pleasure above all others. Grimod implies that the gourmand's "playfulness, his sparkling wit, and his infectious cheerfulness" as well as his exquisitely trained palate entitle him to the choicest morsels.

Grimod not only defined the gourmand and his aesthetic sensibilities but also fashioned a gourmand's code. Many of the rules discussed by Grimod and repeated, sometimes *verbatim*, in nineteenth-century gastronomic essays, establish protocols for the gourmand host as well as for his guests. Grimod surmises the importance of these rules:

> the dining table is a country which, like all others, has its ways and customs, and the Gourmand's Code contains an abundance of rules that one must follow so as to not seem like a savage, but which would lead a reserved gentleman who observed these laws faithfully to die of starvation at a four-course dinner. (28)

On one hand, Grimod codifies dining etiquette in order to train the *nouveaux riches* to pass as men of taste. On the other hand, he states that the gourmand must break these rules if they interfere with his right to pleasure, such as when he is faced with an unaccomplished host who does not "anticipate [his] guests' every wish" (29). Thus, Grimod suggests that the uninitiated must follow an elaborate set of rules not to appear uncouth. The innately born and well-educated gourmand, however, need only follow his own pleasure.

Because of the daily nature of the gourmand's pleasure-seeking, novelty plays a crucial role in the titillation of his palate. According to Grimod, "the sense of taste, the primary one for any reasonable man, needs to be spurred on by change; it thrives on surprises" (33). Thus Grimod applauds those chefs who incorporate foreign dishes, ingredients, and culinary techniques into French cuisine, noting that "our great artists have not hesitated to explore foreign lands, and to draw upon the Culinary Art of an entire Continent, while simply correcting, and adjusting for our taste the dishes brought back from their journeys. This has resulted in an immeasurable increase in the number, and in the very nature of our pleasures" (39). Grimod embraces innovation and transnational culinary exchange, aligning the gourmand with a cosmopolitan sensibility. He also suggests that a well-developed palate must be familiar with the flavors of the world.

Brillat-Savarin

Although Grimod's *Manuel des Amphitryon* and *Almanach des Gourmands* were widely read and highly influential in nineteenth-century France, England, and the United States, they are largely unread by contemporary Americans and English alike. Reasons for their relative obscurity include: their detailed discussion of long disappeared Parisian food purveyors, restaurants, and edibles; an encyclopedic length, in the case of the *Almanach*; and the fact that only small portions of each have been translated into English.[9] Less eccentric, more accessible to the lay reader, and distilled into an easily digestible length and form, Brillat-Savarin's *The Physiology of Taste* (1826) enjoys a comparatively wide contemporary audience. Several of the aphorisms that begin his book are so well known today that they can be justly termed proverbial. Two such examples include: "Tell me what you eat, and I shall tell you what you are" and "The destiny of nations depends on how they nourish themselves" (1).[10] Though Brillat-Savarin did not invent these pithy remarks, versions of which appear in Grimod's writing, his work popularized them.[11] By marrying the physical pleasures of gastronomy with spiritual wisdom and social enlightenment, Brillat-Savarin, like Grimod before him, democratized post-revolutionary gourmandise and worked to create a knowledgeable dining public. Unlike Grimod, however, who hailed from an aristocratic background and bridged pre- and post-Revolutionary France, Brillat-Savarin was decidedly middle class, making him a fitting spokesperson for modern French gastronomy.

In keeping with the gastronomic genre begun by Grimod, *The Physiology of Taste* incorporates a pastiche of styles and approaches, including philosophical reflection, quasi-scientific theories, personal anecdote, mythology, and travelogue. Brillat-Savarin's self-described goal was to define gourmandise, "indulg[ing] in a little autobiography" to illustrate its finer points (Drayton 296). *The Physiology of Taste* extends Grimod's cosmopolitan focus to include tales drawn from Brillat-Savarin's sojourn to America from 1793–1796, where he arrived as an exile, having been denounced during the French Revolution's Reign of Terror. In sections such as "Traveler's Luck," "Exploit of the Professor," "National Victory," and "The Battle," Brillat-Savarin recounts his hurried departure from France along with various adventures during his extended stay in America.

If Grimod fathered food criticism, judging Paris' high-end food purveyors and burgeoning restaurants, Brillat-Savarin penned the precursor to today's gastronomic memoir. In the first section of the book, personal anecdotes take second place to the philosophical and scientific theories, which they illustrate. In the second, or final, section, however, Brillat-Savarin captures

---

9. Giles MacDonogh's *A Palate in Revolution: Grimod de la Reynière and the Almanach des Gourmands* includes a chapter that distills a miniature "dictionary" of Grimod's *bon mots* on topics ranging from "abstemious people" and "aphrodisiacs" to "wine merchants" and "women." Denise Gigante's *Gusto: Essential Writings in Nineteenth-Century Gastronomy* includes a chapter gathering Grimod's thoughts on "Elements of Gastronomic Etiquette."

10. Unless specified as Drayton in the citation, the Brillat-Savarin quotes come from Fisher's translation of his work.

11. In his study "Grimod de la Reynière's *Almanach des Gourmands*," Michael Garval takes Brillat-Savarin to task for not referencing his debt to Grimod. Garval notes that "all the ideas conveyed by Brillat's twenty aphorisms can be found in Grimod's *Almanach,* at least in embryonic form and often developed at length" (61).

"some pleasant memories, and clarifie[s] others that were on the point of fading" (20). In other words, he fashions gastronomic memoir. Brillat-Savarin states outright that this final section takes part in a form of self-construction, or a means of articulating the self in relation to the surrounding world:

> I have found the reward for all my labor in this part of the book where I see myself once more among my friends. It is above all when life is about to escape our grasp that we become important to ourselves, and our intimates are a part of that final I AM. (364)

Central to Brillat-Savarin's project, then, is the fundamental goal of memoir: to capture and to fix memories through narrative and to construct versions of the self in language. For Brillat-Savarin, writing gastronomic memoir served a dual function. First, it enabled him to articulate knowledge about the self and the self in relation to the world that comes from the practice and study of gastronomy. It also enabled him to configure key memories that, taken together, articulate the self as a cosmopolitan, erudite, witty, reflective, eloquent, and authoritative gastronome.

Like Grimod, Brillat-Savarin defined the primary goals of gastronomy as the attainment of aesthetic pleasure and social well-being. As Brillat-Savarin describes: "gourmandism is an impassioned, considered, and habitual preference for whatever pleases the taste" (151). Such pleasures, like the very act of eating, work to dissolve the boundaries between self and other. He explains this phenomenon as follows:

> Gourmandism is one of the most important influences in our social life; it gradually spreads that spirit of conviviality which brings together from day to day differing kinds of people, melts them into a whole, animates their conversation, and softens the sharp corners of the conventional inequalities of position and breeding. (153)

The pleasures of the table foster such conviviality and mutual accord because they nourish "an especial well-being" within the individual, sating, as they do, the hungers of "both soul and body" (189). Whereas physical pleasure arises from "the actual and direct sensation of satisfying a need," spiritual "pleasures of the table are a reflective sensation which is born from the various circumstances of place, time, things, and people who make up the surroundings of the meal" (188).

According to Grimod and Brillat-Savarin, gastronomy not only fosters pleasure and well-being, but also stimulates the intellect and the imagination, imparting knowledge and creative inspiration. In order to establish gastronomy as an art and the gourmand as an artist, one of the primary goals of gastronomic literature, Brillat-Savarin aligns eating with heightened perception, creativity, and self-expression to state that that when a true gourmand experiences a "well-savored meal," "his spirit grows more perceptive, his imagination flowers, and clever phrases fly from his lips" (189). Brillat-Savarin likewise underscores that his own literary endeavor, which includes remarkable skill as a storyteller, keen wit, and eloquent self-expression, has been nourished by his devotion to gastronomy and his well-honed palate.

Just as gastronomy nourishes creative expression, it also imbues the gourmand with a cosmopolitan sophistication. Thus, Brillat-Savarin, like Grimod before him, presents himself as a man-at-home-in-the-world, who embraces international exchange and the globally inflected table. In particular, Brillat-Savarin celebrates the importation of foreign ingredients, dishes, and culinary techniques into French cuisine, a cross-pollination spurred by the rise of the restaurant and the ensuing competition between chefs. As a result of such international exchange,

> new foods have been discovered, old ones bettered, and both new and old combined in a thousand ways. Foreign inventions have been imported; the world itself has been put to use, and contributes so much to our daily fare that in one meal we can trace a complete course of alimentary geography. (330–331)

Brillat-Savarin even offers a brief sampling of the regions and their representative specialties found at the Parisian restaurant table: beefsteak from England; sauerkraut from Germany; garbanzo beans and liqueurs from Spain; Parmesan and sherbets from Italy; smoked eels and caviar from Russia; pickled herrings from Holland; soy and coffee from Asia; Cape wines from Africa; yams and chocolate from America (335). Gourmands become part of the international frontier by embracing and, quite literally, ingesting foreign edibles. In so doing, they hone a worldly palate, familiar with foreign tastes.

The Rise of the English Gastronome

By the mid-nineteenth century, gastronomic literature, along with French cuisine, had earned a popular place in affluent English culture, ending a century of resistance to French gastronomy. Throughout the 1700s and early 1800s, the wealthy English palate had been characterized by a devotion to wholesome, hearty fare, which derived from a partiality toward rural cookery. This partiality contrasted with that of the affluent French, who embraced a more urban, or courtly table. In *All Manners of Food*, Stephen Mennell examines this phenomenon in detail, attributing the greater hold of country cooking on the wealthy English than on their French counterparts to the "higher prestige accorded the country life in England than in France. . . . One effect was that the English gentleman, living at least a substantial part of the year on his estates and involved in the life of the countryside, was content to eat in great degree off the product of his land" (130–131).

After the French Revolution, increasing numbers of French chefs migrated to England, an influx that exponentially increased the rate that French dining trends were absorbed into English culture. The French influence became so pervasive that, as Gigante explains, by

> mid-century it was assumed that to acquire taste was to acquire French eating habits. French restaurateurs for their part considered themselves missionaries of civilization, spreading ideals of cultured taste and acquired appetite beyond the border of France. And because every art has its critic, they were assisted in this project by gastronomical litterateurs. (*Gusto* xxxi)

Gastronomic literature was not the only male-authored food writing to flourish in England. Many of the French émigrés who became highly lauded restaurant chefs also wrote professional cookbooks, which served to codify the culinary arts as practiced in the nation's most elite kitchens—public as well as private. Two of the most famous exemplars of this tradition include Louis Eustache Ude and Alexis Soyer. Tellingly, one of the most prolific and popular English chefs of the nineteenth century Charles Elmé Francatelli fully embraced the French culinary tradition; he studied with Antoine Carême in Paris before starting his illustrious career in London. Although professional chefs and gastronomes focused their attention almost exclusively on the public realm and the elite home kitchen, the occasional gastronome, such as William Kitchiner, or famous chef, such as Soyer or Francatelli, would venture into the realm of middle and working class domestic cookery.[12] By and large, however, male authors of both professional cookbooks and gastronomic literature focused on the public sphere—the gourmand on honing public taste and the professional chef on titillating the gourmand's palate.

The absorption of French dining habits into English culture was accompanied by a noticeable degree of tension and resistance, which courses throughout nineteenth-century English gastronomic literature. A few English gastronomes embraced the French unconditionally, a stance that resulted in remarkably derivative writing, which relied heavily, and often *verbatim*, on Grimod and Brillat-Savarin. In fact, lack of originality and inelegant style characterize much of English gastronomic literature. In order to survive the transplant from France in a lively manner, English-authored gastronomic literature needed to display an appreciation of gastronomy and gastronomic literature as art forms that had been carefully cultivated and nourished by the French. The successful English gastronome also understood, however, that such art forms must be adapted to suit the distinctively English palate in order to enliven English culture. In other words, once on English soil and digested

---

12. William Kitchiner authored *The Cook's Oracle and House Keeper's Manual* (1817). Alexis Soyer wrote *The Modern Housewife* (1849) and *Shilling Cookery Book for the People* (1854). Charles Elmé Francatelli compiled *Plain Cookery Book for the Working Classes* (1852).

by English sensibilities, gastronomic literature needed to be infused with discernible native character in order to thrive as a genre.

As late as 1864, one of the nation's most aesthetically attuned authors of gastronomic literature, A. V. Kirwan bemoaned the disparity between the excellence of English letters and the weakness of its gastronomy and the paucity of its gastronomic literature, reflecting that:

> It may be a humiliating confession, but in England no learned treatises have been written on the art of dining or dinner giving. We are wholly without "meditations" or "contemplations gastronomiques." ... Our inventive powers are not turned in the direction of luxury, nor do we make our bill of fare our calendar, nor measure the seasons by their dainty productions. We talk little of dining or dishes, however much the most luxurious and sensual among us may think about it. ... We have given birth to a Bacon, a Locke, a Shakespeare, a Milton, a Watt; but we are without a Vatel, a Bechamel, a Laguipierre, a Beauvilliers, or a Carème. (50–51)

Kirwan is among those authors who respected the French tradition and shared its dedication to honing an aesthetics of pleasure, yet worked to construct a gastronomic philosophy specifically suited to the English palate.

Well before Kirwan bemoaned the fate of his nation's palate, however, England had developed a highly original and distinctively English form of gastronomic literature—the mock gastronomic essay. Two of the most remarkable contributions to this form actually predate Brillat-Savarin's *The Physiology of Taste*. The pseudonymous Launcelot Sturgeons's *Essays, Moral, Philosophical, and Stomachical* (1822) and Charles Lamb's "A Dissertation Upon Roast Pig" (1823) lampoon the egocentrism and self-indulgence of gourmandise. Among those more straightforward works, the most well written and original that sought to transform French gastronomy into a distinctly English philosophy include Kirwan's *Host and Guest* (1864), Thomas Walker's *Aristology, or the Art of Dining* (originally published as *The Original* in 1835), and Eneas Sweetland Dallas' *Kettner's Book of the Table* (1877).[13] These works stand out for their stylistic flair and their

---

13. Scholars differ markedly in their assessment of the century's most well-written English gastronomic literature. Stephen Mennell finds Thomas Walker's *Aristology* the only truly original work. In *Two "Loaf-Givers,"* Leonard N. Beck states that "Despite its obvious debt to Brillat-Savarin, *The Art of Dining* (1853, 1874) of Abraham Hayward is conceded to be the best English writing of the period" (130). Denise Gigante finds Sturgeon's *Essays, Moral, Philosophical, and Stomachical* the most remarkable contribution and excludes Hayward altogether from her collection *Gusto: Essential Writings in Nineteenth-Century Gastronomy*. The stiffness of Hayward's writing might account for the mixed response he receives. For example, following a chapter on Walker, he writes: "Having now glanced over the whole of Mr. Walker's contributions to the art of dining we shall endeavor to convey some notion, however faint, of the varied and extended interest which the subject may be fairly considered to comprise" (153–154). William

focus on aesthetic pleasure; they work to educate and to enliven the English palate in a manner that owes more debt to Brillat-Savarin than to Grimod. Although it does not compare stylistically to the aforementioned works, Abraham Hayward's *The Art of Dining* (1852) also deserves mention as a book influenced by Brillat-Savarin; it was widely read and quoted by nineteenth-century gastronomes. Unlike the works inspired by Brillat-Savarin, John Cordy Jeaffreson's *A Book About the Table* (1875) exhibits a macabre sense of humor and a sadistic tendency in keeping with Grimod, who "was enormously influential in nineteenth-century Europe" and widely "adapted . . . into English" (*Gusto* 1).

One of the first English works of gastronomic literature, Launcelot Sturgeon's *Essays, Moral, Philosophical, and Stomachical* (1822), was directly inspired by Grimod. Unlike Jeaffreson who shares Grimod's macabre sense of humor, however, Sturgeon transforms the eccentric wit of Grimod into a highly satiric tone that mocks the very genre it imitates. Gigante hypothesizes that such satire results from the tension that surfaces when French and English gastronomic philosophies collide. She explains the phenomenon as follows:

> Throughout the eighteenth century, the English had prided themselves on their common sense as a nation of beef-eating, plain speakers with no patience for foreign (particularly French) ostentation. But the literary genre of gastronomy, perhaps recognizing from its very origins this potential for critical rebuff, evolved its own satiric, self-mocking style. (*Gusto* xxxiv)

Sturgeon's *Essays, Moral, Philosophical, and Stomachical* transforms Grimod's dark humor and egotism into a parodic critique of the solipsistic gourmand. Much of Sturgeon's content is taken directly from Grimod, at times presented in a straightforward fashion. At other times, however, Sturgeon revisits Grimod's work in order to refashion its content with a perverse twist. The repeated juxtaposition of the forthright with the parodic ultimately calls into question the sincerity of the seemingly straight passages. For example, Sturgeon opens with a definition of the epicure drawn straight from Grimod. Once defined, however, the epicure and the code by which his actions are bound are subject to Sturgeon's satiric scrutiny. In the following passage

---

Kitchiner's *The Cook's Oracle* is another work that receives mixed reviews. Gigante includes it in her anthology. It has not been included in the present discussion for two reasons. First, the work's primary concern is with presenting recipes. Second, the introductory material, which leans heavily toward gastronomic essay, displays an awkward, verbose style. To wit, he describes the French attitude toward drink as follows: "They know how, so easily, to keep Life in sufficient repair by good eating, that they require little or no screwing up with liquid Stimuli. This accounts for that *toujours gai* and happy equilibrium of the animal spirits which they enjoy with more regularity than any people: their elastic Stomachs, unimpaired by Spirituous Liquors, digest vigorously the food they sagaciously prepare and render easily assimilable, by cooking it sufficiently" (11).

Sturgeon mocks the gourmand's self-centered devotion to his own pleasure as well as the elitism that permeates Grimod's writing:

> Nothing partakes more of the very essence of high-breeding, than a nonchalant disregard of every thing but your own comfort: therefore, when finger glasses are brought, not only rinse your mouth, but gargle your throat, just as if you were in your dressing room. . . . In fine, if you wish to acquire the character of a thorough-bred man of ton, you must affect—even if it should not be natural to you—the most decided egotism, and total want of feeling: laugh at the distresses of your friends, and pretend not to understand those of the public. (43–44)

By interweaving the basest threads that run throughout Grimod's code of etiquette, Sturgeon satirizes its penchant for incivility, implying that a gourmand who takes the best morsels for himself, insists on levity no matter how serious the surrounding context, and differentiates himself by following elaborate, seemingly random rules fails to fulfill his social duty toward others.

Sturgeon likewise parodies the link gastronomic authors forge between creativity and gastronomy, using mustard as the risible subject, noting how "it expands the mind, exalts the imagination, and sublimates the fancy; it is to its copious use that the remarkable strength and poignancy of the speeches at all public dinners is chiefly to be attributed" (95). At another point, Sturgeon mocks the absurdity of gastronomic fads by praising assaefoetida—a resinous compound also known as devil's dung because of its fetid, sulfuric smell. Of it, he writes: "he is but a mere pretender to the name of epicure who does not prefer its savoury pungency to the mawkish effluvia of attar of roses" (100). He even calls on women to liven up the drawing room by sprinkling assaefoetida on their handkerchiefs, thereby targeting the fact that some of the dishes and ingredients cherished by the gastronome would strike the "uneducated," or less jaded, palate as downright unpalatable and offensive.

Charles Lamb's "A Dissertation Upon Roast Pig" proves another classic of the mock genre and shares the parodic tenor of Sturgeon's *Essays*, a fact that leads some scholars to believe that Lamb himself authored the pseudonymous work.[14] In the following jest at gastronomic literature, Lamb mocks the hyperbolic and hyper-sexualized nature of the genre:

> Pineapple is great. She is indeed almost too transcendent—a delight, if not sinful, yet so like to sinning, that really a tender-conscienced person would do well to pause—too ravishing for mortal taste she, woundeth and excoriateth the lips that approach her—like lover's kisses, she biteth—she is a pleasure bordering on pain from the fierceness and insanity of her relish. . . . (146)

---

14. In *Gusto*, Denise Gigante points out that Lamb owned a copy of the *Essays* and may have been its author.

By employing metaphor and personification in an exaggerated, absurd fashion, Lamb parodies two of the most prominent literary devices of gastronomic literature—the equation of food with women and the projection of the eater's desire onto the food itself. Lamb also mocks the sensuality of gastronomic writing by creating sensually repulsive passages, such as the following one in praise of roasted pigskin:

> Crackling as it is well called—the very teeth are invited to their share of the pleasure at . . . overcoming the coy, brittle resistance— with the adhesive oleaginous—Oh call it not fat—but an indefinable sweetness growing up to it—the tender blossoming of fat—fat cropped in the bud—taken in the shoot—in the first innocence— the cream and quintessence of the child-pig's yet pure food. . . . (135–136)

Here Lamb clearly parodies the sadism that runs throughout gastronomic literature and depicts the gourmand's appetite as gluttonous and revolting. His grotesque mix of metaphors underscores the cannibalistic side of eating.

Whereas authors such as Sturgeon and Lamb developed what might be known as mock gastronomic literature, the majority of English gastronomes practiced a more reverent approach toward gastronomy, sincerely working to develop the English palate as well as English digestion. Such sincere gastronomes figure dining as a fine art that nourishes a capacity to incorporate the world, to feel its pleasures, and to express the self and the self in relation to its surroundings. Like their French counterparts, English gastronomes were also concerned with gourmandise as a means of achieving social communion and generally considered women to be an impediment to reaching this goal.

First published in serial form in 1835 and later collected as *Aristology; or The Art of Dining*, Walker's gastronomic philosophy rests on the inherited belief that "The legitimate objects of dinner are to refresh the body, to please the palate, and to raise the social humour to the highest point" (212). Toward this end, he insists, like Grimod before him, that the diner must have what he wants when he wants it, cautioning that "an attention to this on the part of females, might often be preventative of sour looks and cross words, and their anti-conjugal consequences" (207). Expressing a distaste for women at the table typical of most gastronomes, Walker finds that

> Ladies are very apt to suppose that men enjoy themselves the most when they are not present. They are in a great measure right, but for a wrong reason. It is not that men prefer their own to a mixture of female society, but that females delight in a number of observances, and in forms[,] . . . and upon a certain display and undeviating order,

which conspire to destroy that enjoyment, which they seem to think they are debarred from. The fault is their own. (217)

Walker's disparaging attitude toward women was much in keeping with that of nineteenth-century gastronomes in general, who largely agreed that women lacked the innate capacity to become gourmands. Brillat-Savarin and Abraham Hayward stand out for their appreciation of women's contribution to the table. The former declares: "The leanings of the fair sex toward gourmandism are in a way instinctive, for it is basically favorable to their beauty" (156);[15] Hayward concludes that "women make far the best English cooks" (66).

Although Walker chose to adopt the misogynistic attitude practiced by most nineteenth-century gastronomes, he made a distinguished contribution in his outright appreciation of English cookery, which he argues is more "favourable to physical power" than that of the French. He concludes, nonetheless, that the English table might be improved were it to incorporate select French strengths, such as the ability to produce light, attractive dishes and a reverential attitude toward the vegetable. About the latter, he states:

> Every body of genuine taste is delighted with a display of vegetables of superior order; and if great attention was bestowed upon that part . . . dinners would be at once more wholesome and more satisfactory to the palate, and often less expensive. . . . There is something very refreshing in the mere look of fine vegetables, and the entrance of a well-dressed dish of meat, properly accompanied by them and all their adjuncts, would excite a disposition to enjoyment much greater than can the unmeaning and unconnected courses now placed before our eyes. This is a matter of study and combination, and a field for genius. (214–215)

Here Walker suggests that vegetables, properly prepared and presented, work to harmonize the dinner, leavening the heaviness of the meat, a lightness that, in turn, keeps the appetite in harmony with the body and its digestive functions. His approach toward vegetables concerns itself as much with health and economy as with taste, proportion, and pleasure.

Walker's emphasis on balance, health, and pleasure likewise led him to praise simplicity. Toward that end, he chastises over-ornamentation of the dining table, commenting that white dinnerware is "indicative of a proper feeling and a due attention in the right direction" (216). "Proper feeling" and "due attention" serve as integral components of Walker's gastronomic philosophy because they aid in achieving one of the primary goals of gastronomy—an aesthetic that nourishes pleasure and harmony within the individual, which, in turn, unites the entire dinner party. Walker writes:

---

15. Brillat-Savarin extends his thoughts on women gourmands to surmise that gourmandism in women "agrees with the delicacy of their organs, and acts [as] a compensation for certain pleasures which they must deny themselves, and certain ills to which nature seems to have condemned them" (155).

"For complete enjoyment a company ought to be One; sympathizing and drawing together, listening and talking in due proportions—no monopolist, nor any ciphers" (210). Here Walker echoes Brillat-Savarin who asserts that gastronomy "brings together from day to day differing kinds of people, melts them into a whole" (167).

Published nine years after Walker's gastronomic essays, Kirwan's *Host and Guest* provides an overview of gastronomic literature as a genre, lauding Grimod above all others and bemoaning the scarcity of commendable works in England. He makes an exception for Walker's writing, noting that within England "There is not a more amusing and racy volume than the 'Original' by Mr. Walker" (42). In regard to culinary literature, or cookbooks, Kirwan finds Maria Eliza Rundell's *Domestic Cookery* "perhaps the most popular and practical work of the kind that has ever appeared in England" (45). He is far less kind about William Kitchiner's *The Cook's Oracle* remarking that "it is written in a vain-glorious assuming style and filled with gasconading vulgarisms and obsolete pedantry. The attempts at wit are ludicrously heavy and unsuccessful" (41).[16]

After surveying gastronomic and culinary literature in France and in England, Kirwan compares the French and English tables in order

> to show the respective merits of French and English cookery. Substantial solidity and simplicity are the distinctive marks of the one; variety, delicacy, and harmonious combination is the character of the other. Both are excellent in their way, but a fusion of the two kitchens, rejecting what is coarse and barbarous in the English, and too gross, Gascon, and Provençal in the French, would be the perfection of good living. Though personally no admirer of French manners or French morals[,] . . . I am of opinion that there is much in the French kitchen which might be advantageously transplanted and successfully imitated in this country. (58–59)

Here Kirwan gives French gastronomy its due while maintaining staunch loyalty to England. In keeping with his fellow countrymen, Kirwan expresses an intense concern with health and digestion, noting that the simple national fare of England is "infinitely more nutritious, and to the English stomachs, at least, just as easy of digestion—perhaps, indeed, easier than the more refined and *recherché* fare of our livelier neighbours" (56). Kirwan suggests in this comparison that ease of digestion comes with familiarity, yet he still

---

16. Although concerned primarily with recipes, *The Cook's Oracle* has often been classified as gastronomic literature due to its introductory material, which owes a strong debt to Grimod. In another of his works, *Peptic Precepts*, Kitchiner claims that "the sagacious *Gourmand* is ever mindful of his motto—Masticate, Denticate, Chump, Grind, and Swallow" (*Gusto* 73). This statement encapsulates Kitchiner's simultaneous attunement to gastronomy and outright fixation with digestion, both of which have earned him impassioned detractors and defenders alike.

encourages the incorporation of "foreign" dishes into the English culinary repertoire, noting that "[v]ariety is as necessary to the stomach as change of scene, or change of study to the mind, and that variety should be placed in our day within the reach of as many as possible" (63).

Following the French founding fathers, Kirwan links the ingestion of novel dishes with the mind's expansion. Challenging the palate as a means of challenging the mind would, in fact, become a primary occupation of the nineteenth-century English gastronome, who urged diners to embrace innovation and change within their diet. Kirwan explains that such experimentation leads to knowledge, reflecting that

> Cookery is eminently an experimental and a practical art. Each day, while it adds to our experience, should also increase our knowledge. And now that intercommunication between distant nations has become facile and frequent; [sic] now that we may make an early breakfast in London and a late dinner in Paris, it cannot be permitted that cookery should remain stationary. (60)

By linking experimentation, experience, knowledge, and communication between distant nations, Kirwan adopts a cosmopolitan approach toward the table. He implies that, while the artistically inclined, technically knowledgeable cook can create an aesthetically meaningful dish that stimulates the mind's palate, it takes the enlightened, well-traveled gourmand to consume, digest, and communicate the nuanced meanings conveyed by a given dish as well as the cultural significance of national cookery styles. Kirwan understood that when an individual ingests a foreign nation's cookery, he likewise comprehends a facet of its culture.[17] Thus, while he finds English cookery easy to digest and healthy, he argues that the English palate and gut must become accustomed to unfamiliar flavors and cooking techniques in order to grow apace with the modern world.

More humorous than *Aristology* and *Host and Guest*, *A Book About the Table* by Jeaffreson details ancient dining rituals and menus, relates amusing anecdotes about famous epicures at table, and briefly surveys the world's most curious dishes. In short, he entertains his reader much as the gourmand entertains his host, showing a deep knowledge and skilled mastery of gastronomy and gastronomic literature. *A Book About the Table* likewise displays a tendency to elaborate on animal cruelty, a trait typical of the genre. For example, Jeaffreson clearly took linguistic pleasure in crafting the following list of methods by which the ancients tenderized meat:

---

17. Despite Kirwan's belief in the benefit of international exchange, he does not embrace all national cookery. For example, he lauds Turkish and Indian cookery, but dismisses German and Russian as having little to teach the British. His authoritative and opinionated tone on such matters is typical of gastronomic literature.

It was their custom to kill animals by slow and terrifying processes, in order that their flesh should be made tender by muscular agony and mental distress. The flesh of the hunted hare is said to be more tender than the flesh of a shot hare; and it is probable that the struggles of a creature slowly killed by torture soften its muscles. Anyhow, our forefathers were assured that flesh was tender in proportion to the amount of pain and terror employed in slaying it. Game struck by the terrifying falcon was more toothsome than game killed in a quicker and less alarming manner. . . . In like manner bulls were baited with dogs. . . . To bait an ox with dogs was to soften its flesh for the teeth of old men and children; but to bait the animal with bears was to make the meat so tender and soluble that it would melt in a babe's mouth. The apologist for the brutalizing amusements of our ancestors will see his advantage in this account of the origin and prime purpose of bull-baiting. To show that the barbarity had a commendable object is at least to palliate its worst features, and also to account for the social toleration of its exhibitions. (63–4)

Each time Jeaffreson describes the particular pain an animal feels while being prepared for slaughter, he counters it by describing the gustatory pleasures its tortured flesh provides the gourmand. The more pain the animal has experienced, the more 'tender,' 'toothsome,' 'soft,' and 'soluble' it becomes. According to this logic, sadism transforms the flesh of a living creature into an ideal dish for the gourmand—both palatable and easy to digest. Such juxtaposition of pleasure with pain characterizes much gastronomic literature heavily inspired by Grimod. Unlike Jeaffreson, however, Grimod felt no need to "palliate" the "worst features" of animal cruelty.

The final English work under consideration, *Kettner's Book of the Table*, written by Eneas Sweetland Dallas, does not follow the usual eclectic form of gastronomic writing. Rather, it follows an encyclopedic format, with discussions of select dishes and ingredients, chefs, authors of gastronomic literature, famous hosts, among other gastronomic miscellany arranged in alphabetical order. Each listed dish includes a recipe provided by the London restaurateur Auguste Kettner. Despite its encyclopedic form, the work has been included here for discussion because it so elegantly and clearly expresses one of the primary goals of gastronomic literature: to transform the essence of food and the aesthetic pleasure of its consumption into language. For Dallas, gustatory pleasure, good taste, and elegant, yet economical self-expression are inextricably bound together.

Dallas emphasizes that good taste should, like good cookery, be simplified. This motif, which runs throughout gastronomic literature, originates with the gastronome's drive to differentiate the gourmand from the glutton. As Carolyn Korsmeyer explains, from the time of Plato gluttony has been figured "as a clear enemy of philosophy, the love of wisdom. . . . [B]y implication taste is regarded as complicit in the dangers of appetite. It does, after all, provide much of the enjoyment of eating, and such enjoyment is a temptation to indulgence and gluttony" (15). To avoid the charge of gluttony, gastronomy sought to extract what it deemed frivolous and distracting from the dining table and the meal itself—to distill an aesthetically balanced table setting and menu. Elegance becomes aligned with restraint and proportion. Thus simplicity enables the gourmand to avoid gluttony, with its uncontrolled and uncivilized hunger.

In addition to aligning gastronomy with simplicity, gastronomes also sought to raise the valuation of taste and smell, which had long been categorized as the least valuable of the senses because of their involvement with physical appetite.[18] Toward that end, Dallas notes that, while hearing, sight, and touch work independently,

> taste is made for marriage, and smell is its better half. It loses all its delicacy when it cannot mate with a fine olfactory nerve. Though thus deficient, it is by common consent chosen as the type of all that is most refined in human enjoyment—the worship of the beautiful. This is a feather in the cook's cap. It is the business of his life to minister to the sense of taste—and taste is at once so fine and so potent that it is selected from all the senses to designate the standard of art and the power of detecting all that is loveliest in heaven and earth. (455–56)

For Dallas, taste's dependence on smell heightens its powers and enables it to serve as the model for "all that is most refined in human enjoyment." According to Dallas, just as its communion with smell enables taste to achieve a delicacy unobtainable on its own, so too the communion of diners at the table enables appetite, "a mean thing by itself alone," to rise

> out of itself, inspired with wit and imagination, with romance, and remembrance, with kindness of heart and all the tenderness, it may sometimes be folly, which link us to each other and make up the delight of life and the courtesies of society, that love turns to poetry, and hunger and thirst, as at a banquet of the gods, compel the feast of reason and the flow of soul. (178)

Here Dallas captures the power of gastronomy to transform the satisfaction of a physical need into nourishment for the soul. Like other gastronomes, Dallas underscores that the aesthetic pleasures of gastronomy give rise to communal well-being, which, in turn, nurtures poetic self-expression. In other words, gastronomy nourishes the poetic transformation of food into language.

---

18. In *Making Sense of Taste*, Korsmeyer argues that the debasement of taste and smell within the philosophy of aesthetics continues, with the exception of gastronomic philosophers, up through the end of the twentieth century. Like Dallas, she elegantly reconfigures the conventional hierarchy of the senses to raise taste and smell to an honored philosophical position. In doing so, she aligns herself with the gastronomic tradition. In fact, she draws on such key figures as Brillat-Savarin and M. F. K. Fisher to flesh out and sustain her argument.

The Rise of the American Gastronome

During the first half of the nineteenth century, English gastronomic literature crossed the Atlantic quite readily in book form. Popular works were imported directly from England and such best sellers were often reprinted by American publishers. Original American works of gastronomic literature did not begin to appear, however, until the late 1800s, and they appeared few and far between in comparison to those authored by the English. The rare gastronomic works of note include Theodore Child's *Delicate Feasting* (1890), Joseph Barber's *Crumbs From the Round Table* (1866), and George Ellwanger's *The Pleasures of the Table* (1902). The first of these, Child's *Delicate Feasting*, was not, in fact, even penned by an American; the author was an English art critic residing in Paris who contributed regularly to *Harper's*. *Delicate Feasting* has been included here as an American work, however, because it was specifically addressed to an American audience and was first published in the United States.

Not surprisingly given the author's nationality, *Delicate Feasting* shares the dry wit, elitism, attention to etiquette, and devotion to the aesthetics of taste typical of many English works. It opens with a letter to Child from his 'American friend' P. Z. Didsbury, whom one reviewer called a Dryasdust, indicating that Didsbury is a fictional character created by Child in order to frame his book.[19] In the letter, Didsbury tells his 'friend': "the usefulness of your book will consist largely in awakening a spirit of criticism and in calling attention to the roles of intellect and sentiment in the art of cooking" (viii). This letter differentiates *Delicate Feasting* from the cookbook, which Child notes flourishes in both the United States and England, yet is rarely "based on careful observation or on truly scientific and artistic principles." Didsbury concludes:

> Much, therefore, remains to be done, and I am sure that your dainty volume . . . will greatly help to increase in America a knowledge of the true principles of delicate feasting. If, after reading your pages . . . my countrymen do not become convinced . . . that delicate cookery develops the intelligence and the moral sensibility, the fault will not be yours. (ix–x)

Child works to raise cookery to an art form, noting in one of the book's opening maxims that the cook should approach food with "a sense of dignity and self respect and a certain emotion. . . . The cook who is a real artist and whose dishes are works of art, will experience over his saucepans emotion as poignant as that which Benvenuto Cellini felt when he was casting one of his immortal bronze statues" (3–4).

In addition to his focus on establishing cookery as an art with the power to draw forth aesthetic emotion, Child, like Grimod, outlines a code of

---

19. Jonas Dryasdust was a fictional character to whom Sir Walter Scott dedicated several of his novels, including *Ivanhoe*.

etiquette to safeguard the gourmand's pursuit of aesthetic pleasure. In particular, he proposes that the dining review might be extended from the restaurant to the private table. With such reviews in hand, Child suggests, he could avoid the "terror" that accompanies a dinner invitation from an unknown host. Faced with such an invitation, Child finds himself asking:

> What will befall me? . . . Having invited me to dine, do they know how to dine themselves? Will the temperature of their dining-room be neither too high nor too low? Will the lights be so arranged that my eyes will not be dazzled, and that restful bits of shadow will remain soothingly distributed about the room? Will the chairs be the outcome of reason, or merely of the furniture-maker's caprice? . . . Will the food be real food? (199)

To quell such anxiety, Child proposes "the formation of an International League for the protection of diners-out" against "the slovenly and inartistic ways that are rapidly becoming traditional" (202). The League would gather references that its members could consult before dining "in a strange house."

Such a disdainfully wry tone characterizes much of *Delicate Feasting*, particularly the sections concerned with fashioning a gourmand's code of etiquette. For example, Child derides one author's suggestion that dinner napkins might be ornamented with mottoes and inscriptions in order to stimulate a flagging discussion as "cruel and too ironical," stating: "If people's conversational powers are so limited that they require the motto of a table napkin to help them out, it were better to prohibit conversation at table altogether, and have some one read aloud, as was the custom in the old monasteries" (162). Child's elitist tone typifies the English-authored literature of gastronomy, particularly those works most focused on establishing a code of behavior for the gourmand.

Unlike their English counterparts, Joseph Barber and George Ellwanger convey an enthusiasm and sense of wonder that marks their work as distinctively American. In particular, Barber's *Crumbs From the Round Table* showcases a decidedly American sense of humor and freshness reminiscent of Mark Twain while simultaneously articulating an aesthetic approach toward the table. Barber also stands out in his welcoming approach toward women, remarking that

> It is a Bad reflection on the gallantry of antiquity, that up to the era of Charlemagne ladies were rarely invited to dinner or supper parties, and it should be mentioned, as a fact complimentary to the sex, that, from the period when they took their seats at the festive board, the tone of social life improved.

He likewise praises women as better cooks than men, noting that unfortunately "the *cuisiniers* of the masculine gender have eclipsed the lady artists in fame, although, if we take the latter *en masse,* the former can not hold a candle to them" (15).

Philosophically, Barber inherits the French understanding of gastronomy as an essential component of education, noting "that a refined taste in eating and drinking has generally been a characteristic of well-educated men in all countries. Indeed, the association between literature and good cooking dates back to the dawn of learning" (12). Like his predecessors, Barber asserts that education alone does not make a gourmand. Rather, he is fashioned from "generous instincts, cultivated tastes and talents, and perfect physical organization" (32). Barber implicitly links the refinement of American cookery with the development of the nation's literature, noting that "A poetic temperament refines the appetite, and a fine appetite, well served, tends to sustain and vivify a poetic temperament. Thought cannot soar on a lenten diet; luxuriant (or luxurious) imaginings were never yet born of Spartan fare" (73). Barber provides copious examples of the link between the practice of gourmandise and a poetic imagination, remarking that

> The bran-bread and non-carnivorous thinkers and writers, from Diogenes to Sylvester Graham, do not occupy a large space in history nor figure brilliantly on its pages. Shakespeare in his early youth hankered after the fat bucks in Sir Thomas Lucy's park, and in later life indulged in jolly dinners with rare Ben Jonson at the Mermaid. . . . Milton, notwithstanding his puritanism, is said to have fed his peerless muse with the choicest provender, and to have regarded a banquet missed as a paradise lost. . . . That "solid man" in philosophy, Lord Bacon, loved dainties almost as well as bribes, and one of his biographers asserts that he caught the pulmonary complaint of which he died while engaged in stuffing a capon with snow! (76–77)

Such lists of literary greats who were practiced gourmands abound in gastronomic literature. In fact, they provide key evidence with which authors link gourmandise and eloquent self-expression.

Like other authors of gastronomic literature, Barber critiques his nation's cookery in order to hasten its improvement, lauding certain skills well practiced in England and in France. For example, he urges Americans to imitate the English way with puddings, noting that his countrymen likely prefer pastry over puddings because the former "is more indigestible. If there be any thing an American likes to outrage, it is his digestion. He appears to entertain no respect whatever for his stomach or duodenum, imposing on them the most hopeless tasks and cruel penances" (36). Despite such tirades against American pastry, Barber finds much in his nation's cookery to recommend. In particular, he lavishes high praise on the American breakfast, noting that "'Juno, when she banquets,' has nothing equal to it. What is Olympian ambrosia to buckwheat cakes!" (16). He likewise lauds American broiled spring chicken as "a thing to thank heaven upon with epicurean unction. Done of an amber brown, anointed with fresh butter, and duly seasoned, it is a dish to take the reason prisoner" (16–17).

Although Barber adds little to the aesthetics of gastronomy, primarily ruminating on established ideas, both his style and his tone are notably refreshing. In particular, his sense of humor and infectious enthusiasm considerably elevate his work. Barber's commentary on fishing, for example, showcases *Crumbs from the Round Table* at its best:

> [T]he *brook trout* is the fish for me. It is the sliest, the cutest, the daintiest, the most beautiful, the purest, the most delicious of swimming creatures. Brook trouting is the very poetry of angling. It is an intellectual amusement, too, and requires as much caution, calculation, and prescience as a game of chess; as fine touches of art are necessary to perfect a picture or a statue. . . . Felix Grundy said he was born a veteran—I was born a fisherman. When I read, in Dr. Livingstone's book, of a region in Africa where there was no water, I leaped from my chair in an agony of commiseration, exclaiming, "Miserable aborigines! what do they do for fish?" If age or rheumatism should debar me from visiting the fish-frequented streams, I intend to have an aquarium constructed in my library, and angle in it from an easy-chair. I want to enjoy, as long as possible, the greatest pleasure this world can afford me, not knowing whether there are any fish in the next, or, if there be, whether it is permissible to catch them. (62)

Barber's comic energy and boyish wonder mark *Crumbs from the Round Table* as distinctively American, notably distinguishing it from the dry wit that typifies much of English gastronomic literature.

Despite the fact that it did not appear until 1902, George Ellwanger's *The Pleasures of the Table* clearly participates in and elegantly develops gastronomic literature as practiced in the nineteenth century, a tradition to which it categorically belongs. By distilling the essence of nineteenth-century gastronomic literature, *The Pleasures of the Table* likewise extends the tradition into the twentieth-century, a gesture that inspired the likes of James Beard.[20] From his opening epigraphs by Brillat-Savarin and Abraham Hayward, Ellwanger positions himself as a gastronome. In particular, he states outright that he does not wish to participate in "the practical art" of cookery—"the published works of the past decade alone being too numerous to digest." Rather, he declares that his work will be "more closely concerned with the history, literature, and aesthetics of the table than with its purely utilitarian side" (iii). He devotes several chapters to the history of cooking as well as "Old English Dishes" and expends high praise on Grimod's *Almanach*, finding the "great charm of the work consists in its magisterial tone, as well

---

20. In his introduction to M. F. K. Fisher's *The Art of Eating*, James Beard lauds *The Pleasures of the Table* as "a fascinating volume" and describes Fisher as an American gastronome in the tradition of Theodore Child and Ellwanger.

as in its unbounded enthusiasm, humour, and originality" (130). In the chapter devoted to Brillat-Savarin, Ellwanger notes that

> he is at once the corypheus of good cheer and its most refined expo-
> nent. Few subjects are as difficult to treat without grossness as those
> relating to the gratification of the appetite, the pleasures of eating and
> drinking, which he has handled with such felicitous skill. Accompany-
> ing him along his alluring ambages, whose aisles are naturally redolent
> of truffles and vol-au-vents . . . , all other arts appear secondary to that
> of gastronomy. (175–176)

Ellwanger's reverence for Grimod and Brillat-Savarin familiarized a select group of Americans with the core of the gastronomes' philosophies as well as with their contribution to the study of aesthetic pleasure. In a chapter on "Sundry Guides to Good Cheer," Ellwanger likewise lauds and sum-marizes the key contributions of more recent gastronomes. Fittingly, he ends the section with a passage from the author Elizabeth Robins Pennell, whose *Feasts of Autolycus* claims the honor of the being the first work of gastronomic literature penned by a woman in the English language.

In addition to an expertise regarding the history and literature of gas-tronomy as it developed in Europe and the United States, *The Pleasures of the Table* showcases Ellwanger's wit, finely-tuned aesthetic, elegant self-ex-pression, and cosmopolitan sensibility—traits that characterized the ideal nineteenth-century gastronome. Perhaps even more importantly for the devel-opment of American gastronomy, however, Ellwanger celebrates his nation's passion for the outdoors, the "luxuriant diversity" of its raw materials, and its ingenuity (251). Like Barber before him, Ellwanger becomes especially poetic and animated while roaming the countryside in pursuit of game; the chapter "Spoils of the Cover" stands out as the book's most enthusiastic and effusive, reminiscent—albeit in a decidedly different tone—of Barber's reverie on the brook trout. For example, Ellwanger reflects that "game to the sportsman embodies an aesthetic attribute unknown to the majority, the very associa-tions of sport in themselves conferring the keenest appreciation of the true instincts of gastronomy. The . . . field and the table become merged in ties of mutual affinity" (356). Ellwanger esteems, as Brillat-Savarin before him, the pleasures of hunting America's abundant fowl. Whereas Brillat-Savarin fondly recalls the pleasures of hunting wild turkey in Connecticut, Ellwanger prefers the ruffed grouse, which he find surpasses all other fowl. In a florid, mock-heroic style, Ellwanger pays the following homage to the grouse:

> He is preeminently the bird of the woodlands, supreme in his sturdi-
> ness and his strength. . . . See him as he springs from the tangle of
> the saplings, a shaft of mottled splendour where the sunlight strikes
> his sides; and the hoarse boom of the double-barrel fails to check his
> tumultuous flight. Behold him in the spring while he struts upon his

chosen log with extended tufts and expanded feathers, beating the air with his wings, and sounding his reverberating peal of defiance and love. Consider him amid the rigours of the frost, loyal to his native haunts. . . . Observe him once more when the deadly volley has stopped his career, and he falls upon the russet carpet, in glossy black ruff, and plumage in blended hues of olive, brown, black, and grey—the noblest game-bird that treads the forest aisles!

[N]one may surpass, if equal, him in his wild woodland flavour. His back is the very incarnation of poignancy, while no bird that flies can vie with the whiteness and plumpness of his breast. . . . (365)

Writing in a mock-heroic vein enables Ellwanger to successfully figure the prey as the hero of his gastronomic tale, who sacrifices his "noble" life to nourish the active gourmand's hunting and dining pleasures. Whether boyishly playful, as in Barber's case, or delivered in a mock-heroic vein, as in Ellwanger's, the American tales avoid the sadism that often accompanies the treatment of game in much gastronomic literature, belying a more reverent attitude toward the life taken for the sake of gourmandise.

Not content with celebrating his nation's natural bounty, Ellwanger likewise takes into account the "inventive genius" that has shaped the American palate (250). In particular, he works to raise the cocktail to a revered place at the dinner table, cautioning that it should only appear at carefully planned dinners and be limited to one per guest. If offered to guests and drunk immediately before sitting down to the meal, Ellwanger asserts, the cocktail

is undoubtedly a stimulus to appetite and provocative of good-fellowship. It pitches the company in a pleasant key at the onset, and imparts a zest and an *allégresse* to the first part of the repast that were otherwise lacking. . . . Impelled by its own geniality, the company will take abundant care of itself, and the stream of conversation and ripple of anecdote flow freely along, unimpeded by the boulders of formality or the aridity engendered by a dearth of joyous fluids. (196–197)

Given that the United States, by many accounts, was the first nation to fully embrace the cocktail as a social lubricant, developing mixology into a well-revered craft, it is entirely fitting that an American such as Ellwanger would demand the cocktail's induction into the realm of gastronomy. Not surprisingly, Prohibition did much to dampen the development of gastronomy in the early twentieth century. Nonetheless, with its repeal came a renewed interest, made all the more lively and widespread because of the much bemoaned thirteen-year absence, or furtive presence, of wine, beer, and hard alcohol at the dining table. As a result, the literature of American gastronomy grew exponentially during the 1930s, with 1937 seeing the publication of *Serve It Forth* by M. F. K. Fisher.

NINETEENTH-CENTURY DOMESTIC COOKBOOKS

From the early 1800s women's food writing in the United States, as in our culinary forebear England, was largely composed of domestic cookbooks. Numerous scholars have explored the nineteenth-century domestic cookbook from sociological, literary, and historical angles. However, a brief overview of the explicit goals of seven of the most popular and influential nineteenth-century domestic cookbooks in England and the United States illustrates the domestic ideology that pervaded women's food writing. Three of these works hail from England: Maria Eliza Rundell's *A New System of Domestic Cookery* (1805), Eliza Acton's *Modern Cookery for Private Families* (1845), and Isabella Beeton's *Book of Household Management* (1861). The remaining four hail from the United States: Mary Randolph's *Virginia Housewife* (1824), Lydia Maria Child's *The Frugal Housewife* (1829), Eliza Leslie's *Directions for Cookery* (1837), and Marion Harland's *Common Sense in the Household* (1871). Each author prefaces her work by articulating and reinforcing the increasingly popular alignment of women with an orderly, economically minded, practical, and other-oriented domesticity.

Taken as a whole, domestic cookbooks modeled and reproduced heteronormative domesticity, an ideological dynamic that defined a woman's role as being a wife and mother as well as upholder of the nation's morality. This domestic ideology had become deeply embedded within English and American culture by the late nineteenth century. Its roots, however, can be traced to the best-selling cookbooks of the early 1800s. Maria Eliza Rundell's *Domestic Cookery*, first published in England in 1806, flourished briefly in America where it was published in well over thirty editions from 1807 up to the Civil War (Bowler 11). From the outset of her book, Rundell links the economic success of the family to the housewife when she states: "Many families have owed their prosperity full as much to the conduct and propriety of female management, as to the knowledge and activity of the father" (29). Throughout the nineteenth century and up through World War II, the importance of the housewife's fiscal responsibility in household management would remain one of the common themes of the domestic cookbook. So too would the alignment of women with "conduct and propriety" and men with "knowledge and activity." In this configuration, Rundell explicitly articulates the ideology of separate spheres, which saturated English and American life throughout the nineteenth and early twentieth-centuries. At its core, this ideology designated the private sphere, or home, as women's place and the public sphere as the exclusive domain of men. It also figured the proper woman as pious, nurturing, and other-oriented, characteristics a mother modeled for and bequeathed to her daughters. Rundell herself wrote *Domestic Cookery* for her "own daughters, and for the arrangement of their table, so as to unite a good figure with proper economy" (25).

By and large, the most popular cookbooks in both England and America focused intently on aiding the housewife in running an orderly and economical household. Economy so saturated domestic ideology that it even permeated the style of the typical cookbook. *Domestic Cookery* begins with the claim that the author has "avoided all excessive luxury," a statement that aptly describes Rundell's writing, which borders on terse (25). Aside from the introductory material, Rundell as a personality effectively disappears from the text. Her personal recommendation that "[t]he flavour of broiled hare is particularly fine" proves one of the most ornate commentaries in the book. It precedes the following recipe for broiling and hashing hares, given in its entirety: "The legs or wings peppered and salted first, and when done, rubbed with cold butter. The other parts warmed with the gravy and a little stuffing" (123). While both the style and content of *Domestic Cookery* leave historian Esther Aresty marveling at the popularity of "this undistinguished little book with its stodgy, unappetizing recipes" (164), Rundell achieved a popularity in England not surpassed until 1861, when *Mrs Beeton's Book of Household Management* became a best seller on both sides of the Atlantic, thereby earning its place as "the most famous English cookery book ever published" (Beeton vii).

Between the original publication of Rundell's and Beeton's wildly popular works, however, appeared what many authorities consider to be the foremost English cookbook of the nineteenth century—Eliza Acton's *Modern Cookery for Private Families* (1845). Beeton's *Book of Household Management*, in fact, borrowed copiously from Acton without acknowledging the debt. Elizabeth David would label *Modern Cookery* as one of the two finest cookbooks written in the English language.[21] Unlike the terse style characteristic of Glasse and Rundell, Acton's *Modern Cookery* is gracefully written and conveys an elegant, yet economical style of cookery well in keeping with domestic ideology. For example, Acton begins her section on "Soups" by noting that the "art of preparing good, wholesome, palatable soup, *without great expense*, which is so well understood in France, and in other countries where they form part of the daily food of all classes of the people, has hitherto been very much neglected in England" (21). Here Acton signals her focus on health and economy, yet she adds the bonus of flavor, the discussion of which is often oddly absent in nineteenth-century domestic cookbooks. Acton likewise signals her comparatively cosmopolitan focus. In addition to incorporating French cooking techniques that

---

21. In an article for the *Daily Telegraph*, Elizabeth David noted that *Modern Cookery* "is indeed a very great and original cookery book. Apart from Sir Kenelm Digby's entrancing, posthumous *Closet Opened* of 1669, Eliza Acton's must be the finest in the English language, but after the author's death in 1859, the publisher apparently forgot about her book. Two years later, in 1861, young Mrs. Beeton was not so neglectful. She helped herself to a number of Miss Acton's recipes, publishing them without acknowledgement and in an emasculated form" (*Is There a Nutmeg in the House?* 216–217).

might benefit the English kitchen, *Modern Cookery* includes a final section of "Foreign and Jewish Cookery," that includes a small selection of recipes such as "Jewish Smoked Beef," "A Simple Syrian Pilaw," and "Risotto a la Milanaise."

Acton makes clear, however, that in lieu of "the elegant superfluities or luxurious novelties" with which she might have "more attractively . . . filled [her] pages," she has chosen "the most rational and healthful methods of preparing those simple and essential kinds of nourishment which form the staple of our common daily fare" (1). She iterates her strict alignment with domestic ideology, forcefully, yet elegantly, asserting that

> tables of the middle classes should all be well and skillfully prepared particularly as it is from these classes that the men principally emanate to whose indefatigable industry, high intelligence, and active genius, we are mainly indebted for our advancement in science, in art, in literature, and in general civilisation.
>
> When both the mind and body are exhausted by the toils of the day, heavy or unsuitable food, so far from recruiting their enfeebled powers, prostrates their energies more completely, and acts in every way injuriously upon the system. (1)

In keeping with domestic ideology, Acton suggests that it is the housewife's responsibility to feed the nation's men, who depend on wholesomely cooked meals to nourish their energy and intelligence, upon which the advancement of the nation depends. Though Acton herself would never marry, she promoted the other-oriented, self-effacing economy of the successful nineteenth-century domestic cookbook. In order to do so, she, by her own admission, largely omitted those recipes that might have "more attractively, though not more usefully, filled [her] pages."

Although Acton's *Modern Cookery* "was an immense and deserved success," it was soon to be overshadowed by Isabella Beeton's *Book of Household Management* (David 2000, 216). Beeton based her book on "the many thousands of recipes contributed by readers of the *Englishwoman's Domestic Journal*," a periodical published by her husband, Sam Beeton. Like Hannah Glasse before her, Beeton "borrowed largely and unashamedly" from other authors, including Eliza Acton and Alexis Soyer (Hess, *Art of Cookery* xv).[22]

Though the recipes themselves may not have been original, the way in which *Household Management* folded them into its structure certainly was. As Margaret Beetham concludes in her study of the work, "Beeton

---

22. Soyer was not above using the ideas of another author without attribution. Davidson writes, "To his discredit, [Soyer] represented himself as author of a major historical work, the *Pantropheon*, which had apparently been written by a French teacher, Adolphe Duhart-Fauvet, resident in London, who received money for it but not the credit he rightly expected" (279).

transformed the material she borrowed and she did this through its systematic presentation. . . . In organizing her material the way she did, Beeton demonstrated the task of management which she advocated" (21). Such systemic organization became central to the domestic cookbook and, in turn, the Victorian housewife, because, as Beetham surmises:

> Managing the domestic . . . meant keeping in place not only material objects (kitchen utensils, glasses, flowers for the table), not only meals appropriate to the time of year and the family's income, but also [the housewife's] body and the bodies of her household with their appropriate cultural meanings. . . . At the level of the social this meant the mistress was responsible for protecting the boundary between the world of the domestic circle and the public world. (28)

This drive to contain women's bodies entailed the suppression of women's physical hungers, a suppression that has been eloquently explored by numerous scholars of the Victorian era.[23]

Yoking an appetite for food with an appetite for sex, middle-class Victorians believed hunger to be naturally modest in women and robust in men. Equating spices, red meat, sweets, coffee, and rich food in general with sexual drive, Victorians gendered these foods male and perceived them as inappropriate for a woman to eat except in moderation. As a result, cravings for these "inflammatory foods" were thought to indicate "dangerous sexuality" in girls. Because appetite was linked so tightly with sexuality, "both mothers and daughters were concerned about its expression and control. It was incumbent upon the mother to train the appetite of the daughter so that it represented only the highest moral and aesthetic sensibilities" (Brumberg 166). Thus, within the Victorian era, a "portrait of the appropriately sexed woman . . . emerges as one who eats little and delicately. She is as sickened by meat as by sexual desire" (Michie 17). The drive to control female appetite became so strict, at times, that girls often suffered from chlorosis and anemia. Because social convention defined the proper woman as an "object of desire" but never as an agent of desire, a desiring woman was considered greedy, excessive, and a threat to the stability of "home and the community" (Levy 106). The lack of pleasure in nineteenth-century women's food writing attests to the imbrication of female desire with excess and greed. By figuring the housewife as an orderly, contained, and other-oriented individual,

---

23. Just a few such scholars whose work has been instrumental in detailing the nineteenth-century suppression of women's appetite and desire include Helena Michie (*The Flesh Made Word*), Susan Bordo (*Unbearable Weight*), Joan Jacobs Brumberg ("The Appetite as Voice"), Tamar Heller and Patricia Moran (*Scenes of the Apple*), Anna Krugovoy Silver (*Victorian Literature and the Anorexic Body*), and Anita Levy (*Other Women: The Writing of Class, Race, and Gender, 1832–1898*).

domestic cookbooks helped to define female propriety and to delineate the domestic bounds within which the proper woman was expected to perform.

Across the Atlantic, such ideology can be traced to the founding works of American cookery. In the preface to the first regional American cookbook, *The Virginia Housewife* (1824), Mary Randolph defines the housewife's role as follows:

> The prosperity and happiness of a family depend greatly on the order and regularity established in it. The husband, who can ask a friend to partake of his dinner in full confidence of finding his wife unruffled by the petty vexations attendant on the neglect of household duties . . . will feel pride and exultation in the possession of a companion, who gives to his home charms that gratify every wish of his soul. . . . The sons bred in such a family will be moral men, of steady habits; and the daughters, if the mother shall have performed the duties of a parent in the superintendence of their education, as faithfully as she has done those of a wife, will each be a treasure to her husband. (iv)

Here Randolph articulates the ideological function of the housewife: to "gratify every wish of [her husband's] soul"; to birth and rear sons who turn into "moral men"; and to raise daughters who "will each be a treasure to her husband." In other words, the declared goal of the cookbook is to help women achieve, maintain, and perpetuate a heteronormative family dynamic.

Published five years later, in 1829, Lydia Maria Child's *The Frugal Housewife*, "dedicated to those who are not ashamed of economy," includes classic American recipes such as baked beans and Indian pudding along with concoctions to sooth the sick and hungry such as "Dyspepsia Bread" and "Gruel." In addition to its focus on cookery and household management, *The Frugal Housewife* provides the following critique of female education:

> The difficulty is, education does not usually point the female heart to its only true resting-place. The dear English word 'home,' is not half so powerful a talisman as 'the world.' Instead of the salutary truth, that happiness is *in* duty, they are taught to consider the two things totally distinct; and that whoever seeks one, must sacrifice the other. (Child 101)

Here, Child collapses 'the world' into 'the home' and 'happiness' into 'duty,' implying that a woman's world should be the home and that her happiness will arise from performing household duties. Child's assertion that the happy female is one who performs her duties selflessly within the domestic realm falls firmly in line with the ideology of separate spheres. Cookbooks such as Child's promoted these ideals and clearly delineated the parameters within which the housewife was expected to perform by aligning women's other-oriented domesticity with the health of the family and, in turn, the nation. Child states outright that the mother who is drawn outside of the domestic sphere and travels into "the world" risks the ruin of her children who "are perhaps left with domestics, or strangers; their health and morals, to say the least, under very uncertain influence" (Child 106).

Even though Child's cookbook took part in a domestic ideology heavily concerned with promoting women's devotion to their household duties, as Barbara Haber succinctly points out, Child "remained childless her whole life, and lived a public life at a time when women were routinely relegated to the kitchen" (Haber 214). Child made a name for herself as a novelist dealing with such controversial topics as a white woman's marriage to a Native American before authoring *The Frugal Housewife* at the age of twenty-six. Despite Child's youth and the fact that she had no children, "the book projects an image of the author as a middle-aged housekeeper with a large brood of children" (214). Child was not the only cookbook author who led a public life while promoting a more domesticated plan for her readers. Beeton herself enjoyed a powerful position within the publishing world as an author, editor, and magazine columnist. When Mary Randolph's family began to suffer financially, she opened a boardinghouse, which became one of the most popular dining destinations for travelers to Richmond, Virginia.

Whereas Randolph wrote to help the "inexperienced housewife" become "a methodical cook" and Child catered to the "Frugal Housewife," Eliza Leslie wrote for a reader concerned with turning out tasty and elegant meals. This may explain why her *Directions for Cookery*, first published in 1837, surpassed even Randolph's and Child's best-selling works to become the most popular American cookbook of the nineteenth century (Arndt 239). *Directions for Cookery* charges the housewife to hone her palate. Leslie asserts that "no man (or women either) ought to be incapable of distinguishing bad eatables from good ones, yet, I have heard some few ladies boast of that incapacity. . . . Let no man marry such a woman. If indifferent to her own food, he will find her still more indifferent to his" (7). Leslie differs from her predecessors by emphasizing that a woman should develop her own palate, a gesture that urges women to recognize and obtain gustatory pleasures. By suggesting, however, that the goal of achieving such pleasures should be to obtain and keep a husband, Leslie's preface nonetheless reinforces an other-oriented domestic economy.

Like Eliza Acton, Leslie herself never married. That a single woman found it necessary to dedicate her book to the instruction of aspiring housewives and to direct male readers to avoid the lure of women with unpracticed palates draws attention to the social constraints against undomesticated female behavior. Like Randolph before her, Leslie ran a boarding house after falling on hard times, an occupation that scholar Jan Longone notes was "respectable enough to *do* perhaps, but obviously not respectable enough for Miss Leslie to mention in print" (ix). Rather, she must promote the art of cookery as a means by which the housewife can earn the adoration of her husband, despite the fact that Leslie parlayed her culinary acumen into writing in order to maintain her financial independence.

One of the frankest and most refreshing cookbook prefaces appears in Mary Virginia Hawes Terhune's *Common Sense in the Household* (1871). Like many of the most popular nineteenth-century domestic cookbook authors, Terhune was a novelist. In response to the didactic and formal tone of many popular cookbooks, Marion Harland, Terhune's pen name, begins *Common Sense in the Household* by appealing to the weary housewife, whose daily duties could fill her with despondency. To earn her reader's confidence and trust, she tells her "I wish it were in my power to bring you, the prospective owner of this volume, in person, as I do in spirit, to my side on this winter evening. . . . I should perhaps summon to our cozy conference a very weary companion" (13). Harland expresses sympathy for the reader who might often find herself "heart-weary with discouragement" and with a "despondent looking forward to the monotonous grinding of the household machine." Harland empathizes with the newlywed who says to herself "in bitterness of spirit, that it is a mistake of Christian civilization to educate girls into a love of science and literature, and then condemn them to the routine of a domestic drudge" (14). Harland's large dose of sympathy leads to one of the most bizarre moments in nineteenth-century domestic food writing, one in which she reflects on her own harrowing introduction to household management. As a bride, Harland recalls being given five popular cookbooks, all of which she pored over diligently

> seeking to shape a theory which should grow in accordance with the best authority. . . . My wrestling begat naught save pitiable confusion, hopeless distress, and a three-days' sick headache, during which season I am not sure that I did not darkly contemplate suicide as the only sure escape from the meshes that girt me. (18)

Luckily, Harland is saved by a knowledgeable friend who counsels her to disregard the cookbooks and tells her "ninety-nine out of a hundred" of them "are written by people who never kept house" (18). From that day forward, Harland began to fashion her own. Thus she passes on *Common Sense in the Household* to help save the weary, distraught, overwhelmed, and under-prepared housewife.

After having cajoled, nurtured, and gained the trust of her inexperienced reader, however, Harland firmly puts her foot down, dispensing advice and platitudes well in keeping with the domestic ideology of her counterparts. She takes a decidedly gentler tone, yet the message remains the same, as she asks her reader:

> would you mind if I were to whisper a word in your ear I don't care to have progressive people hear?—although progress is a grand thing when it takes the right direction. My dear, John and the children, and the humble home, make your sphere for the present, you say. Be sure you fill it—*full!* before you seek one wider and higher. There is no better receipt between these covers than that.

Harland acknowledges that her reader may wish for a life more fulfilling than housework. Yet she nonetheless provides her with a manual on how to become the ideal housewife. Although Harland serves as a matronly persona created by the real Terhune to nurture the self-confidence and competence of her readers, Terhune herself shared her narrator's belief that a woman's first duty was to manage the domestic realm efficiently, economically, and dependably. If, and only if, she had energy and time left over should she pursue interests outside the home. Terhune herself had ample energy to devote to such tasks, authoring well over forty books of fiction, short stories, domestic non-fiction, travel writing, and biography. She also became the first woman elected to the Virginia Historical Society. Married to a Presbyterian minister, Terhune "considered herself fortunate that [her husband's] parishioners tolerated her writing career" (Arndt 203). Like Beeton, Child, Randolph, and Leslie, Terhune had an "active, lucrative career during an era when women stayed home, but saw no contradiction in glorifying a purely domestic role for women" (204).

That female cookbook authors who were accomplished in the public realm—as abolitionists, editors, poets, and novelists—felt the need to pass as full-time housewives when writing about household management, attests to the conservative nature of the domestic cookbook, which developed alongside the notion that women bear full responsibility for feeding the family and for managing the domestic realm. By implication, the woman who ventured out of the home to work in the public realm was felt to put the family structure at risk. As a result, though domestic cookbook authors often led successful, rewarding lives outside the domestic realm, they nonetheless felt compelled to promote a heteronormative ideology founded on the housewife's domestication. In so doing, such professionally successful authors encouraged their readers to contain their physical, psychological, and intellectual selves within the private sphere.

FASHIONING A PUBLIC VOICE

Although Acton, Rundell, Beeton, Randolph, Child, Leslie, and Terhune wrote their advice during the nineteenth century, the constraints against woman's hunger to enter the public sphere remained firmly entrenched within U.S. and English culture well into the twentieth century; such constraints violently impacted the hungriest and most vociferous of women—the suffragists, many of whom, imprisoned for obstruction of traffic (in other words, picketing), chose the hunger strike as a means of refusing participation in a system that denied them public voice as well as legal control over their own bodies. The hunger strikers' message rang so loudly in the nations' ears that officials attempted to drown it out altogether through the literal act of force-feeding, a gesture that not only smothered the suffragette's cry for public recognition but also violated the body she was striking to gain control over, both legally and politically.

The violence of the government response derived in part from the fact that, as Linda Schlossberg notes, "woman's everyday eating practices were imagined to be directly linked to her reproductive capacities, and hence her ability to propagate the race" (92).[24] According to ideological conventions, women with properly domesticated appetites were considered the most fit to bear and raise a strong, moral nation. The proper woman must also place three healthy meals a day on the family table. Otherwise she risked the ruin of her family and, by extension, the nation. Much anti-suffrage propaganda eddied around this ideology, often depicting starving husbands and children abandoned by shrieking and unkempt pro-suffrage wives; one poster titled "Beware of Suffrage," shows a suffragist with a cord wrapped tautly around her neck and an enormous pair of shears slicing through her extended, serpent-like tongue.[25] As such images and force-feeding attest, the fear of women gaining public voice unleashed a violent backlash aimed at keeping women's power tightly contained within the domestic sphere.

Alongside and in response to such attempts to silence female power arose the domestic science movement, which established home economics departments in colleges and universities across the United States and Britain. Participants in the movement worked to raise the public's perception of women's work by transforming food preparation and other household duties into a science, which could be taught to the increasing numbers of women entering higher education. Like the suffragists, many of whom supported the rise of home economics, domestic scientists wanted to gain more power for women, albeit by raising the intellectual stature of housework. Although ultimately not as pervasive in Britain as in the United States, the domestic science movement first became institutionalized in 1874 and 1875, when cookery schools sprang up in London, Liverpool, Leeds, and Edinburgh (Bird 121). The United States quickly followed suit, founding the New York Cooking School in 1876 and the Boston Cooking School in 1879 (Schwartz 82). The latter was founded by Mary Lincoln, although its most famous principal turned out to be Fannie Farmer, whose version of *The Boston Cooking-School Cook Book* remains one

---

24. In addition to Schlossberg's essay "Consuming Images: Women, Hunger, and the Vote," the following scholarship analyzes the dynamics of force-feeding, which was prevalent in both the United States and England: Lisa Tickner's *The Spectacle of Women: Imagery of the Suffrage Campaign 1907–1914*; Rosemary Betterton's "'A Perfect Woman': The Political Body of Suffrage" found in *An Intimate Distance: Women, Artists and the Body*; Caroline J. Howlett's "Writing on the Body? Representation and Resistance in British Suffragette Accounts of Force Feeding" found in *Genders* 23.

25. In *The Spectacle of Women*, Lisa Tickner provides a thorough analysis of the anti-suffrage depictions of pro-suffrage women and vice versa. Her work likewise features numerous reproductions of the imagery used by both sides of the campaign, including "Beware of Suffragists," found on page 52.

of America's all-time bestselling cookbooks, which has remained in print since it was first published in 1896.

By the early 1880s, the domestic science movement had begun to play an influential role within the cookbook industry, especially within the United States. In keeping with domestic ideology, domestic science continued to yoke domestic cookery, morality, and the health of the nation. However, it simultaneously strove to professionalize household management by transforming it into a scientific practice. In order to aid in this transformation, "Books written by the movement's adherents discuss food substances as bodily fuels and employ sociological language to emphasize the importance of good nutrition for the health and future of the entire nation" (Humble 60). As Laura Shapiro points out in *Perfection Salad*, the enjoyment of food impeded the fundamental goal of the domestic science movement—the transformation of food preparation into an intellectual and moral pursuit. Through this pursuit, domestic scientists believed they might expunge the baser appetite for physical pleasure. As Shapiro observes,

> Of necessity, [domestic scientists] were proud of their lifeless plates. . . . Domestic scientists were inspired by the nutritive properties of food, by its ability to promote physical, social, and, they believed, moral growth. . . . They did understand very well that many people enjoyed eating; this presented still another challenge. Food was powerful, it could draw forth cravings and greedy desires which had to be met with a firm hand. (6)

In their drive to jettison desire from food preparation and to raise the value of women's work by codifying domestic management as an exact science, domestic scientists reinforced cultural strictures against female pleasure, extending them well into the twentieth century. Fueled by the nationalism that arose during the first and second world wars, the link between home cooking, morality, and national health remained a prominent feature of the cookbook well into the 1950s. One might argue that not until the 1960 publication of Peg Bracken's *I Hate to Cook Book*, which sold over three million copies worldwide, would the cult of female domesticity officially be ousted as the reigning influence over domestic cookbooks.[26]

THE RISE OF THE FEMALE GASTRONOME

Although domestic ideology continued to play a foundational role in women's food writing well into the 1950s, a more subversive form of self-expression took isolated form every now and again—one that unapologetically

---

26. In their study of English food writing, "Food Writing and Food Cultures: The Case of Elizabeth David and Jane Grigson," Steve Jones and Ben Taylor make a similar argument stating that "even by the early 1960s the gender divide between cookery writing and gastronomic literature remained institutionalized" (176).

encouraged women to embrace gustatory pleasures and to understand the palate's education as a key component to a woman's self-knowledge. In the introduction to *Breakfast, Dinner, and Tea: Viewed Classically, Poetically, and Practically* (1859), the American author Julia C. Andrews states that her project "aims to be rather more than a mere cook book; since it contains much curious and instructive matter in relation to the gastronomic habits and peculiarities of all times and all countries" (iii). Hardly a modest undertaking, and one directly inspired by the male-authored genre of gastronomic literature. Andrews achieves her goal of surpassing the "mere cook book" by elegantly interweaving recipes with gastronomic reflection, thereby bridging the gendered divide of food writing in order to "provide gratification for the palate" as well as for the "imagination and memory" (338). In addition to the usual array of English dishes, *Breakfast, Dinner, and Tea* includes a section culled from a variety of travelogues and cookbooks devoted to the "Table Habits and Peculiar Dishes of Various Nations," which range from "Food of the Artic Regions" to "Native Cooking and Eating in the Pacific Islands." Andrews also displays a deep familiarity with culinary and gastronomic literature, discussing the recipes and cooking styles of Soyer, Ude, and Carême; quoting from Brillat-Savarin's *Physiology of Taste* and Charles Lamb's "A Dissertation Upon Roast Pig"; and showcasing the poetry of the appetites, including works by Ben Jonson, Milton, Byron, Pope, Virgil, Shakespeare, and Robert Burns. She also addresses food's capacity to nourish language, a key motif in gastronomic literature. To wit, she reflects: "As poets, though often a half starved race, have yet like other mortals had their favorite dishes, it has sometimes happened, that warmed by the genial influences of a plentiful repast, they have made cookery and its accessories the theme for their muse" (iv). Here Andrews touches on one of the primary benefits of gastronomy as defined by the nineteenth-century gastronome, namely that the aesthetic pleasures of eating have the capacity to transform food into language.

Another nineteenth-century work largely influenced by gastronomy, Catherine Owen's *Culture and Cooking; or, Art in the Kitchen* (1881) steers clear of the domestic ideology espoused by the most popular cookbook authors of the century. Writing under the pen name of Owen, American author Alice Matthews Nitsch, like many of the nineteenth-century females examined here, wrote novels as well as cookbooks. Unlike most domestic cookbook authors, however, she aligns herself with a long line of gastronomes. To wit, the title page includes an epigraph taken from Brillat-Savarin's *Physiology of Taste* and the first chapter begins with a comparison of Owen's own goal in writing with that of Alexandre Dumas. Like Dumas, Owen wishes "to be read by all the world." Unlike Dumas who writes to aid "professors of the culinary art," however, Owen wishes to aid "those whose aspirations point to an enjoyment of the good things of life, but whose means of attaining them are limited" (1). To aid those with limited means approach cookery as an art form, Owen concerns herself as much with elegance as with simplicity and economy of table, quoting noted gastronomes to illustrate that the culinary arts do not align with luxury and excess. According to Owen:

Nine out of ten, when they call a man an epicure, mean it as a sort of reproach, a man who is averse to every-day food, one whom plain fare would fail to satisfy; but Grimod de la Reynière, . . . authority on all matters culinary of the last century, said, "A true epicure can dine well on one dish, provided it is excellent of its kind." (3)

After calling on Grimod, Owen draws on Thackeray to align economy with the gastronomic arts, noting that the famous author and gourmand defined the epicure as "one who never tires of brown bread and fresh butter" (3). Owen explains that she defines the art of "good living," which lies at the heart of the gastronomic and culinary arts, as neither "expensive living or high living." Rather, "good living" entails turning out an elegant table balanced by simplicity and economy. Such emphasis on simplicity as key to an elegant table is firmly in keeping with gastronomic literature; gastronomes repeatedly link gastronomy with simplicity and proportion in order to distance gourmandise from the excess of gluttony. Like the male gastronome, Owen also draws an explicit connection between cookery and poetic self-expression by linking famous French authors with the culinary arts. For example, she cites Charles Baudelaire as having surmised "'that an ideal cook must have a great deal of the poet's nature'" (7). Finally, like the nineteenth-century gastronome, Owen encourages her reader to maintain an open mind toward the unfamiliar dish or ingredient as well as toward the cookery of other nations.

In keeping with her gastronomic bent, Owen does not, as do most popular nineteenth-century cookbook authors, lure the reluctant housewife toward the kitchen with domestic ideology. Rather, she acknowledges that "there exists a feeling, not often expressed perhaps, but prevalent among young people, that for a lady to cook with her own hands is vulgar." To help her reader overcome such prejudice, she calls up Lord Bacon, Talleyrand, and Machiavelli as individuals with a passion for cookery. In so doing, Owen aligns domestic cookery with power and success. Thus, unlike the vast majority of domestic cookbooks that urge readers toward the kitchen by sounding the importance of woman's moral duty to the family and to the nation, *Culture and Cooking* entices its readers by depicting cookery as an art practiced by powerful men. This shift in focus from duty toward artistry marks *Culture and Cooking* as well ahead of its time; domestic cookbooks would not begin to seriously link cooking with artistry for another forty years. This shift toward artistry likewise signals the author's attunement to the change in status of hands-on cookery, which began to noticeably decline in the latter half of the nineteenth century. This change in status suggests, at least on some level, a growing resistance of young women to domestic ideology.

Such resistance to domestication courses throughout Elizabeth Robins Pennell's *Feasts of Autolycus* (1896), the most powerful nineteenth-century expression of aesthetic pleasure in women's food writing. In flagrant opposition to mainstream domestic ideology, which tried to eradicate women's greedy desires, Pennell began writing a column for London's *Pall Mall Gazette* that sought to aestheticize women's approach toward the table and to celebrate female appetite. Although she wrote the column for a London newspaper, Pennell was born in Philadelphia, where she became a notable author with the publication of *The Life of Mary Wollstonecraft* in 1884. That same year Pennell moved to London with her husband, the artist Joseph Pennell. She soon established herself as a journalist, art critic and a cosmopolitan new woman who traveled the continent by bicycle. For five years, she wrote a food column for the *Pall Mall Gazette*, selections of which appeared in book form in England as *Feasts of Autolycus* in 1896 and in the United States as *The Delights of Delicate Eating* in 1901.

Rather than working to separate gastronomy from gluttony as did the majority of gastronomes, Pennell followed the lead of Alexandre Dumas, who conflates the art of eating with gluttony. One of Pennell's favorite authors, Dumas is most known to lay audiences as author of *The Three Musketeers* and *The Count of Monte Cristo*. Within the gastronomic realm, however, he became legend for his posthumously published *Le Grand Dictionnaire de Cuisine* (1873). In it, he divides gluttony into three categories.[27] The first, which he urges should be avoided, is epitomized by the Roman god Saturn's cannibalistic drive to devour his own children. The second, which Dumas lauds without reproach, entails the gluttony of "delicate souls" which is "exemplified by the host who gathers together a few friends . . . and does his utmost to distract their minds and cater to their tastes. The finest modern examples of this type of gluttony are men like Grimod de la Reynière and Brillat-Savarin" (8). The third type of glutton, whom Dumas "can only deplore," consists of "those unfortunates who" refuse to eat and thereby suffer from an "insatiable hunger . . . ; they are martyrs" (9).

From the outset of her book, Pennell decries the fact that women are more well-practiced in the gluttony of martyrs than they are in the gluttony of "delicate souls," noting that

> where the fanatic had fasted that his soul might prove comelier in the sight of God, silly matrons and maidens starved, or pretended to starve, themselves that their bodies might seem fairer in the eyes of man. And dire, indeed, has been their punishment. . . . [G]radually,

---

27. Although enormously revered by late nineteenth- and early twentieth-century gastronomes, Dumas' *Le Grand Dictionnaire de Cuisine* is respected more today for the literary flourish of its anecdotes rather than its accuracy or originality. *The Oxford Companion to Food* puts it most bluntly: "The book, which contains about 750,000 words, is poorly organized and heavily weighted down with recipes from other sources and quotations, not always acknowledged, from other writers such as Brillat-Savarin. The information which it offers is frequently inaccurate . . ." (259–260). Despite its flaws, Pennell found the work captivating, claiming that "[t]he anchorite in the desert could not dip into it without hailing the first camel, abandoning his dates and dry bread, and making straight for the nearest town in search of the master's dishes" (quoted in Colman 1).

so it is asserted, the delicacy of women's palate was destroyed; food to her perverted stomach was but a mere necessity to stay the pangs of hunger. (10)

Pennell charges herself with the task of educating women to contemplate and to seek "the joys of eating." In order to accomplish this goal, Pennell needed to address gastronomy's hostility toward women. She also needed to confront social constraints against women's pleasure, especially given that her own position as a woman who wrote about the pleasures of eating, as opposed to domestic cookery, meant that she would be culturally marked as greedy from the outset. Rather than choosing to defend herself from such a freighted label, however, Pennell turns social convention on its head by giddily celebrating her own gluttony and acknowledging that "the great interest of the following papers lies in the fact that they are written by a woman—a greedy woman" (8). By drawing attention to the fact that a woman who ate or cooked with an aim toward sensual pleasures—either erotic or aesthetic—was defined as greedy and by celebrating her own gluttony, Pennell takes control over the charge that critics might level against her, thereby deflating any attack on her appetite.

Like Dumas, Pennell defines a middle road for gluttony, one untainted by the excessive hunger that characterizes Saturn's cannibalistic appetite or the self-devouring hunger of the ascetic. To wit, Pennell explains "Gluttony is a vice only when it leads to stupid, inartistic excess" (16). Pennell's drive to dissociate gluttony from excess is inseparable from her drive to elevate female hunger to the realm of gastronomy. She works toward these goals by articulating an educated, aesthetically nuanced female appetite, one that iterates, extends, and challenges the philosophical foundations of gastronomic literature by giving voice to the female gourmand. Toward this end, she attempts to transform the perception of female pleasure from one of condemnation into an unapologetic embrace—if not within culture at large, at least within the realm of her essays.

To establish her credentials as a female gourmand and to support her aesthetic philosophy, Pennell draws on the founding French fathers of gastronomic literature. As Grimod did before her, she asserts that the gourmand is an artist and as such "needs no code to guide him. He knows instinctively what is right and what is wrong, and doubts can never assail him" (74). She likewise quotes extensively from Brillat-Savarin to support her claim that women make natural gourmands, noting in her own words that "for the gourmande, or glutton, duty and amusement go hand in hand. Her dainty devices and harmonies appeal to her imagination and fancy; they play gently with her emotions; they develop to the utmost her pretty sensuousness. Mind and body alike are satisfied" (12). Pennell reconfigures women's duty to include the pursuit of sensual pleasures and challenges her female readers to practice gastronomy because "love of good eating is an incentive to thought, a stimulus to the imagination" and develops genius (135–136).

By lauding women's gustatory pleasures and the creativity that these pleasures inspire, Pennell, in the words of scholar Helena Michie, "humorously and categorically explodes the central myths of Victorian femininity" (17). Recently scholars have also pointed out that Pennell's unabashed declaration of female appetite exceeds the bounds of the domestic cookbook and aligns her with the aesthetic movement.[28] In her essay "The Importance of Being Greedy," Talia Schaffer describes Pennell's aesthetic project as follows:

> Pennell aimed to reconfigure meals as high art, turning eating into an act of intellectual appreciation. She wanted to contest the prevailing assumption that an interest in food denoted a debased bodily appetite. At the same time, however, Pennell hoped to reclaim women's appetite as a natural and valued bodily response. (105)

Schaffer places Pennell among the female aesthetes who wrote "light, comic, apolitical" literature as a "deliberately self-protective strategy; their obvious self-parody and oblique and artificial descriptions deflected critical scrutiny" (106). Pennell's choice of style was natural given that she and her husband hosted a weekly salon that included such renowned aesthetes as Oscar Wilde, Violet Hunt, Aubrey Beardsley, and Max Beerbohm.

Schaffer compares Pennell's work to such classic Victorian cookbooks as Isabella Beeton's *Book of Household Management*, remarking that "Pennell worked out a style which compromised between the cookbook and the [aesthetic] critique, teasing the reader with partial recipes withdrawn at the last moment in favour of artistic effusions about food" (110). As Schaffer argues, when read as an aesthetically oriented cookbook, *Feasts of Autolycus* appears to compromise between two genres. This study argues, however, that when read as gastronomic literature, the collected essays showcase Pennell as a woman who altogether refused to participate in the more domesticated cookbook genre and as a woman who wrote about the art of eating, a project previously reserved for men. Pennell's work as an art critic made her particularly well suited to write gastronomic literature, a genre concerned with defining public taste.

In addition to enjoying a deep familiarity with Grimod, Brillat-Savarin, and Dumas, responding to and critiquing each of them in her collected essays, Pennell was an avid collector of culinary and gastronomic literature, owning, among 1,000 volumes, Dumas' *Le Grand Dictionnaire de Cuisine* and an original edition of Grimod's *Manuel des Amphitryon*. In the introduction to her collected essays, Pennell announces her choice to participate in the aesthetic discourse of gastronomic literature rather than in recipe writing:

---

28. In particular, Talia Schaffer and, most recently, Jamie Horrocks have situated Pennell's work against the Victorian domestic cookbook.

The collection, evidently, does not pretend to be a "Cook's Manual," or a "Housewife's Companion": already the diligent, in numbers, have catalogued *recipes*, with more or less exactness. It is rather a guide to the Beauty, the Poetry, that exists in the perfect dish, even as in the masterpiece of a Titian or a Swinburne. Surely hope need not be abandoned when there is found one woman who can eat, with understanding, the Feasts of Autolycus. (8)

By defining herself as a woman who can dine knowledgeably on the Feasts of Autolycus, Pennell claims the rewards of gastronomy. Like the guests of Autolycus who dined with Socrates in Xenophon's *Symposium*, Pennell has imbibed the words of her fellow philosophers. Having done so, she stands prepared to contribute to the discourse on gastronomy.

Like other authors of gastronomic literature, Pennell lauds the cook, the gourmand, and the dinner host as artists. She also equates writing with gastronomy, remarking that "To the artist in words, superfluous ornament is the unpardonable sin. And so with the lovers of Gasterea, the tenth and fairest of the Muses. Better by far Omar Khayyam's jug of wine and loaf of bread if both be good, than all the ill-regulated banquets of a Lucullus" (44–45).[29] As an "artist in words," Pennell transforms sensual pleasures into language, using lush, evocative prose to paint a verbal picture. For example, she describes the market in Marseille:

The air is hot, perhaps, but soft and dry, and the breeze blows fresh from over the Mediterranean. . . . In sunlight and in shadow are piled high the sea's sweetest, choicest fruits; mussels in their somber purple shells; lobsters, rich and brown; fish, scarlet and gold and green. Lemons, freshly plucked from near gardens, are scattered among the fragrant pile, and here and there trail long sprays of salt, pungent seaweed. (98–99)

The visual emphasis in the passage showcases Pennell's training as an art critic. Yet the passage also evokes the texture and temperature of the air along with the penetrating odor of the seaweed. Like *Feasts of Autolycus* as a whole, however, this passage avoids describing the sensual pleasures evoked during the actual act of eating. This passage stands out in the collection, nonetheless, for its straightforward tone. The collected essays are

---

29. Again, Pennell references Brillat-Savarin who proclaims "Gasterea is the tenth muse: she presides over all the pleasures of taste. She could claim to rule the world itself, which is nothing without the life in it, and that life in turn dependent upon what it eats. She is happiest in places where the grapevine grows, where the truffle waxes and wild game and fruits may flourish. When she condescends to appear, it is as a young girl: around her waist she winds fire colored ribands; her hair is black and her eyes are like blue sky, and her limbs are full of grace; beautiful as Venus, she is also everything that is pure loveliness" (148).

more typically characterized by self-deflection, self-parody, and playfully nuanced critiques of gastronomic literature.

Schaffer surmises that the "outrageously flamboyant style" adopted by Pennell is "a deliberate performance of self-abandonment that both participated in, and parodied, aestheticism," while simultaneously working to reclaim women's appetite (110). This project extends Schaffer's argument to add that *Feasts of Autolycus* not only participates in the aesthetic movement, but also clearly engages in the self-parodic vein of gastronomic literature. In fact, the tone of Pennell's work shares much in common with the mock gastronomic literature of Launcelot Sturgeon and Charles Lamb. Thus, just as her "outrageous, flamboyant style" participated in and parodied aestheticism, enabling her to level "an indictment of cultural assumptions about women that aestheticism was very much responsible for perpetuating," so too it mocks gastronomic literature while simultaneously participating in it (Schaffer 110; Horrocks 4).[30] Self-parody enables Pennell to concurrently mock and embrace the cultural alignment of women's desire with greed, thereby celebrating the appetite typically denigrated in women. In doing so, she inserts herself and women's appetite into a traditionally misogynistic genre.

Pennell finds much to emulate in Grimod and Brillat-Savarin, but she doesn't shy from taking them to task. She mocks Brillat-Savarin's effusive description of a tuna omelet by quoting him directly and then tacking her own commentary (in italics below) onto his words. Pennell embeds Brillat-Savarin's quote into her own essay as follows: "to quote again so eminent an authority, let the omelette 'be washed down with some good old wine, and you will see wonders,' *undreamed of by haschish or opium eater*" (168; italics added). Here Pennell gently mocks Brillat-Savarin by extending his effusive quote to a humorous extreme. As in this passage, *Feasts* frequently parodies the hyperbolic tenor of gastronomic literature. In one case, Pennell takes up the cause of the mushroom, which she urges her readers to fully appreciate: "To say that you do not like [mushrooms] is confession of your own philistinism. Learn to like them; *will* to like them, or else your sojourn on this earth will be a wretched waste. You will have lived your life in vain if, at its close, you have missed one of its finest emotions" (154). The amplified emotionality of this passage not only draws attention to the hyperbolic nature of gastronomic literature, but also underscores that, like the aesthetic movement, gastronomy is driven and sustained by aesthetic emotion.

Pennell likewise gently mocks the exaggerated self-importance and authoritarian nature of the gastronome as epitomized by Grimod, who

---

30. Schaffer argues that Pennell "was not the first to apply aesthetic criteria to cookery," but drew inspiration from Elim D'Avigdor, whose *Dinners and Dishes* (1885) "pioneers an aesthetic reformation of cuisine by emphasizing the need for connoisseurship in both cooking and consuming food" (109). As this study demonstrates, neither D'Avigdor nor Pennell pioneered such an aesthetic reformation. Rather, each author participates in the well-established genre of gastronomic literature.

becomes an easy target not only because of his characteristic egotism but also because the gastronomic content and linguistic play of his writing directly inspired Pennell's own. In her essay "The Triumphant Tomato," Pennell makes a tongue-in-cheek nod to Grimod whom she finds a fitting namesake for a stuffed tomato: "Prepare . . . sausage meat, garlic, parsley, tarragon, and chives, and the tomatoes so stuffed you may without pendantry call *à la Grimod de la Reynière*" (175). In this passage, Pennell employs one of Grimod's favorite forms of word play—the *double entendre*. On one level she implies that Grimod, like the tomato, is stuffed full of himself. On another level, she reverses the equation of women with food, to serve Grimod up in the manner of a tomato.

In addition to such *double entendres*, which Grimod himself institutionalized within gastronomic literature, Pennell employs another common conceit of the male-authored genre—namely, the equation of desirable women with delectable dishes. Within these comparisons, Pennell occasionally embeds social commentary, as she does in the following description of how to bind a partridge: "Truss your birds in seemly fashion, when, as if in birdlike emulation of Hedda Gabler, they cry for vine leaves on their breast" (119). Her comparison of Henrik Ibsen's volatile female protagonist who longs for freedom with a pheasant being trimmed for dinner implies that women have been trussed by society just as they have been within gastronomic literature.[31] Pennell employs another Ibsen character to make this point even more explicitly. In the following passage, she compares a fish with Nora, the protagonist of Ibsen's *A Doll's House,* which levels a scathing critique of Victorian domesticity: "Not one yearns to such infinite purpose as the sole; not one is so snubbed and enslaved. A very Nora among fish, how often must it long to escape and to live its own life—or, to be more accurate, to die its own death!" (90). In her comparisons of Hedda Gabler to a partridge and of Nora to a sole, Pennell mocks the equation of women with food while simultaneously replacing the sort of women who appear within gastronomic literature. Alongside the ubiquitous, nameless virgin, Pennell inserts female protagonists who draw attention to the suppressed intellectual and emotional needs of women.

In addition to Nora and Hedda Gabler, characters who challenge the domestication of women, Pennell showcases the allure of a powerful woman. To wit, the following passsage on salad:

Make it of tomatoes, scarlet and stirring, like some strange tropical blossoms decking the shrine of the sun. . . . It is a salad that vies with

31. In "'Bribery with sherry' and 'the influence of weak tea': Women Critics as Arbiters of Taste in the late-Victorian and Edwardian Press," Meaghan Clarke addresses the progressive role that Pennell played as a female art critic, pointing out that "it was not possible for women critics to adhere to the perceived etiquette of demure or absent looks, rather they were *employed* to look" (141). To extend this notion further, I would argue that, in *Feasts of Autolycus,* what on first glance appears "demure" often turns out "to look" critically at women's roles in society.

Cleopatra in its defiance to custom. Love for it grows stronger with experience. The oftener it is enjoyed the greater the desire to enjoy it again. (31)

Here Pennell reverses the equation of delectable food with virginal women to prize the defiant, sexually experienced Cleopatra. Such moments that prize the experienced woman, however, are rare in Pennell's writing. Her writing does, though, repeatedly value what Pennell describes as "exotic," "strange," "elusive," "mysterious," "bizarre," and "piquant" flavors. Each of these adjectives apply equally well to Pennell's own writing and capture its ambiguity and refusal to be trussed down by interpretation. Vacillating from straightforward iteration to mockery, from social critique to self-parody, and from veiled allusion to flamboyant performativity, *Feasts of Autolycus* defies categorization. It also, in the end, defies commitment.

Inarguably, Pennell's collected essays are nothing short of extraordinary in their embrace of the female appetite for intellectual and physical pleasures. As Schaffer points out, however, "Pennell's prose is shaped by the bodily shame associated with food, an unbecoming gluttony that she must either reclaim as virtue, or sublimate into art" (123). She ultimately falls short in her drive to aestheticize the appetite of the female gastronome, in large part, because her prose vacillates so wildly that, at times, it careens out of control. Thus a celebration of female appetite can morph into a devaluation of women, a move that iterates, rather than challenges, the misogynistic tendencies of gastronomic literature. Such morphing occurs, in part, because Pennell relies on the same figurative devices used by the male authors that she critiques in order to articulate the pleasures of gastronomy. These figurations not only include the comparison of women to food, but also the notion that food, like women, should be exquisitely prepared for male consumption and male pleasure. Thus, while Pennell successfully inserts strong female characters into gastronomic literature, these women still figure in relation to delectable dishes aesthetically composed for male consumption.

As a result, Pennell encounters difficulty imaging female desire in a way that does not simultaneously constrain the very appetite that she works to express. For example, in the following passage Pennell both parodies and reinforces the equation of desirable food with female virginity:

[T]he tiny, round radish, pulled in the early hours of the mornings still in its first virginal purity, tender, sweet, yet peppery, with all the piquancy of the young girl not quite a child, not yet a woman. . . . Do not spoil it by adding other *hors d'oeuvres*; nothing must be allowed to destroy its fragrance and its savour. (19)

On one level, this image parodies the fixation with female virginity shared by the gastronome and society at large. It does so, however, in a manner that iterates rather than alters the devaluation of learned women typical of gastronomic literature. In Pennell's configuration, the radish tastes best when gathered in the morning; then it remains unspoiled, like the virgin, who is pure, "tender, sweet, yet peppery." By equating the rosy radish to a "young girl not quite a child, not yet a woman," Pennell suggests that the most desirable female, like the most delectable radish, is the "piquant" yet "pure" virgin. Such comparisons appear throughout Pennell's book, effectively showcasing virginity in a way that repeats the cultural constraints on female sensual pleasure and erotic sophistication that she sets out to combat. She inserts Cleopatra in one passage, yet showcases—albeit parodically—the nameless virgin in another.

In addition to adopting gastronomic literature's tendency to equate food with women, Pennell also inherited the genre's silence on female desire. As a result, rather than articulating her desire by writing about her own appetite for and sensual response to food, Pennell often displaces her desire onto the food itself, a common move within gastronomic literature. In her playful mockery and iteration of such displacement, however, Pennell avoids honing a language with which to capture and convey her own appetite. For example, in the chapter "Stirring Savoury," ingredients clamor to be transformed into delectable dishes: "ham and tongue pray eagerly to be grated and transformed into bewildering *croûtes*. The ever-willing mushroom refuses to be outsped in the blessed contest, but murmurs audibly, '*Au gratin* I am adorable;' while the egg whispers, 'stuff me, and the roses and raptures are yours!'" (221). While such highly erotic discourse parodies the sexualized prose of gastronomy as well as of the aesthetic movement, it also elides Pennell's appetite for the food itself. Thus, although Pennell claims, by way of Brillat-Savarin, that a woman "is bewitchingly lovely in the very act of eating," she avoids depicting herself in this 'very act' (14). In the end, strive as she might to articulate the nuances of her own gustatory pleasures, she cannot quite find the voice to do so. She does, however, begin the work needed to inspire other female writers to successfully figure women who are at home in the world, powerful, and desirous in the act of eating.

2   Forging a Space for Female Desire
M. F. K. Fisher on the Art of Eating

Mary Frances Kennedy Fisher published her first book, *Serve It Forth* (1937), at the age of twenty-nine. Three more books followed in quick succession: *Consider the Oyster* (1941), *How to Cook a Wolf* (1942), and *The Gastronomical Me* (1943). These four books, along with *An Alphabet for Gourmets* (1949), were collected in *The Art of Eating* in 1954, a work that stands alongside *Here Let Us Feast* (1946), *With Bold Knife and Fork* (1969), and *Among Friends* (1971) in securing Fisher's reputation as one of America's most eloquent gastronomes. Through her memoirs and essays, Fisher articulates a gastronomic philosophy developed from the belief that how we gather, prepare, and eat food is inextricably linked to the quality of our lives. The most celebratory scenes in Fisher's writing showcase the wisdom and pleasure gained from putting this belief into practice and articulate an aesthetics of female desire grounded in gastronomic pleasure. They also foreground eating as a powerful source of creativity, communion, and erotic pleasure.

With her first book, *Serve It Forth*, Fisher established herself as a well-educated gastronome, a goal she clearly adopted from the male-authored genre of gastronomic literature. She ventures further than the traditional gastronome, however, in her investigation of the bond between psychological and physical hungers and in her articulation of the psychological nuances of 'hunger satisfied' and 'hunger left unfed.' In so doing, Fisher practices a form of literary gastronomy that pushes women's food writing into a subtly nuanced and psychologically rich territory never before explored. Fisher depicts eating as an act of self-construction and as a celebration of the self in communion with others. She does so, in part, by articulating those moments when the boundaries between self and other are dissolved during the act of eating. She also explores the transformative potential of such moments, their capacity to reconfigure our perception of the self and of the self in relation to others.

In order to embrace the aesthetic pleasures of gastronomy, Fisher departed from the women's food writing tradition to take Brillat-Savarin as her mentor. Nevertheless, she still recognized the domestic tradition's influence on her as a female writer. The domestic tradition not only established the boundaries that her own writing would reconfigure but also provided a vision of unfulfilled female desire that she strove to sate within her own life's writing. Fisher also credited the asceticism of her late-Victorian maternal grandmother with her own passion for gastronomy, reflecting that "if Grandmother had not been the small stout autocrat, forbidding the use of alcohol, spices, fats, tobacco, and the five senses in our household, I might never have discovered that I myself could detail their uses to my own delight" (*To Begin Again* 58–59). As Fisher acknowledges, her development as a writer owed as much to the domestic food writing tradition and to the late-Victorian asceticism of her grandmother as it did to the gastronomic tradition; Fisher's rebellion against the domestic constraints that held women's appetite in check led her to claim the gastronomic pleasures available to men, thereby forging a space for female desire within the women's food writing tradition.

AMERICAN DOMESTIC FOOD WRITING BETWEEN THE WARS

Although gastronomy would not begin to play a lasting, definitive role within women's domestic cookbooks until the second half of the twentieth century, a pleasure-oriented streak developed within women's food writing during the 1930s, sparked in part by the end of the First World War. It came to fruition within a range of books that would herald the arrival of M. F. K. Fisher's *Serve It Forth* (1937), a work in which Fisher defines herself as a gastronome and pays tribute to her favorite food writers. Many of the pleasure-oriented authors of the 1930s worked to present cookery as a creative outlet while simultaneously holding onto the more traditional view of cookery as a duty. *Mrs. William Vaughn Moody's Cook-Book* (1931), which earns repeated mention in Fisher's own writing, illustrates the overlap of the practical, economical, and other-oriented approach toward cookery epitomized by the domestic science movement with an aesthetically driven approach toward cookery. In fact, Moody conflates these two approaches, noting that "[f]ood must meet the need of the body to be nourished, fortified, replenished, and protected. It must meet the need of the spirit to be charmed and comforted. . . . The first of these requirements may be regarded as the science, and the second as the art of food" (4).

As scholar Jessamyn Neuhaus explains in her study of cookery instruction in the United States *Manly Meals and Mom's Home Cooking*, during the 1920s and 1930s cookbook authors increasingly emphasized cooking as a creative outlet, in part, due to the disappearance of servants from the middle-class home. Whereas nineteenth-century authors such as Eliza Leslie assumed that her readers employed a cook, Moody had to assume a readership that turned out three meals a day without the aid of a servant. Working to convince middle-class housewives that a duty formerly assigned to domestic workers—cooking three meals a day, 365 days a year—was a fulfilling task,

> cookbooks in the 1920s and 1930s aimed to give cooking an image overhaul and to reinvent it as an amusing and delightful occupation; [*sic*] an occupation suitable to the artistic, creative sensibilities of white

middle-class ladies and not a laborious task best relegated to the working classes. (Neuhaus 55–56)

Toward this end, Moody clearly takes Americans to task for their dismissive attitude toward food and encourages her readers to understand cookery as an art, noting that

> Contempt for or indifference to the culinary art appears to be largely confined to America. It is surprising that a people as progressive as Americans should have been slow in awakening to the subtleties of this art. On the contrary, there has been from the first a Puritanic rejection of it as not deserving thought and love.
> ... Quick as the American woman often is in detecting the false from the true, in literature, music, and art, she is often hopelessly deficient in discriminating between the pure and the impure, the elegant and the inelegant, in the important matter of food. (6)

On one hand, Moody's sentiment holds much in keeping with gastronomic literature and portends the budding gourmet trend that would gain discernible momentum in the 1940s, the founding decade of *Gourmet* magazine. On the other hand, authors of the 1920s and 1930s also held onto the foundational ideology of the domestic cookbook—namely, that cooking was a woman's duty, one upon which the family structure, and even a stable society, depended. Although challenged by select authors in the interwar years, this ideology would monopolize cookery instruction once again during World War II, a monopoly it continued to hold into the 1960s.

During the interwar years, however, *Moody's Cook-Book* was typical in its simultaneous depiction of cookery as duty and as creative outlet. Less typical, however, were a select group of authors who rebelled wholeheartedly against the clinical precision, sternness, and economy of the domestic science movement to address cookery exclusively as an art form. One remarkable example of this rebellion took form as *Recipes of All Nations* (1935) by Countess Morphy, the pseudonym of Marcelle Azra Forbes. Counting in at over 800 pages, *Recipes* outweighs some of the heaviest domestic science manuals such as Fannie Farmer's *The Boston Cooking-School Cook Book*. It also covers a far greater geography of study. Unlike domestic science cookbooks, which provide exhaustive instruction on all-American fare and include a few foreign dishes altered to suit the average American palate, *Recipes of All Nations* includes instruction for such dishes as *awara* (palm fruit) soup and *fricasée* of iguana from Guinea; potato gnocchi and *osso bucco* from Italy; *udon* and *miso* from Japan; and *chapati* and beef *korma* from India. A native of New Orleans, Morphy traveled extensively and lived as an expatriate in London during the 1930s. In keeping with its author's trans-Atlantic background, *Recipes of All Nations* was published in both the United States and England, with the

American version including a section on English cookery and the English version including one on cookery in the United States.

Throughout her cookbook, Morphy articulates an aesthetic philosophy far more in keeping with gastronomes than with domestic cookbook authors. The chapters, largely divided by nation, begin with a brief introduction in which Morphy distills a key aspect of a country's or a region's approach toward cookery. Italians "are blessed with the divine gift of enthusiasm which alone leads to the creation of great works of art—and to gastronomic achievements of the highest quality" (121). "Spanish cookery is reminiscent of bull fights of Spanish dancing and of Goya. It is vivid, highly colored, sometimes Quixotic, brilliant, and often enchanting" (195). Morphy approaches cookery as an artistic medium that nourishes aesthetic pleasure. Tellingly, like Elizabeth Robins Pennell before her, Morphy wrote her book after moving from the United States to England, where early twentieth-century women penned more aesthetically grounded and structurally avant-garde food writing than their American counterparts.[1]

As Pennell does with her gastronomic essays, Morphy displays a cosmopolitan palate and, with the occasional exception, showcases a nuanced appreciation of foreign cookery, often gained first-hand from her travels. In the chapter on India, which introduces a section devoted to Eastern cookery, Morphy begins:

> It is difficult for the American mind to grasp the attitude of the East towards food and cookery. The older the civilization the more we find that food and the preparation of it are part of the ritual life of the people, and their reverence and idealism towards it make even the most refined European gourmet appear in the light of a mere sensuous enjoyer of the good things of the earth. (701)

Morphy states outright that her goal is to teach the modern American housewife how "'[e]very woman cooks and eats in other countries—not the highly skilled professional cook, but just the ordinary middle class woman with limited means" (9). In doing so, she hopes to help "the average woman" overcome her fear of foreign cookery as "'messy,' 'over-rich,' or beyond her capabilities as a cook" (8). Ironically, however, Morphy consulted with professional chefs rather than with home cooks to vet the recipes she gathered for the American housewife.

Alongside authors who focused their sights on cookery beyond the United States, another sort of food writer began to travel the country in order to

---

1. A few such English works of note include Hilda Leyel and Olga Hartley's *Gentle Art of Cookery*, Agnes Jekyll's *Kitchen Essays*, and Dorothy Allhusen's *Book of Scents and Dishes*. These cookbooks, although lighter in scholarship, might be understood as precursors to the gastronomic cookbooks of Elizabeth David and Patience Gray.

gather, record, and compile its regional dishes. Sheila Hibben devoted much of her career to collecting recipes from around the United States, which represented "the grace of American cooking" captured in "a farm wife's most secret way with a pie and a seafaring man's trick with a chowder" (*American Regional* iii, i). As early as 1932, Hibben worked to combat the nation's over-reliance on pre-packaged foods and the growing "craze for food out of season" by championing native ingredients. She praised the abundant delicacies that provide the U.S. with "better materials to work with than any other people in the world: pompano, Oregon oysters, swordfish, canvasback duck, terrapin, maple syrup, Celeste figs, green corn, alligator pears, yams. What country on the globe has a better list to delight the heart of the discriminating glutton?" (*National Cook Book* xi). She authored *The National Cook Book* (1932), *The Kitchen Manual* (1941), and *American Regional Cookery* (1946), the latter of which drew largely on *The National Cook Book*. In the 1930s, Hibben began a thirty-year relationship with the *New Yorker*, serving as its first food writer and penning its first restaurant column.

Like Hibben, Grace and Beverly Smith traveled throughout the United States to capture its regional dishes. Their *Through the Kitchen Door* (1938), which was co-authored by Charles Morrow Wilson, provides a refreshing tour of the country and its home cooking. The book embeds recipes within a personable, humorous, and entertaining travel narrative, which explains how the voyagers reach each destination, how they locate the region's best dishes, and their encounters with the myriad locals from whom they learn each recipe. The first-person travel narrative makes *Through the Kitchen Door* a novelty of the 1930s. It would be another twenty years before Duncan Hines wrote *Food Odyssey*, a gastronomic memoir about his travels around the United States by automobile.[2] The authorship of each chapter in *Through the Kitchen Door*, however, remains disappointingly obscure. In the introduction, Wilson states

> The Smiths—Beverly and Grace—did most of the eating. They spent the over-length year making an eating tour of the United States.... Having done most of the eating it is no more than poetic justice the Smiths also did most of the writing. I was merely drafted as general compiler and referee. (5)

Despite this introductory explanation, however, the next chapter on New England cookery is written from the first-person perspective of a nameless narrator who refers repeatedly to "his wife." Wilson was never married to Beverly or Grace Smith. The remaining chapters are narrated by an author traveling with Grace, who notes at one point that "the ladies" discussed the food while Mr. Orr "told me of the never-to-be-forgotten day when he ... had seen Jesse James, the very man, ride past with another horseman"

---

2. A traveling salesman, Hines compiled a list of recommended restaurants for fellow travelers. His *Adventures in Eating*, which first appeared as a slim paperback in 1936, was revised annually until 1962.

(110). Despite the indeterminate authorship, however, *Through the Kitchen Door* stands out as well ahead of its time, showcasing a humorous, all-American blend of food journalism and travel narrative, which owes a large part of its fruition to the travels, the palates, and the research of Beverly and Grace Smith.

A definitively female-authored work, which Fisher lauded in her own writing, Della Lutes' *The Country Kitchen* (1936) might claim to be the nation's first work of culinary autobiography. Lutes' autobiographical sketches revolve around her favorite dishes, which were prepared and eaten on the Michigan farm where she grew up in the late 1800s. Lutes embedded cookery instruction within the narrative flow and included an index of recipes to guide her readers. Given the novelty of its form in the 1930s, reviewers struggled to categorize *The Country Kitchen*, which the American Booksellers Association named "Most Original Book of the Year" in 1936 (Dawson xix). Christopher Morley, perhaps, came closest to an accurate designation, when he defined the book as "gastronomic autobiography," a term that Lutes felt "just about fit" (Dawson xx). As with most works of gastronomic and culinary literature, *The Country Kitchen* does not deal solely with eating or with cooking; the two are inextricably mingled. The book, nonetheless, draws its major sustenance from the kitchen, where Lutes watches, and eventually helps, her mother prepare the meals that form the core of each chapter. Lutes' father serves as the book's gourmand, or "simple epicure" as she calls him; his impish antics, impatient hunger, and infectious delight at the dinner table drive the narrative action and sustain the comic tone that runs throughout the book. Ultimately, however, the kitchen nourishes the heart and soul of the stories, a fact that defines *The Country Kitchen* as more culinary than gastronomic literature.

The fact that Christopher Morley defined the book as gastronomic, as opposed to culinary, autobiography, however, proves instructive. Although today's critics would define *The Country Kitchen* as culinary autobiography, such a term did not yet exist, at least in common literary parlance, in 1936. In the early twentieth-century United States, the term "culinary" connoted cookbooks proper, while the term gastronomic applied to far less structured first-person forms of writing. A cookbook undoubtedly revolved around the kitchen and might entail a few stories about the author, the author's credentials as a cook, or the dinners at which the author served a given menu, but not the personal detail of an autobiography or memoir. For Christopher Morley, the first-person narrative flow and the freedom of self-expression marked *The Country Kitchen* as more in keeping with male-authored gastronomic literature than with domestic cookbook. It falls, in fact, somewhere in between. Lutes' focus remains undeniably domesticated throughout, and the recipes around which each chapter is centered are those handed down and prepared by women. Recounted from the perspective of a child, the narrative "I" rarely features as a central protagonist of the stories. For that matter, neither does the mother. That honor belongs to the father, whose role as "a simple epicure" coupled with the mother's and daughter's place in the kitchen iterates the heteronormative dynamic of nineteenth-century food writing.

In a remarkable way, however, Lutes' narrative claims itself as transgressively modern. In between humorous vignettes about her father and lovingly detailed recipes that showcase her mother's culinary acumen, Lutes slips lush, erotic prose. These moments, which inevitably revolve around the narrator's recollection of an especially delightful dish, capture an aesthetics of pleasure that marks Lutes as one of America's most evocative food writers. In the following passage, Lutes recalls a day at the county fair as well as the chicken pie that she and her family shared:

> I remember as if it were yesterday the strident sound of the "music" of the merry-go-round. . . . The shouts of children as they chased pell-mell across the dusty lot where, my father said, the balloon was being filled . . . , and the distant bellowing of bulls. . . . But even more clearly do I recall the taste of that chicken pie. . . . The crust, as the sharp knife slid smoothly through its rich texture, parted almost flake by flake, so perfectly was it blended, crisply browned on top and unctuously mellowed on the other side with hot, steaming gravy, deeply cream in color and with a fragrance peculiar to the most popular bird in the world. It was a crust such as must have concealed the four and twenty blackbirds which sat before the king, for only queens in their household right could make such a crust. [3] (165–166)

The voluptuousness of Lutes' prose arises from its evocation of a finely tuned sensuality, albeit one that remains carefully contained within the narrative guise of a six-year-old's sensibility. By framing the passage, on one end, with the sounds of her father's voice and children at play and, on the other end, with a tribute to her mother's culinary acumen, Lutes domesticates her aesthetic pleasure. She neutralizes the self-indulgence of gastronomy by embedding its sensuality within an other-oriented economy. At the same time, however, Lutes lauds her mother's cookery as fit for a royal household, underscoring the artistry with which her mother nourishes the family. In so doing, she links domestic cookery with artistic expression, praising her mother as an artist in her own right.

THE MAKING OF A FEMALE GASTRONOME: M. F. K. FISHER AND HER FAVORITE FOOD WRITERS

One year after *The Country Kitchen* was published, M. F. K. Fisher entered the field of food writing with her first book, *Serve It Forth* (1937). The book so successfully evades the other-orientation of the women's food writing tradition that one reviewer, journalist and renowned gourmand Lucius

---

3. This passage is remarkably similar to one that appears in Fisher's *Gastronomical Me*, in which Fisher recounts the pleasures of eating a peach pie while on a picnic with her father and sister. See pages 83–84 for further discussion.

Beebe, assumed it had been written by a man. From the first word, Fisher declares her place as a food writer by positioning herself within and against existing genres of culinary and gastronomic literature. In the opening chapter "To Begin," Fisher divides food writing into "books about eating" versus "books about what to eat" (5). A portion of the "books about eating," or gastronomical literature, focus specifically on "those who eat," which is a subcategory that Fisher often finds "pompously nonchalant" (6).

The "books about what to eat," or cookbooks, Fisher subdivides as well. The first category are those inspired by domestic science, which she describes as: "stodgy, matter-of-fact, covered very practically with washable cloth or gravy-coloured paper, beginning with measurements of food values and ending with sections on the care of invalids. . . . They are usually German, or English or American." The second type of cookbook "begin[s] with witty philosophizing on the pleasures of the table, and end[s] with a suggested menu for an intimate dinner given to seven gentlemen who know his wife, by a wealthy old banker who feels horns pricking up gently from his bald skull. These books are usually French" (5). Having divided food writing into books "about eating and about what to eat and about people who eat," Fisher states outright that she will "do gymnastics by trying to fall between these three fires, or by straddling them all" (6). In other words, by refusing to be neatly contained within the existing categories, she intends to fashion a new form of food writing in which she will "humbly recognize" Brillat-Savarin and his philosophy "about eating," yet will work to avoid flitting too close to those works about "what to eat" or "about people who eat."

As Fisher's first foray into food writing, *Serve It Forth* takes tentative steps toward developing a new genre. On one level, though, Fisher works too hard at refashioning the standard territory, depending on such standbys as ancient dining habits, the chef Vatel's suicide, the rise of gastronomy and gastronomical literature, and a definition of the ideal dinner. She undoubtedly succeeds in reexamining such regular features of gastronomic literature from a fresh, wry perspective, but such material itself is far from novel. Fisher does venture into new territory, however, in her attempts to illuminate the seam that binds physiological and psychological hungers—a goal that would become foundational in her later food writing, gaining its most powerful expression in *The Gastronomical Me* (1943).

Although Fisher lauds *The Country Kitchen* in her discussions of food writing and clearly drew inspiration from its narrative flow as well as from Lutes' remarkably lush prose, she reserves her most ebullient praise for Brillat-Savarin's *Physiology of Taste*. Fisher would consider her translation of his *Physiology of Taste* to be one of her finest books. Fittingly, Fisher's first work of gastronomic literature, *Serve It Forth*, begins and ends with a discussion of Brillat-Savarin and his gastronomic philosophy. Of Brillat-Savarin's contribution to food writing, Fisher observes:

> It is difficult to write about physical pleasures without being either coarse or over-delicate, vaguely sentimental or dry and scientific. *The*

Physiology of Taste is none of these. It is as near perfection as we yet know it, and a constant wonder. The temptation to quote from its clear, pungent prose is hard to resist. Infinitely better, however, is the companionship of the book itself, for there is no superfluous word in it, no dull page. (*Serve It Forth* 93)

Physiology provided Fisher such meaningful companionship over the years that by the time she wrote *With Bold Knife and Fork* in 1969, she would "count [Brillat-Savarin] among [her] most trusted friends" (210). Tellingly, she claims Brillat-Savarin as opposed to Grimod de la Reynière as her literary mentor, only infrequently referencing the latter in her discussions of gastronomy and food writing. Whereas Grimod reveled in self-styled egotism, elitism, and misogyny—traits that make for highly engaging, if not always agreeable, commentary—Brillat-Savarin stands out among gastronomes for his belief in and praise of female gourmands as well as for his comparative modesty. His female-friendly and humble self-presentation made Brillat-Savarin the ideal mentor for a budding American gourmand such as Fisher.

In addition to Brillat-Savarin, Fisher drew inspiration from two early twentieth-century gourmands—Paul Reboux and André Simon. A novelist, drama critic, and *bon vivant*, Reboux believed: "Cookery is an art with a philosophy and an aesthetic of its own" and that "monotony and uniformity . . . must be avoided at all costs" (*Food for the Rich* 105). Toward that end, Reboux embraced the "fantastic and bizarre," such as turquoise macaroni, tinted with methalyn blue (24, 42). In keeping with Grimod's sense of humor, he dedicates his *Plats Nouveaux* to, among others, "Fontenelle, who, gazing at a flock of sheep, lost himself not in bucolic reverie, but in speculating on the tenderness of their flesh" (*Food for the Rich* vii).[4] He urges his readers:

For heaven's sake, let's have a little curiosity. Let's be on the alert, not slumbering in a bed of habit: let's give new flavours and unfamiliar combinations the benefit. . . . [W]hen a new harmony greets your palate. . . . [a]nalyse the sensation, disentangle the flavours, try to identify each note of the symphony. In this way you will educate your palate, you will enjoy new pleasures. (24–25)

Fisher shared Reboux' dislike of monotony and his affinity for surprise at the table, an affinity that greatly influenced her own philosophy as a host. She reflects that the meals she cooked in her youth always included "an element of surprise, if not actual danger" (17). As an adult, she felt that

---

4. Paul Reboux' *Plats Nouveaux* was translated into English as *Food for the Rich* in 1958. Passages are quoted from this edition, translated by Margaret Costa.

One of the best things I could do for nine tenths of the people I knew was to give them something that would make them forget Home and all it stood for, for a few blessed moments at least.

I still believe this, and have found that it makes cooking for people exciting and amusing for me, and often astonishingly stimulating for them. My meals shake them from their routines, not only of meat-potatoes-gravy, but of thought, of behavior. (*GM* 101)

This philosophy provides a mirror reflection of the goal of nineteenth- and early twentieth-century American domestic cookbooks, which focused on creating predictable, economic, and balanced meals. Fisher eschewed familiarity and comfort in order to "excite" and "amuse" herself and to "stimulate" her guests. By including such a description of her own goals as a host, Fisher challenges her readers to break out of their domesticated patterns and to open themselves to the pleasures of gastronomy along with the self-reflection and knowledge it inspires. Fisher likewise encourages her readers to detect and to nourish their own hungers, both physical and spiritual—a goal that drives much of her food writing.

Fisher links gastronomy with spirituality to articulate a philosophy almost in perfect alignment with that of André Simon, whose *Art of Good Living* (1929) elegantly distills a modernized definition of gastronomy. Simon writes that the art of good living

introduces a measure of spirituality and idealism into materialism, reminding humans that they are not animals. At the same time, Art acts as a corrective to ascetic aestheticism, reminding the noblest soul that it is but a guest and that it must not ignore nor despise its host, the body and its claims. . . . The Art of Good Living is a living art: its body, that which all may see and acquire, is called *Gastronomy*; its soul, that which giveth life to the body, a gift from heaven, which no money can buy, is a form of the living spirit of Charity; it is called *Hospitality*. (16–17)

Here Simon extends nineteenth-century gastronomy into the twentieth century and underscores one of the key motifs in Fisher's writing—a reverent approach toward "the body and its claims."

Whereas Fisher makes an occasional nod toward Reboux and Simon in her books, quoting a recipe or describing their oeuvre, she embraces Brillat-Savarin far more overtly. From the first sentence of *Serve It Forth*, Fisher acknowledges the centrality of Brillat-Savarin's *Physiology* to her own gastronomic philosophy as well as to her first book. Like Brillat-Savarin, Fisher engages with gastronomy as a means of analyzing and reflecting on politics, national character, civilization, the aesthetics of pleasure, the art of conversation, sexuality, and much more. Fisher, however, delves further into the subjective realm than any previous gastronome. She not only examines those moments when physical pleasure nourishes intellect, a task undertaken by most serious gastronomes. She also studies those instances when gastronomy nourishes and fulfills emotional hunger. Exploring gastronomy as a means of nourishing intellectual and emotional growth enables Fisher to figure eating as a powerful form of self-construction. In particular, Fisher illuminates how the pleasures of gastronomy transform psychological and physical hungers into an aesthetic emotion. This aesthetic response, in turn, nourishes a feeling of symbiosis with the surrounding world. Fisher describes these moments "as much a matter of spirit as of body. Everything is right; nothing jars. There is a kind of harmony, with every sensation and emotion melted into one chord of well-being" (*Serve* 83). Like male gastronomes, Fisher lauds such moments of harmony and hones her gastronomical knowledge in order to nourish them. Fisher exceeds her male predecessors, however, in her investigation of the emotional nuances that enable such moments of harmony.

GIVING VOICE TO FEMALE DESIRE

Over the course of the six years between *Serve It Forth* and *The Gastronomical Me*, Fisher fashioned a form of food writing that articulates the pleasures of gastronomy as well as an aesthetic philosophy much in keeping with the tradition of gastronomic literature.[5] Fisher, however, tempers the sensual pleasures and attention to aesthetics of gastronomy with the practicality of the domestic cookbook.[6] The influence of domestic cookbooks on Fisher's development as a writer can be seen most clearly in works such as *How to Cook a Wolf* (1942), *An Alphabet for Gourmets* (1949), and *With Bold Knife and Fork* (1969). These books neatly fit Traci Marie Kelly's definition of culinary memoir, "which presents a personal story interlaced with reminiscences about cooking, dining and feasting" (255).

The majority of Fisher's memoirs, however, including *Serve It Forth* (1937), *Consider the Oyster* (1941), *The Gastronomical Me* (1943), *As They Were* (1982), and *Long Ago in France* (1991) deal far more with the art of eating than they do with cookery. Articulating an aesthetic philosophy in keeping with gastronomic literature, these works are best categorized as gastronomic memoir. In particular, Fisher creates a form of memoir that celebrates female desire and investigates the expression of female appetite in both public and private spaces.

5. In addition to *The Physiology of Taste*, Fisher incorporated a range of nineteenth-century gastronomic literature into her own writing, including Grimod de la Reynière's *Almanach des Gourmands*, Charles Lamb's "Dissertation on Roast Pig," Thomas Walker's *Original*, and Elizabeth Robins Pennell's *Feasts of Autolycus*, which she calls a "mannered and delightful book" (577).

6. In addition to *Moody's Cook-Book*, Fisher listed Marion Harland's *Common Sense in the Household*, Fannie Farmer's *Boston Cooking-School Cook Book*, Lizzie Black Kander's *Settlement Cook Book*, Sheila Hibben's *National Cook Book* and Irma Rombauer's *Joy of Cooking* among her favorite cookbooks.

In her first two books, *Serve It Forth* and *Consider the Oyster* Fisher begins to explore gastronomy and gastronomical writing as a form of self-construction, borrowing heavily from the traditional structure of gastronomic literature in order to do so. In *Consider the Oyster*, however, Fisher ventures more boldly into uncharted literary territory. In particular, she celebrates the eroticism and danger inherent in eating. Before Fisher, Pennell had drawn a strong connection between sexuality and gastronomy. She had done so, however, through parody and self-deflection. Fisher uses less self-protective measures, crafting a nuanced approach that celebrates female appetite for sensual pleasure, both aesthetic and erotic. More than any of Fisher's other works, *Consider the Oyster* articulates an aesthetic of sensual pleasure that conflates eating with sex. Insisting that "it is impossible to enjoy without thought," Fisher recalls a particular passage from a book

> in which Jean-Louis Vaudoyer speaks of a woman he once watched eat something especially delicious. She savored her enjoyment with a carefully sensual slowness, and then she sighed, as it came to its inevitable end, "Ah . . . what a pity that I do not have little tastebuds clear to the bottom of my stomach!" Such a remark could not seem anything but gross to an ascetic man, partly because a woman said it and partly because all such frank gastronomic pleasures are inexplicable to him. . . . And yet to a man who has once eaten something and taken thought about it . . . not merely digested it and remembered that, but eaten, digested, and then *thought* . . . such a blatantly sensual remark . . . is not only comprehensible but highly intelligent. (34, 57)

This passage articulates two of the key motifs in Fisher's writing; it addresses the cultural constraints against female pleasure, and it illustrates woman's considerable hunger for the pleasures and wisdom of gastronomy.

As in her discussion of the woman who wished for "tastebuds clear to the bottom of [her] stomach," Fisher repeatedly claims the female right to gustatory pleasure. Toward this end, she images herself as a female gourmand, a hungry woman with a sophisticated, curious, and robust appetite. At one point, she recalls drinking

> Pouilly-Fuissé, various kinds of champagnes *nature*, a pink Peau d'Onion, and both bottled and open wines of Anjou with oysters in France, and whether or not they were correctly drunk or not, I was. Nobody knew it except for my own exhilarated senses and my pleased mind, all of which must enter into any true gastronomic experience. (55)

By articulating herself as a well-educated, sensually sophisticated, and witty gastronome, as comfortable quoting Grimod and Reboux as she is Swinburne and Shakespeare, Fisher creates a space for female desire as well as for female intellect within gastronomic literature. She likewise creates a language of female appetite that celebrates both alimentary and sexual hungers. In "Eating Our Way Toward Wisdom: M. F. K. Fisher's Oysters," the poet and scholar Lee Upton elegantly summarizes the importance of this accomplishment:

> Obliquely, *Consider the Oyster* contemplates habitual assumptions about gender. The oyster is, of course, associated with women, the female genitals, and erotic prowess. . . . The oyster's very connection to women and erotic force presents Fisher with remarkable possibilities for insinuation. . . . She considers the oyster with boldness, presenting oysters as more various, dramatic, and more appetitive than we may have supposed. Women, so frequently associated with the oyster, emerge as beyond categorization and thus containment. (199)

As Upton remarks, Fisher articulates a female appetite for food, sex, and knowledge that exceeds the domesticated bounds of women's food writing. By venturing into the public realm of gastronomy to investigate the sensual and intellectual pleasures of dining, Fisher claims a space where female appetite can be artfully and publicly sated.

OVERCOMING AN ASCETIC INHERITANCE

Victorian Hangover

Fisher frequently juxtaposed the benefits of a liberated appetite with one deformed by repression, often addressing the toll such repression took on the female and on the deadening of the American palate. As academic studies have shown and Fisher illustrates in her own writing, the American concern with containing the female body and its appetites became a prominent part of middle-class ideology during the Victorian era.[7] Scholars Tamar Heller and Patricia Moran address the cause and effect:

> An outgrowth of the rise of capitalism, domestic ideology segregated home and workplace to a hitherto unknown extent, . . . emphasizing fundamental differences between male and female nature. While the association of women with the private sphere, or with distinctive

---

7. Just a few such scholars whose work has been instrumental in detailing the nineteenth-century suppression of women's appetite and desire include Tamar Heller and Patricia Moran (*Scenes of the Apple*), Helena Michie (*The Flesh Made Word*), Susan Bordo (*Unbearable Weight*), Joan Jacobs Brumberg ("The Appetite as Voice"), Anna Krugovoy Silver (*Victorian Literature and the Anorexic Body*), and Anita Levy (*Other Women: The Writing of Class, Race, and Gender, 1832–1898*).

characteristics, was not new, domesticity deployed these associations to disembody women to a greater extent than ever before, elevating an ideal of womanhood that deemphasized female sexuality even as it emphasized women's spiritual power as moral guide within the home. If this ideal apparently redeemed women from the long-standing misogynist tradition of seeing them all as greedy and lustful Eves, it did so by displacing appetite from the virtuous woman within the home to the fallen women outside it. (22)

The disembodiment of the Victorian woman both arose from and fueled the middle class belief that the proper woman should carefully control "her physical appetites (including, but not limited to, her hunger for food and, relatedly, her sexuality)" (Silver 27). In turn, the notion that the proper woman must control her appetites led to the gendering of foods. Those foods that were thought to enflame desire, such as red meat as well as spicy or rich foods, were gendered male and considered inappropriate for women to consume except in modest amounts. As scholar Anna Silver surmises, "[t]he idea that women should eat only small amounts of food, or particular kinds of food, as a sign of their purity ironically implies that one cannot take women's innocence for granted" (49–50). Thus, the desiring, hungry woman becomes culturally laden with negative connotations ranging from greed and excess to monstrosity and perversion. As a result, middle-class Victorian culture encouraged a female asceticism that arose from and reinforced a cultural fear of women's sexual appetite. Female sexual desire, in fact, was understood as a threat to the integrity of the family structure. As scholar Anita Levy explains, middle-class Victorians conceived of the female "as a desired object . . . [who] had the power to preserve the home and the community" (106). This dynamic also worked powerfully in reverse: "as a desiring subject, [a woman's] unregulated desires threatened the stability of both social formations."[8] Consequently, the respectable middle-class woman was defined by her capacity to repress and to control the "primitive" desires lurking within.

Taught to renounce sensual pleasure yet in charge of home cookery, middle-class Victorian women often practiced a form of asceticism meant to keep their own and their daughters' physical hungers in check. Within her food writing, Fisher explores the repercussions of this attitude, constructing her maternal Grandmother Holbrook as a figure who embodies the cultural fear of female appetite. According to Fisher, "the flatter a thing tasted, the better it was for you, Grandmother believed. And the better it was for you,

8. As Levy explains, middle-class Victorians defined themselves, in part, by denigrating the lower classes and the racial Other. In turn, they created a "model of psychosexuality" in which "desire in the middle-class female actually bore all the same features as desire in the working-class woman and the savage," ensuring the production of a "body that distinguished what was docile and desirable in a woman from what was degenerate and desirous" (106, 109).

she believed, the more you should suffer to eat it" (*To Begin Again* 53–54). Not surprisingly, when overseen by her grandmother, cooking in Fisher's family involved the same lack of pleasure that eating did. Fisher recalls how her grandmother "made it clear that helping in the kitchen was a bitter heavy business forbidden certainly to men, and generally to children" (*GM* 4). When she made strawberry jam, "the process consisted of "stir, sweat, hurry. It was a pity." As Fisher recalls, her grandmother "stood like a sacrificial priestess in the steam." The fact that Grandmother Holbrook felt cooking a "bitter heavy business" yet insisted on making jam like a "sacrificial priestess" illustrates the cultural expectation that the proper woman accustom herself to self-sacrifice.[9] As philosopher Susan Bordo succinctly explains:

> The rules for [the] construction of femininity (and I speak here in a language both symbolic and literal) require that women learn to feed others, not the self, and to construe any desires for self-nurturance and self-feeding as greedy and excessive. Thus, women must develop a totally other-oriented emotional economy. In this economy, the control of female appetite for food is merely the most concrete expression of the general rule governing the construction of femininity: that female hunger—for public power, for independence, for sexual gratification—be contained, and the public space that women be allowed to take up be circumscribed, limited.[10] (171)

The repercussions of participating in an economy that represses female appetite vary from anorexia to hysteria to the asceticism practiced by Grandmother Holbrook. These repercussions, in turn, impacted the dinner table, where bland, overcooked meals became a byproduct of the self-denial practiced by "respectable" middle-class women.

Fisher situates Grandmother Holbrook's attitude toward cooking, eating, and the body within the broader context of middle-class domesticity when she writes that "The Nervous Stomach was to Grandmother and to her 'sisters' in the art of being loyal wives and mothers . . . a heaven-sent escape" from the cultural expectations that they undergo "a period of dogged reproduction, eight or twelve and occasionally sixteen offspring, so that at least half would survive the nineteenth-century hazards of colics and congestion" (*To Begin* 51–52). As Fisher implies, the physical abnegation practiced by women such as her maternal grandmother stemmed largely from the fact that two of the main functions performed by a housewife—bearing

---

9. Contemporary studies of Western women show that they still cook to please the tastes and distastes of their husbands and children rather than to satisfy their own palates. See Roy C. Wood, *Sociology of the Meal*, 56.

10. While I've applied this quote to late-Victorian and Edwardian middle-class women, Bordo argues that this remains true in contemporary society.

and feeding children—centered around the same body she was taught to renounce. The tension surrounding this contradiction encouraged an almost phobic fear of the body, one that Fisher's grandmother indulged fully during her self-sanctioned escapes from domesticity, which led either to religious retreats or to Dr. Kellogg's Battle Creek Sanitarium.

Yoking sexual abstinence with "a strictly healthy diet," Battle Creek provided the ideal sanctuary for Grandmother Holbrook's worship of asceticism. Dr. Kellogg's strictures against pleasure were so strong, in fact, that he advocated circumcising men without anesthesia and experimented by pouring carbolic acid on a woman's clitoris to halt sexual arousal, which he records it successfully did (Haber 74). Open from 1866 to 1931, Battle Creek became "the largest and best-known health resort in the United States," a fact that suggests just how firmly entrenched the need to control bodily appetite had become in middle-class American culture (Haber 71).

In *The Gastronomical Me*, Fisher explores how this repression of the body and its fears influenced American cookery and drained pleasure from mealtime. She also illuminates how the attitude with which one approaches food greatly influences the spiritual sustenance that it provides. Meals prepared or eaten with a disdain for "the body and its claims" not only demean the cook and her work, but also denigrate those for whom she cooks. Throughout *The Gastronomical Me*, Fisher equates asceticism with a disrespect for the body and its needs and equates gastronomy with self-nourishment. At one point, she explores this correlation by comparing the American and French treatment of a basic ingredient—the potato. She recalls that in her own home, potatoes were "mashed, baked, boiled. It was shameful, I always felt, and stupid too, to reduce a potentially important food to such a menial position . . . and to take time every day to cook it, doggedly, with perfunctory compulsion" (51). Because Fisher equates the treatment of food with the treatment of the self, reducing potatoes to a "menial position" is "shameful" because it likewise reduces the people who prepare and eat the potato to a "menial" stature. Rebelling against such dogged, "perfunctory compulsion," Fisher approached the art of eating as a source of intellectual and physical fulfillment. In doing so, she worked to raise the body, food, and the home cook from a menial and shameful position to one of honor.

While the potato's treatment as "shameful" and its position as "menial" belie a pleasureless approach toward food and cooking, Fisher encountered quite a different attitude upon her arrival in France, where her first husband, Al, worked for his doctorate at the University of Dijon. As newlyweds who had just arrived in Paris, Fisher and her husband are on their way to settle in Dijon when they encounter a potato soufflé in what marks "one of the fine moments" of Fisher's life. She describes the incident:

> I forget now what we ate, except for a kind of soufflé of potatoes. It was hot, light, with a brown crust, and probably chives and grated Parmesan

cheese were somewhere in it. But the great thing about it was that it was served alone, in a course all by itself. I felt a secret justification swell in me, a pride such as I've seldom known since, because all my life, it seemed, I had been wondering rebelliously about potatoes. . . . I almost resented them, in fact . . . or rather, the monotonous disinterest with which they were always treated. I felt that they *could* be good, if they were cooked respectfully. . . . And now, here in the sunny courtyard of the first really French restaurant I had ever been in, I saw my theory proved. It was a fine moment. (51)

Fisher's pride at witnessing the potato artfully prepared comes from the knowledge that even the most fundamental components of life *can* and *should be* treated with care and imagination.

The Gendered Duties of World War II

Fisher explores the correlation between respect for the food one eats and self-respect most forcefully in her third book, *How to Cook a Wolf* (1942), a work written in rebellion against the wartime cooking advice distributed by the government and by such popular domestic cookbooks as *Thrifty Cooking for Wartime*. Whereas the government and many wartime cookbook authors promoted the notion of food as fuel for the body, Fisher's *How to Cook a Wolf* directly challenges governmental manuals and popular advice on constructing three "balanced" meals a day, many of which Fisher holds up as "shocking example[s] of gastronomical panic" (184). In contrast to government rhetoric, *How to Cook a Wolf* philosophizes on how to feed the unrationed mind, showcasing a way to live gracefully during a time of scarcity. As one critic astutely surmises: "Against the government's call to eat on behalf of the nation and its military-industrial complex, Fisher calls on her readers to eat selfishly" (Carruth 778).

In contrast to Fisher's call "to eat selfishly," the United States government promoted domestic self-sacrifice as essential to the war effort. Like England, the United States adopted the notion of the home front as a war front and meals as munitions to arm the family body against enemy ideology. As Amy Bentley illustrates in her World War II study *Eating for Victory: Food Rationing and the Politics of Domesticity*, the United States Committee on Food Habits suggested that altering the American meal structure to accommodate food shortages "might make Americans vulnerable to easy acceptance of fascist ideals" (Bentley 63). According to such logic, the housewife who nourished her family with three "square meals" a day helped to create a national body firm enough to keep the enemy's mind and body at bay.

Meats and sweets became especially indispensable during wartime, not only because they were part of the standard national meal structure, but also because they symbolically embodied the extreme ends of the gender divide; meat became so hyper-masculinized during the war, in fact, that the United States Office of Price Management distributed pamphlets stating

American meat is a fighting tool . . . it helped the Americans drive the Japs from Guadalcanal; It helped sustain the heroic British 8th Army in its blistering drive from Egypt to Tunisia. . . . [Meat] is as necessary to soldiers as bullets. . . . Submarine crews hunting down Japs in the Pacific could not do their job on a diet of beans. (quoted in Bentley 96)

Soldiers were supplied with one pound of meat per day to keep them in fighting shape. Correspondingly, during wartime, "the connection between baking and female nurturing . . . intensified" (105). One reason such gendered ideology intensified during World War II derives from the fact that women were taking on many of the jobs formerly assigned to men currently fighting abroad; "between 1940 and 1945, the number of women workers surged from 12 to 18 million" (Schenone 305). The more the war challenged the traditional gender divide by bringing women into the workforce, the more the government attempted to assure the nation that its traditional family structure would not be compromised. Toward that end, it depicted the patriotic woman as one who could work outside the home while still performing her traditional wifely duties of cooking, cleaning, and caring for the children.

Published the same year that Fisher's *How to Cook a Wolf* appeared, Alice Winn-Smith's *Thrifty Cooking for Wartime* (1942) outlines the housewife's patriotic duties in a way that resolutely echoes governmental advice:

With the grim realities of war at our very shores it behooves all Americans to grit their teeth, tighten their belts, and wade through the unpleasant job of cleaning up the mess. . . . [I]n order to do her part the housewife, like the soldier, needs a new set of rules. . . . Just as necessary as shouldering a rifle, is the shouldering of our responsibilities in the home. It is a "commanding job." Gratitude for all that we have to use and to give will overcome any martyrdom, and the discipline necessary will be good for ourselves and our families. . . . American Housewives—Generals at Home Defense—I salute you! (vii–x)

Following this introductory material appear chapters such as "Meatless Dishes for Victory Dinners" and "Soup—The Real 'All-Out-For Defense' Meal." In this context, food becomes a weapon and cooking a martial practice needed to "arm" the family stomach for war; cooking three meals a day likewise becomes the housewife's indispensable duty, a burden that she must "shoulder" for the nation's welfare. Tellingly, *Thrifty Cooking* was eagerly imported from its native United States into England. The approach toward cooking as a practice that requires regulation, martyrdom, and discipline was hardly new to the American or the English housewife; such an approach had been espoused by domestic science cookbooks for almost a century. The image of the housewife as a military commander was made famous by the most popular cookbook of the nineteenth century, Isabella Beeton's *Book of Household Management* (1861), which begins with the words: "As with the Commander of an Army, or the leader of any enterprise, so is it with the mistress of the house" (7). The notions of thrift, economy, duty, and self-sacrifice ominpresent in nineteenth- and twentieth-century cookbooks, however, were taken to an all-out extreme during wartime.

In rebellion against such an economy, Fisher wrote *How to Cook a Wolf*. During a time when cookbooks were fueled by patriotic fervor and characterized by a rhetoric of thrift, Fisher proffered advice on how to "live with grace and wisdom," "intelligence and spirit" (6, 84). The only way to keep the wolf firmly at bay, Fisher suggests, is to discern your own hungers and to work hard to see that they are met. Fisher was not alone in her wartime rallying cry for gastronomy. She took part in what Jessamyn Neuhaus describes as "the new gourmet movement that, somewhat paradoxically, emerged full force in the United States during the 1940s" (104). The first issue of *Gourmet* magazine was published in 1941 and "a thriving gourmet industry emerged in New York during the war," spurred, in part, by the dreary recipes that proliferated in manuals such as *Thrifty Cooking for Wartime* (Carruth 777). Although Fisher defiantly condemns such popular domestic cookbooks, *How to Cook a Wolf*, more so than any of Fisher's other works, tempers the aesthetic pleasures of gastronomy with a practicality derived from nineteenth-century domestic manuals, which often included recipes for cleaning supplies, home remedies, and fabric dyes. Alongside the aesthetically inspired recipes of Escoffier, Paul Reboux, and Ambrose Heath, Fisher includes recipes for making soap and stuffing pincushions.

At points in *How to Cook a Wolf*, most often when discussing wartime cookery, Fisher adopts a tone best described as wry, defiant, self-mocking, and flippant. At other points, she conveys a more self-reflective, philosophical approach toward gastronomy, musing on how to live with "grace and dignity" during times of rationing. For example, in her chapter on "How to Be Cheerful Though Starving," Fisher recalls a woman named Sue who fed large groups of people on weeds gathered from the seaside and transformed them into

> salads and stews, . . . blended and cooked so skillfully that they never lost their fresh salt crispness. She put them together with thought and gratitude. . . . I doubt she spent more than fifty dollars a year on what she and her entranced guests ate, but from the gracious abstracted way she gave you a soup dish full of sliced cactus leaves and lemonberries and dried crumbled kelp, it might as well have been stuffed ortolans. . . . Sue had neither health nor companionship to warm her, but she nourished herself and many other people for many years, with the quiet assumption that man's need for food is not a grim obsession, repulsive, disturbing, but a dignified and enjoyable function. (84–85)

As Fisher reflects, the most nourishing meals come from kitchens that treat food with respect. Whereas collections such as *Thrifty Cooking for*

Wartime approach food as a weapon and introduce the notion of gratitude as a means of overcoming the martyrdom inherent in "making do," Sue approaches food and cooking with gratitude for the pleasure it brings to the mind and the body. In her recollection of Sue's cookery, Fisher illustrates that weeds, respectfully treated and graciously served, can be transformed into a stimulating, enjoyable, and profoundly satisfying dish. Fisher underscores that it is not so much what one cooks, but rather the attitude with which one approaches cookery that flavors the spiritual sustenance it provides.

In order to shake Americans out of their rigid insistence on three square meals a day, Fisher suggests serving them just one ample dish of soup with buttered bread or perhaps a delicately constructed vegetable casserole in order to "startle" them out of their well-entrenched habit of eating a meat, starch, and vegetable followed by dessert at every meal. Fisher not only urged her readers to rebel against government and domestic science advice on eating three square meals a day, whose monotony she found deadening to the mind and to the body, but also openly decried the American attitude toward the sensual pleasures of eating. She challenged the American habit of teaching children

> not to mention food or enjoy it publicly. If we have liked a meringue, or an artful little curl of pastry on a kidney pie . . . we have not been allowed to cry out with pleasure but instead have been pressed down, frowned at, weighted with a heavy adult reasoning that such display was unseemly, and vulgar, and almost "foreign." . . . For too many nice ordinary little Americans the devil has been drowned, so that all their lives afterwards they eat what is set before them, without thought, without comment, and, worst of all, without interest. (164)

In *How to Cook a Wolf*, Fisher demonstrates the benefit of voicing pleasure in food; it allows her to gain sustenance from what she calls her "mind's palate." Fisher devotes the book's final chapter to providing her readers and herself with just such sustenance. Toward that end, she writes of "half-forgotten luxuries and half-remembered delicate impossible dishes" and describes such remembrance as "necessary, now and then, to your soul, and your body, too" (191). She encourages her reader to

> Sit back in your chair. . . . Drop a few years from your troubled mind. Let the cupboard of your thoughts fill itself with a hundred ghosts that long ago, in 1939, used to be easy to buy and easy to forget. Permit your disciplined inner self to relax, and think of thick cream, and fat little pullets trotting through an oak grove rich with truffles, "musky, fiery, savory, mysterious." Close your eyes to the headlines and your ears to the sirens and the threatenings of high explosives, and read instead the sweet nostalgic measures of these recipes, impossible yet fond. (192)

Fisher continues the chapter by describing the rich, mysterious dishes that once fed her body and now feed her "mind's palate." In doing so, she illustrates how reading and writing about food can nourish psychological hungers.

TRANSFORMING HUNGER INTO FULFILLMENT AND PLEASURE

Fisher dealt explicitly with psychological hunger within her memoirs, often exploring how she satisfied or failed to satisfy her own need for comfort, warmth, and safety. She also worked to capture the dynamics of such hungers in writing, often revisiting the same moment in life from varying angles of approach in order to do so. One such moment revolves around a particularly rough time in Strasbourg, where she lived for a short period with her first husband, Al, who was conducting research at the University. When her husband left for the University each morning, Fisher tried to write in their rundown flat, so poorly heated that icicles formed on the kitchen spigot. Her fingers numbed by the cold and her spirits dashed by the dingy surroundings, Fisher found herself unable to write. To fill the time, she would stare out the window, identifying with the caged animals in the zoo across the street. One particularly bleak February day, Fisher reached such depths of despair that, as she describes in *Serve It Forth,* she and Al moved "bag and baggage to the most expensive *pension* in the city. It was wonderful—big room, windows, clean white billows of curtain, central heating. We basked like lizards" (25–27). Fisher depicts one accounting of the events in *Serve It Forth* and six years later presents another perspective on the incident in *The Gastronomical Me.* A comparison of these two passages illuminates how Fisher figures psychological hungers—and the capacity or failure to nourish them—through the act of eating. They also show Fisher's development as a writer, her maturing ability to linger over moments of vulnerability, refracting the angles of loneliness, anguish, pain, and fear from which they are fashioned.

In the first version of the Strasbourg incident, which appears in *Serve It Forth,* Fisher delivers a comparatively lighter perspective that emphasizes her relief at moving from a dingy flat into a luxurious *pension.* She does so by interweaving her plight "in a cramped dirty apartment across from the sad zoo" with that of the "animals and birds frozen too stiff even to make smells" (26). She contrasts such despair with the "subtle and voluptuous" experience of eating dried tangerine sections while watching passersby from the warmth of a hotel window. To underscore the sensual pleasure she finds luxuriating in the comfort of the hotel room, Fisher recounts how the maid came in to plump the pillows as Fisher tore "delicately . . . those white pulpy strings that hold tangerines into their skins" then left them on the radiator to dry and forgot about them.

Later that afternoon Fisher finds that "On the radiator the sections of tangerines have grown even plumper, hot and full." She eats them slowly throughout the afternoon. By nightfall, she reflects: "[t]he sections of tangerine are gone, and I cannot tell you why they are so magical. Perhaps it is that little shell, thin as one layer of enamel on a Chinese bowl, that crackles so tinily, so ultimately under your teeth. Or the rush of cold pulp just after it. Or the perfume. I cannot tell" (28). In this passage, Fisher conveys the sensual gratification of eating the tangerine sections. Yet she likewise underscores that such gastronomic pleasure remains inextricably linked to the security and relief she felt safely nestled in the clean, light, and airy *pension* after months freezing in a rundown flat. The sating of her anxiety, the relief of her psychological hunger for comfort and warmth, nourished the "subtle and voluptuous and quite inexplicable" pleasure she found biting into the tangerine slices.

In the version of the story that Fisher includes in *The Gastronomical Me*, she underscores the loss of creativity and depths of despair that she faced in the dingy flat, where "she tried to write," but couldn't because her "hands and head were too cold." Here, the zoo animals feature more prominently. Rather than watching them from the window, Fisher describes visiting the zoo, where she would

> stand and stand, waiting for some sign of life from the rumpled creatures on the other side of the bars, but even the guinea pigs were too stiff to carry out their usual haphazard copulations. The storks, symbol of Alsace, would stare bleakly at me and occasionally drip a languid feather into the frozen filth, and I would turn back to my home, stumbling a little in my haste to get there before the fire went out again. (115)

Fisher's wry sense of humor, which leavens the anguish of this passage, sharpened during the six years between *Serve It Forth* and *The Gastronomical Me*. Such humor enabled Fisher to delve more forcefully into dark moments without losing her sure footing as a writer. She provides her readers a breath of humor before diving into the famished depths of her psyche. As fitting a gastronomic memoir, Fisher anchors her recollection with a tamale pie that Al had cooked for their supper. She describes:

> It was probably one of the best that has ever been made, anywhere in the world where anyone would bother to make one, and I hope it was the only one I shall ever eat.
>
> Of course, it was not the concoction itself that broke my spiritual back. I know that well. But a little while after I finished eating it . . . , I began to cry. It was the first time Al had even seen a tear in either of my eyes. Now there were thousands. . . .
>
> I sat in the gradually chilling room, thinking of my whole past the way a drowning man is supposed to, and it seemed part of the present, part of the gray cold . . . and the moulting birds frozen to their own filth . . . I know now I was in the throes of some small glandular crises, a sublimated bilous attack, a flick of the whip of melancholia, but it was terrifying . . . nameless. (116)

By anchoring her breakdown with tamale pie, Fisher suggests that the pie triggered such melancholy because it failed, as did the apartment, to fulfill her basic needs for safety and warmth. Without these needs met, Fisher found herself unable to write. Once comfortably settled in the *pension*, however, and nourished by the restaurant's "wild-boar meat[,] . . . . peas, lentils, potatoes, [and] chestnuts, rubbed to a suave paste," Fisher once again felt her creativity revive (117).

Fisher's shift in focus from *Serve It Forth* to *The Gastronomical Me* exemplifies the writing process itself as a form of self-construction; Fisher configures the same series of events in disparate ways. The first emphasizes her relief at escaping a run-down apartment; the second illuminates her hunger for safety and warmth as well as the melancholy she feels being unable to write. Such a shift in perspective illuminates the function of memoir, which fixes a given memory in writing in order to crystallize a particular version, or aspect, of the self. In this way, memoir participates in a form of self-construction, or what Jeanne Perreault defines as autography. According to Perreault, autography "makes the writing itself an aspect of the selfhood the writer experiences and brings into being" (191). It becomes a "self-in-the-making." As a memoirist, or autographer, Fisher does not attempt to recount the facts of her life story. Rather, she articulates a given set of memories, which have been refracted through a subjective lens. In turn, she draws, expands on, and, at times, embellishes those particulars, which reflect the self or self-in-relation-to-the-world she wishes to write into being.

Because *Serve It Forth* was Fisher's first contribution to the literature of gastronomy, she focuses the story on the "subtle and voluptuous" pleasures of eating the tangerine sections in the comfort of a hotel room. As she does throughout *Serve It Forth*, Fisher figures herself as a gastronome. By the time she writes *The Gastronomical Me*, Fisher has established herself as one of America's premiere gastronomes, thus she no longer focuses on determining her credentials, which include a deep familiarity with gastronomic literature, a finely tuned and well-educated palate, and an elegant and evocative written voice. Rather, she fashions a gastronomic memoir that illuminates female desire—for food, for love, and for the pleasures of a life well-fed. Within *The Gastronomical Me*, Fisher lingers on her despair in Strasbourg in order to portend the impending failure of her first marriage. Thus she images a vulnerable and frightened woman who has lost the will to write and whose lack of purpose has left a void "terrifying, nameless." Soon after the incident, Fisher meets the man who would become her second husband, "the love of her life," beginning a period in which she felt "all her hungers fed" (189).

From an early age, Fisher wrote daily, often reflecting on language and the importance of writing to her identity and to its ongoing formation. In a letter to her sister Norah, she describes the flow of language in her thoughts: "Words shift and reform themselves in the mind, folding onto themselves and begetting new connotations like colored glass in a kaleidoscope or cells in a plant" (*Stay* 31). The same could be said of memory as it functions in her memoirs. The life events and subjective states that she experiences continually shift the primary meaning and illuminate new facets of a given memory. In turn, Fisher freezes the kaleidoscopic movement through a prose configuration that articulates a particular theme, belief, idea, or emotion.

As a writer who used gastronomy as a grounding metaphor, Fisher pondered the difficulty of describing moments "of complete gastronomic satisfaction," remarking that "[s]ometimes they are too keen to be bandied in conversation, too delicate to be pinioned by our insufficient mouthings" (*Serve It Forth* 83). But, she notes:

> Occasionally, in a moment of wide-flung inebriation or the taut introspection of search for things past, a person hits upon his peak of gastronomic emotion. He remembers with shock, almost, and with a nostalgic clarity that calls tears to his inward-looking eyes.
>
> If you can surprise him at such quick times, and make him talk, you are more than fortunate. It is as tricky a business as to watch a bird of paradise at play. (83)

In order to capture blissful moments of "gastronomical satisfaction" Fisher often describes those instances when eater and eaten converge, instances when the boundaries between inside and outside, self and other are temporarily dissolved. These moments entail an intermingling of bodies that disrupts stasis, allowing for intellectual and emotional growth. Fisher articulates the psychological effects and subtle transformations that occur during such exchanges. She effectively translates these "liminal" moments into language by using food as a metaphor through which to express a subjective, existential process.

In one passage from *The Gastronomical Me*, Fisher recalls a picnic she shared at the age of ten with her father and sister Anne. Her description underscores the intermingling of communal pleasure, flavor, and memory:

> Anne and I both felt a subtle excitement at being alone for the first time with the only man in the world we loved. . . . That night I not only saw my Father for the first time as a person[,] . . . I saw the dimples in my little sister's fat hands in a way that still moves me because of that first time; and I saw food as something beautiful to be shared with people instead of as a thrice-daily necessity. I forget what we ate, except for the end of the meal. It was a big round peach pie. . . . It was deep, with lots of juice, and bursting with ripe peaches picked that noon. Royal Albertas, Father said they were. The crust was the most perfect I have ever tasted, except perhaps once upstairs at Simpson's in London, on a hot plum tart. . . . And still the warm round peach pie and the cool yellow cream we ate together that August night live in our hearts' palates, succulent, secret, delicious. (7–8)

In this scene, the shared moment of recognition of and by the other infuses the act of eating with profound significance. Because Anne, Fisher, and their father are joined together as a threesome for the first time while eating the peach pie, the "succulent, secret, delicious" pie flavors the aesthetic core of Fisher's memory. Because the pie imprints the moment on their "hearts' palates" during the act of incorporation, the memory of the pie embodies the shared pleasure of a communal moment; the pie's flavor does not simply represent the communion felt that day, but rather, in effect, contains it.

In *An Alphabet for Gourmets*, published in 1949, Fisher recalls the same plum tart she references in the aforementioned passage. She describes how the tart she ate "at Simpson's in London" arrived at her table "hot, bathed in a flood of Cornish cream, steaming and flowing in the ample plate! How rich it was, how sweet and revivifying to my cold and enervated and above all *young* body! How its steam and savor engulfed and comforted me!" (*Art of Eating* 657). The tart triggers a feeling of communion, or integration, that resembles Fisher's peach pie eating experience. It does so, in part, because the flavor of its crust resembles that of the peach pie, a resemblance that evokes the memory imprinted on what Fisher calls her "heart's palate." In turn, this intermingling of flavor and memory enables Fisher to experience the tart as an agent that "engulfs" and "comforts" her, effectively dissolving the boundaries between self and other, present and past, eater and eaten, inside and outside.

As with the peach pie, Fisher often wrote about the pleasures of eating as an implicit metaphor for emotional intimacy; the most evocative gastronomic moments in Fisher's memoirs often occurred when she was intimately involved with a lover. Quite often the quality of the dishes Fisher recalls eating during a given period of time directly reflects the intensity of her romantic passion—the more in love she felt, the more likely she was to encounter an unforgettably tasty dish.[11] Honeymooning with her first husband, Al, in Paris, Fisher dined on "hot chocolate and the rich croissants" for breakfast. She describes them as

> the most delicious things, there in bed with the Seine flowing past me and pigeons wheeling around the gray Palace mansards that I had ever eaten. They were really the first thing I had tasted since we were married . . . tasted to remember. They were part of the warmth and excitement of that hotel room, with Paris waiting. (48)

In a like manner, Fisher memorializes the meal that she and Al ate to celebrate their first evening in a new apartment in Dijon and to mark their one-month anniversary. That evening, as Fisher recalls,

---

11. This equation also works in reverse. Those dishes that fail to satisfy often correspond to a lack of romantic fulfillment or even a time of loss and despair in her own life.

we ate the biggest, as well as the most exciting, meal that either of us had ever had. . . . Everything that was brought to the table was so new, so wonderfully cooked that what might have been with sated palates a gluttonous orgy was, for our fresh ignorance, a constant refreshment. . . . [W]e felt as if we had seen the far shores of another world. We were drunk with the land breeze that blew from it, and the sure knowledge that it lay waiting for us. (*GM* 58–59)

The meal along with the emotions it stirs (here wonder and fulfillment) speak not only to the satisfaction of a hunger for food but also to the delight of being in love. Fisher explains: "when I write of hunger, I am really writing about love and the hunger for it, and the warmth and richness and fine reality of hunger satisfied . . . and it is all one" (*GM* ix). Infused with hunger for warmth and love and hunger satisfied, *The Gastronomical Me* illuminates how sensual pleasures construct and nourish female identity. The memoir also showcases how the aesthetic pleasures of eating nourish Fisher as a writer.

In *The Gastronomical Me*, Fisher recounts her sensual awakening and charts the development of her belief that how one handles, prepares, and eats food is inextricably linked to how one approaches life. This belief was honed in large part during time spent in France and Switzerland, where Fisher passed what she considered the best years of her first and second marriages. She began living with the man who would become her second husband, Dillwyn Parrish, in 1937.[12] The couple settled in Switzerland, where they began a brief idyll that Fisher recalls as the best part of her life.[13] They lived off the land, growing, harvesting, cooking, and eating their meals. Fisher recounts working with

the oldest soil either of us had ever touched. . . . [I]t seemed almost bursting with life. . . . We grew beautiful salads, a dozen different kinds, and several herbs. There were shallots and onion and garlic. . . . In one of the cellars we stored cabbages and apples and tomatoes and other things on slatted shelves, or in bins. And all the time we ate what we were growing. (152–153)

She and Parrish lived in harmony with the land, practicing a life firmly grounded in the soil, as well as in the body. This harmony echoed Fisher

---

12. Initially Fisher and her first husband, Al, lived with Dillwyn Parrish in Switzerland. As Parrish and Fisher's passion for one another became increasingly obvious, Al left the couple to return to the United States.

13. After Parrish's death in 1941, Fisher wrote that "Dillwyn was life for me. Life is sex, and sex life" (*Life in Letters* 85). Although Fisher was eventually remarried and divorced and had many subsequent lovers, she states in an interview conducted forty years after Parrish's death that "if he had lived, I'm sure we'd still be together. He was the love of my life" (Lazar 64).

and Parrish's symbiotic rapport, one in which the couple "not only made love but *Talked* almost steadily for almost the ten years [they] knew each other" (*Life In Letters* 110–11). Fisher felt "beautiful, witty, truly loved[,] . . . the most fortunate of all women, past sea change and with her hungers fed" (*GM* 189).

Fisher's self-described "bliss" with Parrish was brutally interrupted by the amputation of one of his legs, which had become gangrenous following an embolism that traveled from his calf to his pelvis. He was eventually diagnosed with a terminal circulatory disease, which left him incapacitated with pain. Fisher wrote her second book, *Consider the Oyster*, in part, to entertain and distract her dying husband. Two years after Parrish's death in 1941, Fisher became pregnant with her first child, whom she formally presented as an adopted child. She spent her pregnancy in hiding. During this reclusive period, she wrote *The Gastronomical Me*, which recounts her growing capacity to detect and to nourish her own hungers. The memoir ends with a trip that Fisher took to Mexico to heal from Parrish's death. As Fisher's biographer Joan Reardon describes, *The Gastronomical Me* "can be seen as an effort to put the past into some kind of context before [she] assumed the responsibilities of a single parent" (156).

Parrish's death marked the beginning of a twelve-year period during which Fisher would lose most of her closest loved ones—her husband and brother each committed suicide, and both her parents died. She married and divorced her last husband, Donald Friede, who spent much of their marriage in and out of mental hospitals. Experiencing such tragedy, Fisher found herself unable to write, confessing to her psychiatrist that "writing for me was (is?) a form of making love. I have nobody to make love to" (*Life in Letters* 22). Fisher figures writing as a form of communion that echoes her gastronomic philosophy in its emphasis on intimacy. Because Fisher envisioned eating, as well as writing, as a form of communion arising from embodied pleasures, her world-view was challenged by the loss of appetite she experienced after the death of her loved ones. From 1950 to 1955, Fisher found herself unable to write.

When she began to write again toward the end of this five-year period, Fisher did so assured that she would "never write as casually, easily, nonchalantly again" (*Letters* 147). This ease did return temporarily, however, in 1957, when she found herself "alive and nourished by an active and very satisfying *actuality* of man-woman love" (*Letters* 158).[14] She explained in a letter to a friend that "[b]eing in love again has loosened my tight dry muscles, and I am writing easily" (*Letters* 159). The romance did not last long, however, and twelve years would pass between *An Alphabet for Gourmets* and her next book, *A Cordiall Water*, subtitled *A Garland of Odd and*

---

14. According to Fisher's biographer, Joan Reardon, the man-woman love Fisher refers to was in actuality a woman-woman love; from 1957 to 1960, Fisher carried on an affair with Marietta Voorhees.

Old Receipts to Assuage the Ills of Man and Beast. The radical shift from gastronomy to curatives suggests that, no longer able to write as a form of making love or as a means of paying tribute to the lost "love of her life," Fisher began to write as a form of healing.

Fisher's next substantial project, *Map of Another Town* (1964), provides a blueprint for the writing process as a means of working through emotional trauma. The book, which recounts Fisher's year-long sojourn in Provence with her daughters, would be Fisher's first memoir since *The Gastronomical Me*, written over twenty years before. Unlike *The Gastronomical Me* which recounts those years in her life before she had lost most of the people she loved, a time when she felt "the most fortunate of all women, past sea change and with her hungers fed," *Map of Another Town* examines her "self-inflicted development as a ghost" (189, 63).

Driven abroad by the need to recuperate from twelve years of devastating loss that left her "scarred," "almost disintegrating," Fisher reflects on the journey:

> I was alone in Europe for the first time in my life really; always before I had been the companion of someone well loved. . . . Now I was single, with two small daughters, and a world war and some private battles had come between the two women of myself, so that I felt fumbling and occasionally even frightened (59).

Rather than nourishing herself with food, as she does in *The Gastronomical Me*, Fisher practices the art of disappearance, a feat "that takes practice. . . . It is mainly a question of withdrawing to the vanishing point from the consciousness of the people one is with" (10).[15]

The woman Fisher depicts in *Map of Another Town* contrasts dramatically with the woman who connects with and participates in foreign cultures in Fisher's more gastronomically grounded works. These "two women"— one driven toward connection and the other toward disappearance—capture the dialectic between feeding well and self-denial, between agency and its repression. They also capture the struggle between the emotional ends of eating—well-being and pleasure versus disgust and fear. Whereas Fisher's early works celebrate an appetite for food and for love, *Map of Another*

---

15. In "M. F. K. Fisher and the Embodiment of Desire," Julie Campbell quotes this passage, concluding that "[t]his ability to assess a moment, by being in it but not necessarily part of it, and to withdraw from it at will, suggests that Fisher has achieved the foreigner's 'self-confidence of being, of being able to settle within the self with a smooth, opaque certainty' which [Julia] Kristeva compares to 'an oyster shut under the flooding tide or the expressionless joy of warm stones'" (200). In contrast, I argue that, when examined alongside her eating pleasures, Fisher's 'ghostly' presence in *Map of Another Town* indicates a troubling disembodiment that attests to disabling psychological pain.

Town articulates the feeling of disintegration and fear that both arises from and feeds her loss of appetite.

One of the few dining scenes included in the memoir finds Fisher eating what "seemed the longest meal I had ever endured. . . . [I]ts rich tedious courses bit like acid inside me, metamorphosed by anger and ennui. . . . All this was good for me. It made me accustom myself to acceptance of my slow evolution as an invisible thing, a ghost" (67–68). This scene provides a polar reflection of Fisher's time abroad recounted in *The Gastronomical Me*. Rather than nourishing intimacy and pleasure, dining becomes a corrosive against which Fisher must shield herself by "withdrawing to the vanishing point from the consciousness" of those around her.

That Fisher's memoirs written about her travels abroad in the company of her first two husbands center around the intimate pleasures of eating while *Map of Another Town* finds her a self-described ghost attests to the disembodiment and disintegration that accompanies mourning; her lack of appetite within the memoir indicates a psychological disengagement with her body and with the surrounding world.[16] Fisher's shift away from gastronomy also indicates that she found a drive to create memoir that replaced her drive to write as a "form of making love"; she wrote as a form of grieving. Articulating the psychological wounds that haunted her journey to France in 1954 enabled Fisher to work through her grief. Fisher's return to gastronomy in her next memoir indicates that she successfully restored her appetite for life as well as for food writing.[17] One of Fisher's most celebratory endeavors, *With Bold Knife and Fork* (1969) demonstrates that Fisher succeeded in reconstituting her "disintegrating" self, albeit in an altered form; the ghostly woman who haunts *Map of Another Town* has become embodied once again and is able to celebrate the physical pleasures of preparing and eating her favorite recipes. Fisher lauds her "sensual and voluptuous gastronomical favorites-of-a-lifetime" and urges her readers "with bold knife and fork, eat well of forbidden fruits!" (135).

The most notable change between Fisher's earlier food writing and *With Bold Knife and Fork* lies in her increasing reliance on the food writing of others and on the writing process itself to nourish her hungers. The memoir shows Fisher nourishing herself with words, relying on language to recall the memory of former pleasures. Commentary on American and

---

16. Significantly, the other memoir in which Fisher recounts her travels to France while single, *A Considerable Town*, 1970, is also relatively sparse on alimentary anecdotes, clearly falling into the travel writing genre.

17. While *The Cooking of Provincial France* came out in 1968, it has not been included in the discussion of Fisher's motives as a writer because, like *The Story of Wine in California*, it was solicited and constricted by an outside source. Commissioned by Time-Life, *The Cooking of Provincial France*—whose contributors include Elizabeth David and Julia Child—was so heavily edited that Fisher attempted at one point to have her name withdrawn from the project. She found the end result "one more status-symbol of quasi-literacy" (*Life In Letters* 244).

French cookbooks and gastronomic literature abound. Fisher also reflects on the power of memory to nourish both physical and psychological hungers; she has mastered the skill of feeding the body through the intellect so well that she can "savor" the "strange familiarity" of "flavors once met in early days" on what she calls her "mind's palate" (100–101). This reference to the "mind's palate" echoes the passage from *The Gastronomical Me* in which Fisher recalls eating a peach pie with her father and sister. The moment from her childhood was marked by a feeling of communion, the memory of which remained imprinted on her "heart's palate, succulent, secret, delicious" (8). A striking change marks the difference between the earlier and the later passages—a shift in the source of nourishment. Fisher once fed her creativity with embodied pleasures, nourishing her mind with her body. In later years Fisher nourished creativity by savoring her favorite foods and food writing on her mind's palate, feeding her body with memories of former pleasures.

The most powerful articulation of Fisher's gastronomic philosophy appears in her final work, the posthumously published *Last House*. In the following scene, Fisher recounts the events of an evening struggling with a stubborn illness:

> I coughed steadily in a small, dry, exhausting way until the speed and sound of the cough changed, and up into my throat moved my soul. . . . The soul, smooth and about the size of a small truffle or scallop or a large marble, rose firmly into my upper throat. . . . I knew what it looked like, for I had seen it long ago. I knew its color and its contours and its taste. . . . I told it, in a flash of our first meeting, and of the mystery and respect, and indeed affection I had battened on from that day. I was about five, maybe four. . . . [A]ll I remember is that my young, small soul rose into my throat and then came out. . . . It was about as big as a little hazelnut or chickpea, of the subtlest creamy white, like ivory but deeper. . . . I recognized it fully, without any doubt or timidity, as my own soul. Then I put it gently into my mouth, bit into it, and chewed and swallowed it. . . . I made sure that none had stayed in my mouth and that all of it was well down my throat, for it was important that it reassemble itself and stay there inside me, to grow. . . . I never wondered about its next visit, but I knew there would be one. (28–31)

By imaging her soul as a "truffle" or "chickpea" that she chews and swallows, Fisher dissolves and reconstitutes the boundaries between inside and outside, self and other, eater and eaten, soul and body, incorporation and expression. Fisher is not disturbed and alienated by the embodiment of her soul because she "recognizes" herself with "affection." With this imagery, Fisher not only dissolves boundaries, but she also effectively converges opposites by imaging inside *as* outside, self *as* other, eater *as* eaten, the soul *as* embodied, and incorporation *as* expression. Fisher symbolizes a self-construction based on mutual incorporation and expression, one in which external and subjective realities are conjoined through communion; she incorporates, chews and swallows a part of herself, a part that has become externalized and reconfigured, so that it "can reassemble itself . . . inside" and "grow." By figuring her soul as both inside and outside, self and other, Fisher images a realm of mutual construction, one in which she incorporates and is incorporated by the external world. This passage literalizes one of Brillat-Savarin's most quoted aphorisms: "Tell me what you eat, and I shall tell you what you are" (1). Fisher not only *is* what she eats, but she *eats* what she is.

By telling her "expressed" soul about "the mystery and respect and indeed affection" that she feels for it, Fisher feeds her soul with words so that it can, in turn, nourish her body. Fisher underscores that speaking, like eating, provides spiritual *and* physical nourishment; eating and language mutually construct the body and the soul. Because the feelings of pleasure and integrity that arise from these communal moments are by nature short-lived, they carry with them a poignant reminder of the anxiety and alienation that also inhabit the scale of human emotions. Fisher's gastronomic memoirs show, however, that nurturing a vision of the self in symbiosis with the surrounding world encourages a form of self-construction in which the pleasures of eating, whether embodied or expressed in language, wield the power to assuage anxiety, loneliness, and fear by nourishing moments of identification, communion, and pleasure.

3   A Queer Appetite
The Alice B. Toklas Cook Book

Since its publication in 1954, *The Alice B. Toklas Cook Book* has enjoyed a cult readership among American food lovers, many of whom have prepared its recipes, which span from the sensible "Restricted Veal Loaf" to the extravagant "Young Turkey with Truffles" to the controversial "Haschich Fudge."[1] As much as the recipes themselves, the reminiscences into which they are embedded have long drawn readers eager to learn more about Toklas' adventures with her partner Gertrude Stein. Only recently, however, has the *Cook Book* begun to garner serious attention from literary scholars, who had previously gleaned it for information about Stein and her relationship with Toklas before setting it aside.

One notable and eloquent exception dates back to Paul Schmidt's "As If a Cookbook Had Anything To Do With Writing," published in 1974. Schmidt examines four of the most preeminent American food writers, Julia Child, Adelle Davis, M. F. K. Fisher, and Toklas to argue that the latter pair belong to a tradition of food writing that can be traced back to Jean Anthelme Brillat-Savarin and are, "like him, amateurs of the table," who rely on an intermingling of anecdote, memory, and flavor (180–181).[2] After Schmidt's article, over a quarter century would pass before critics would begin to address the genre-blurring nature of Toklas' *Cook Book*. One of the first to do so, Traci Marie Kelly happened upon it quite by "accident"

---

1. For a first-hand account of cooking from Toklas' cookbook when it was first published, before the advent of Julia Child, see Janet Malcolm, "As the French Do."

2. More particularly, Schmidt examines Toklas, Fisher, Julia Child, and Adele Davis to argue that these women "belong to two traditions of writing about food that we can trace to two great monuments of France: *La Physiologie du Gout* by Brillat-Savarin, and *Le Guide Culinaire* by Escoffier. In this heritage, Alice B. Toklas and M. F. K. Fisher are Savarinists, and like him, amateurs of the table; Julia Child and Adelle Davis are Escoffians, and like Escoffier, both are professional cooks." Schmidt states that, like Brillat-Savarin, the Savarinist relies on "anecdote stimulated by food, the memory of taste awakened by anecdote" (180–181). In "'Consider the Menu Carefully': The Dining Room Tales of Alice B. Toklas," Salvatore Marano likewise links *The Alice B. Toklas Cook Book* with *The Physiology of Taste*. His brief comparison finds the two texts share an "anecdotally digressive manner" and a mastery of "the three stages of the cultural process of production, preparation and consuming of food" (176).

while researching Gertrude Stein. Kelly went on to analyze the *Cook Book* in an essay, published in 2001, that defines three major categories of culinary autobiographies: the culinary memoir, the autoethnographic cookbook, and the autobiographical cookbook. This latter category, to which Kelly assigns *The Alice B. Toklas Cook Book,* is "a complex intermingling of both auto-biographical and cookery traditions. . . . Such texts do not necessarily favor one element or the other; rather, the authors try to balance and illuminate the inter-elemental nature of how the recipe reveals the life story" (257).

Even more recently, Anna Linzie not only locates the *Cook Book* "at the borders of several genres or categories: cookbook, autobiography, and liter-ary experiment," but also draws attention to its gender-blending content (140). She observes:

> In the *Cook Book* as a whole, the unconventional use of the quint-essentially (male) modernist 'war story' genre not only alongside but thoroughly mixed up with the description of trivial, domestic aspects of life such as cooking and recipes works to collapse, or at least un-dermine the strongly hierarchical distinction between the martial and the domestic arts. . . . [t]he boundaries between public and domestic concerns have been unsettled or partly erased. (160)

Noting that the *Cook Book* has been dismissed by scholars because "it has typically been read and categorized, if at all, simply as a trivial cookbook," Linzie examines it as a genre-bending and gender-blending text through the lens of autobiographical theory to "conceptualize the *Cook Book* as a ren-egade autobiography," which challenges "an autobiographical tradition that presupposes heterosexuality" (148, 139, 51). As such, she reads the cook-book as a "queer" text, a term used by scholars and activists to designate that which challenges, questions, and disrupts heteronormativity. In turn, "to queer" as a scholarly pursuit means to delineate how texts and contexts destabilize "normative" notions of gender and sexuality as fixed or essential in order to underscore their fluidity.[3] I would like to extend Linzie's analysis of the *Cook Book* as a text that destabilizes the heteronormative ideology of autobiographical writing by shifting the focus from autobiography onto food writing. Taking up where Schmidt left off in his discussion of Toklas' debt to Brillat-Savarin, I argue that Toklas incorporates key tenets of gastronomic literature into her cookbook, a gesture that disrupts the heternormative domestic food writing tradition by ideologically queering its convention-ally gendered bounds. By simultaneously addressing Toklas' *Cook Book* as a queer text and situating it within a highly gendered food writing tradition,

---

3. In the words of queer activist, writer, and scholar Thomas Glave, the term 'queer" has "been used much in recent years as both verb and adjective by many . . . scholars. . . . With such linguistic and intellectual fluidity and expansiveness, almost anything can be 'queer'-ed or 'queery'-ed: text. . . , public and private spaces, ideological, cultural, historical, and national narratives . . . , metaphors, allegories, and so on" (246).

this study works to interweave and extend the disparate strands of Toklas scholarship in order to illuminate the power of genre-bending food writing to transgress and reconfigure conventional gender ideologies.

Published a decade after *The Gastronomical Me*, M. F. K. Fisher's pioneering celebration of female appetite, *The Alice B. Toklas Cook Book* blurred the boundaries that separated gastronomic literature from the domestic cookbook by merging these genres into one book. Like Fisher before her, Toklas adopted the French appreciation of cooking and dining as art forms. She also revered and nurtured the aesthetic pleasures that lead to gastronomic knowledge and articulated such pleasures in writing. But unlike *The Gastronomical Me*, which is comprised entirely of gastronomic memories, or memoir, Toklas' *Cook Book* revolves mnemonically and organizationally around recipes, which are addressed to the American and English home cook. By interweaving her recipes with a travelogue that charts her undomesticated adventures dining throughout the United States and France, Toklas inserts herself and her pleasure into an other-oriented, self-denying genre. In doing so, she flouts the heteronormative ideology that discouraged women's self-expression and pleasure in eating.

Blending the sensuality and self-expression of gastronomic literature with the attention to domestic detail of the American cookbook, Toklas positions herself as a gourmand and as an exceptionally skilled and aesthetically attuned home cook. In other words, Toklas figures herself as a queer modern epicure—equally at ease in the home kitchen as in the most elite restaurants. Her self-presentation calls into question and reconfigures the nineteenth- and early twentieth-century ideologies that defined gastronomy and gastronomic tourism as male pursuits and domestic cookery as a feminine endeavor.

THE MASCULINE PALATE: MALE-AUTHORED DOMESTIC COOKBOOKS AND GASTRONOMIC TOUR GUIDES

The seeming effortlessness with which Toklas bridges the gendered divide between men's and women's food writing stands out in sharp contrast to the tension that surfaces in the domestic cookbooks that American men began to author in the late 1930s. Whereas Toklas discoursed with ease on the traditionally male pursuit of gastronomy, American men often displayed a defensive masculinity upon entering the feminized realm of the home kitchen. Such defensiveness attests to their discomfort, which, at times, became so pronounced that it led to what Barbara Haber describes as "ludicrous posturing" (213).[4]

---

4. In *From Hardtack to Home Fries*, Barbara Haber examines the posturing of male cookbook authors from the 1930 to the 1960s. She also traces this posturing back to women cookbook authors of the nineteenth century, who often worked to "hide the fact that they may have been more interested in politics and social justice" than in domestic management (213).

Unlike their British counterparts who had long been writing the occasional book on household management and felt comfortable advising the housewife on cookery instruction, American men had rarely written for the female home cook. Rather, they penned professional cookbooks, gastronomic literature, or disquisitions on the scientific and moral principles of healthy eating—genres traditionally gendered male. Unlike the realm of gastronomy and professional cookery, the home kitchen and home cookery were perceived as female domains. As a result, the American man who wrote domestic cookbooks was inherently conscious of his potential feminization. In her study of cookbooks and gender in the twentieth-century United States, Jessamyn Neuhaus examines a range of domestic cookbooks written by men to find that "authors and editors took pains to depict men as essentially different kinds of culinary creatures than women in order to safeguard the masculinity of the male hobby cook" (76). Some authors differentiated themselves from the female home cook by declaring themselves innate gourmands who, like their nineteenth-century predecessors, wanted to help their readers hone an aesthetically nuanced palate. Others simply denigrated women's cookery skills, often resorting to disparaging rhetoric.[5] As Neuhaus documents, for example, George Frederick's *Cooking as Men Like It* (1930) attributes the relative decline in marriage to woman's "incompetent cookery," noting that "few things move man to manslaughter more than does poor cookery" (82). Robert Loeb dedicates his popular and playful *Wolf In Chef's Clothing* (1950) "To my father, and my father's father, and my father's father's father, right back to Adam, all of whom spent their lives as the passive victims of feminine culinary caprice—from the first apple to the apfelstrudel" (7).

Gentler authors sought to depict men as artists in the kitchen who enjoyed an innate creativity not shared by women. For example, in the preface to his *The Best Men are Cooks* (1941), Frank Shay notes that "[m]en should be good cooks, for they have a greater feeling for food than women have; . . . they are adventurous and are willing to take chances. . . . Women have reduced cooking to a science while men cooks are working to restore it to its former high estate as one of the finer arts" (vii).[6] Like Shay, male authors frequently depicted men as more adventurous and imaginative in the kitchen than women. They also took pains to define themselves and their palates as more aesthetically refined and attuned to pleasure than the female home cook with her uninspired taste.

---

5. Neuhaus points out that with the onset of World War II and the rise in patriotic propaganda that linked the nation's well-being to mom's home cooking, "fewer authors felt inclined to attack women's fundamental lack of cookery ability" (153).

6. Shay did not maintain such a gentle tone toward women throughout, however. As Barbara Haber points out, "He snidely refers to the British Mrs. Beeton, the most famous woman cookbook author of her day, as 'the nineteenth-century lady who put the blight on English cuisine'" (212).

Many male authors differentiated themselves by using the words "gourmet," "king," or "chef" in their titles and by firmly aligning themselves with the nineteenth-century gourmand, presenting their cookbooks as gustatory criticism and themselves as arbiters of good taste. For example, in *Gourmet Dinners* (1941), G. Selmer Fougner blends gastronomic essay, domestic cookbook, and professional cookbook in one work. A wine writer for the *New York Sun*, Fougner clearly defines himself as a gourmand in the elite sense of the term—well-traveled, well-heeled, well-connected, a well-respected dining critic, and in much demand as a dining companion. In the forward to *Gourmet Dinners*, he states outright that

> his function in the field of gastronomy, as he sees it, is limited to the role of the widely traveled gourmet who describes the culinary marvels he has found in his search after epicurean adventure throughout the world. And with the description, he passes along to his readers the recipes for the fine dishes which have been set before him in the various epicurean groups . . . of which he has been, in a manner of speaking, the moving spirit.
>
> The author, then is not a cook. But greatly mistaken indeed is he who believes that to criticize a dinner it is necessary to be an expert chef. (vii)

On one level, Fougner's assertion that he "is not a cook" enables him to avoid association with the home kitchen and its accompanying feminization. On another level, Fougner's claim that he "is not a cook" echoes that made by many nineteenth-century gourmands who defined themselves as consumers, rather than producers, of the culinary arts.

As self-defined critics of the culinary arts, the nineteenth-century gourmand "represented the public pursuit of sensory pleasure," unlike women who concerned themselves with "the private satisfaction of physiological needs" (Ferguson 93). Drawing on tradition, Fougner dissociates himself from the practice of domestic cookery, claiming an authority as a gourmand, or dining critic, with a discriminating palate. Like the nineteenth-century gourmand, or man of good taste, Fougner likewise writes in order "to interest those who like to read about good food" (xiii). In other words, his book fits into what Stephen Mennell describes as the "ill-defined margin at which the gastronomic essay gradually shades into the cookery book." Such works "seem intended to be read as literature" as much as for practical instruction (271). Fougner states outright that "[s]ome of the recipes are intended purely for experts," thereby excluding them from the practical domain of the home cook, who, he implies, will read them as a form of vicarious gourmandism (xiii).

William Rhode takes a similar tack in *Of Cabbages and Kings* (1938), for which he gathered recipes from European royal kitchens run by chefs who "reduced their work to the simplest, most subtle practices—just as great painters . . . achieve their finest effects in simplicity" (8). He did so in order to offer the modern housewife "the experience of the great, simple artist who really knew food and cooking," encouraging his readers to "[l]ook into [such] experience and get the 'hang' of what makes fine food—not the women's magazine 'pap' of today" (8). Like Fougner, Rhode firmly differentiates his "domestic cookbook" from the women's tradition of home cooking by aligning himself with artists, chefs, and kings.

Appearing a year after Rhode's gastronomic cookbook, Merle Armitage's *Fit for a King* (1939) combines gastronomic essays with recipes to nourish the "cultivated palate" of his readers. In his introductory chapter, Armitage differentiates male gourmands from female home cooks, noting that

> Man has proven that even in an over-refined civilization he can retain an enthusiasm, amounting to gusto, for food and eating. Probably because he *can* enjoy food without inhibitions he best can prepare dishes for the epicure. Far too many women find cookery a drudgery, an inescapable, dull routine. It cannot be from lack of practice then that women, by and large, have not made good as cooks. . . . Cooking is a thing women *have* to do. Remove the daily necessity, and you would, undoubtedly, remove most of the indifference, making room thereby, for lively interest. (12)

Unlike many of his male counterparts who declare that men enjoy an innate gusto absent in women, Armitage provides a cultural explanation for the discrepancy between men's and women's palates. He excuses women's alleged lack of gourmandize by acknowledging that placing three meals a day on the family table leads to "drudgery, an inescapable, dull routine." By presenting cookery and gourmandize as pursuits "Fit for a King," Armitage encourages more men to enter the home kitchen. With this gesture he suggests a future in which men might enjoy preparing the occasional meal themselves, thereby relieving the housewife of a portion of her weekly cooking duties. Although he does not disparage women outright, however, Armitage still takes their inferiority in the kitchen for a given.

The puffery of men who authored domestic cookbooks in the 1930s clearly attests to their discomfort at entering a culturally feminized realm. Men, however, weren't the only ones struck by anxiety when they entered the domestic realm of cookery. Women found the potential emasculation of men who entered the home kitchen worrisome as well. In *The Mystery Chef's Own Cookbook* (1934), John MacPherson states outright that he adopted the pseudonym to protect his mother who "was horrified when she first heard that I had taken to cooking as a hobby" (viii). Not surprisingly, MacPherson makes a concerted effort to justify home cooking as a respectable occupation for men:

> To me it is not strange that I should find pleasure in cooking. What does seem strange to me is that so few people do find pleasure in it or know that many of the world's greatest men have found pleasure and

relaxation in the art of excellent cooking. They are surprised to hear that Alexandre Dumas was a wonderful cook, and that the last book he wrote was a cookbook. . . . I have in my possession the favorite recipes of over two hundred of the world's greatest men. Among those who have made cooking their hobby are . . . Whistler, Clemenceau, King Edward VII, the Right Honourable Arthur J. Balfour, former Prime Minister of Great Britain. . . . I could almost fill this book with their names—kings, prime ministers, princes, presidents, cardinals, great generals, admirals, scientists, great painters, authors, musicians, sculptors. (vi)

As such examples attest, bridging the rigidly gendered spheres of domestic food writing was no easy task for American men. One notable standout who felt no need to disparage women or to justify his passion for cookery proved to be none other than James Beard, whose first book *Hors d'Oeuvre and Canapés* (1940) provides rules of etiquette and recipes for hosting the ideal cocktail party, which Beard viewed "as the twentieth-century salon" (2). Wanting to encourage more men to take up domestic cookery, Beard chose manly topics for his next two cookbooks, *Cook it Outdoors* (1941) and *Fowl and Game Cookery* (1944). Although these books were geared more toward the male as opposed to the female home cook, Beard does not devalue women or women's cooking in order to justify men's entry into the home kitchen. By 1949, Beard hit his stride as the "Dean of American cookery" in *The Fireside Cookbook*, addressed equally to men and women.

By the time Toklas wrote her cookbook, another genre of food writing had taken root in the United States—the gastronomic tour guide. Whereas England saw the publication of Lieutenant-Colonel Newnham-Davis' *Dinners and Diners: Where and How to Dine in London* in 1899 and France began using its first Michelin guide in 1900, the United States would not witness the publication of its own gastronomic guide book until the 1920s, when the first city restaurant guides, such as George Chappell's *Restaurants of New York* (1925), came into being (Smith 352). The first national guide, Duncan Hines' *Adventures in Good Eating*, appeared in 1936. Providing an annotated list of restaurants for travelers throughout the United States and updating it annually, Hines became a national celebrity. International guides began to appear at the end of World War II, when record numbers of Americans began traveling to France. The more well-heeled were guided by Samuel Chamberlain's "An Epicurean Tour of the French Provinces," first published serially in *Gourmet* magazine from 1949 to 1952. Chamberlain first encountered France when he served in the military during World War I and again as a civilian in the 1920s. Before his return to the United States in 1934, he befriended a number of American expatriates, including Toklas and Stein.

In 1952, Chamberlain's series for *Gourmet* appeared in book form as *Bouquet de France*, preceding Toklas' groundbreaking cookbook by two years. Unlike Hines' guidebook, which provides brief, informative reviews of America's restaurants, *Bouquet de France* offers an histori-cal overview of French provincial cooking, a guide to regional inns and restaurants, as well as recipes gathered "from the best provincial and Parisian chefs in France" (viii). Chamberlain undoubtedly drew inspi-ration from two of the founding fathers of French gastronomic tour-ism—Curnonsky (pseudonym of Maurice Edmond Sailland) and Marcel Rouff.[7] Beginning in 1921, Curnonsky and Rouff began publishing *La France Gastronomique*, a twenty-seven volume series on French pro-vincial cooking, which recommends inns and restaurants to discerning French travelers. In doing so, they created a series that "merges travel in France with the cooking found in her provinces" (Curnonsky 13).

Like Curnonsky and Rouff before him, Chamberlain pays tribute to Brillat-Savarin, his home province of Bugey, and his hometown of Belley, even including a fondue recipe concocted by the gastronome's biographer and great-nephew Lucien Tendret. Tendret, a gourmand in his own right, wrote *La Table au Pays de Brillat-Savarin*. Tendret's grandson gave Toklas and Stein a copy of the book, which the couple so well adored that they discussed translating it into English. Like Chamberlain, Toklas derived much inspiration from Brillat-Savarin, Lucien Tendret, and gastronomic guidebooks such as Curnonsky and Marcel Rouff's twenty-eight volume *La France Gastronomique*.

THE MAKING OF A LESBIAN GASTRONOME
AND HER COOKBOOK

Toklas herself grew up in San Francisco to inherit the domestic responsibili-ties expected of a married woman at the age of twenty; when her mother died in 1897, she was bequeathed the domestic management of a home filled with men, including her grandfather, father, uncle, and younger brother. As one family friend remarked, "Alice was looked upon 'only as a housekeeper, provider of food and of general comfort'" (29). Another friend recalled eat-ing at Alice's family home: "'Alice and I sat meekly swallowing our food, never attempting to venture an opinion, nor were we encouraged to do so; quickly we fled at the first opportunity to Alice's room to reestablish our lost identities'" (21). When Alice did offer an opinion, as biographer Linda Simon notes, her "ideas were ignored or dismissed with a laugh."

---

7. In *All Manners of Food*, Stephen Mennell explains that Curnonsky and Rouff "seized the opportunity of linking gastronomy and tourism, and thus initiated a great interest in a vogue for French regional cookery. . . . The alliance of tourism and gastronomy was particularly to the advantage of tyre companies like Michelin and Kléber-Colombes, who began to publish their celebrated guides to the restau-rants and hotels of France. Curnonsky and his friends [Rouff, Louis Forest, Austin de Croze, Maurice des Ombiaux] had links to them, but also wrote their own guides" (276).

During the ten years she spent caring for her family, Toklas struggled to cope with her lesbianism within a *fin de siécle* culture that experienced a fundamental shift in its attitude toward women's intimate relations. On one hand, the tail end of the nineteenth century brought a select group of women access to higher education and to pioneering career opportunities; Toklas herself attended the University of Washington, where she earned the equivalent of an associate degree in Music, a decidedly more conventional route than Stein's decision to study psychology by attending Johns Hopkins Medical School for five years. Having achieved intellectual independence, such women were often loath to marry men who "expected them to become dutiful wives, attending the home" (D'Emilio 191).[8] For many of these women, "the choice to continue or pursue relationships with other women was a natural one. . . . [T]hese partnerships, which were sometimes labeled 'Boston marriages,' were visible to the outside world, and accepted by society" (192). Simultaneously such "overly educated" women were beginning to feature in medical literature. In particular, renowned doctors such as S. Weir Mitchell, Edward Clarke, and John Harvey Kellogg argued that women who pursued intellectual endeavors risked the ruin of their mental and physical health. Male practitioners commonly believed that women were especially at risk from puberty through eighteen years of age, the period during which their ovaries were developing; doctors believed that mental exertion would inhibit ovarian growth, resulting in sterility.[9]

In addition to its growing concern with women's higher education, the medical community was also beginning to examine same-sex relationships and to define them as indicative of mental and physical degeneration. Some suffrage opponents went so far as to yoke a woman's drive for the vote with sexual frustration and homosexual desire. In the words of one doctor, "the driving force in many agitators and militant women who are always after their rights, is often an unsatisfied sex impulse, with a homosexual aim. Married women with a completely satisfied libido rarely take an active interest in militant movements" (Simmons 57).[10] According to this logic,

---

8. As John D'Emilio and Estelle Freedman state in their book *Intimate Matters: A History of Sexuality in America* "[o]f women educated at Bryn Mawr between 1889 and 1908, for instance, fifty-three percent remained unwed. For Wellesley and the University of Michigan, the figures were forty-three and forty-seven percent. The proportion among those who went on for advanced degrees was even more lopsided: three-quarters of the women who received Ph.D.'s between 1877 and 1924 remained single" (190).

9. Not surprisingly, women educators made strong counterarguments as did Mary Putnam Jacobi, one of the nation's most influential and respected female doctors. The belief that a woman's higher education could lead to her mental and physical degeneration, however, continued to prevail within the medical community until well into the twentieth century. See Helen Lefkowitz Horowitz, "The Body in the Library."

10. Dr. John Meagher quoted in Christina Simmons, "Companionate Marriage and the Lesbian Threat."

the best way to silence an activist would be to marry her off to a sexually attentive man. As such thinking attests, the unmarried woman underwent intense scrutiny by the medical community, which was not only beginning to define same-sex relationships as homosexual but also to construct "images of lesbians. . . . around notions of illness, perversion, inversion, and paranoia" (Benstock 11).

Such hostility toward women achieving higher education and toward same-sex desire spoke loudly to the fragility of middle-class heteronormative conventions at the turn into the twentieth century. In the words of one scholar: "In constructing viable lives without motherhood, female couples offered an implicit challenge to the delicate structure of middle-class civilized morality" (D'Emilio 201). Thus, Toklas grew up during a time when public response toward women's same-sex relationships was undergoing a revolutionary shift from one of acceptance to one of disgust and hostility. Simon summarizes Toklas' plight as a lesbian living in the early twentieth-century United States: "Unable to fulfill the expectations of marriage and children, limited to those very few friends who understood her, Alice looked forward to a lonely future" (34). Her only hope lay in an escape from her familial duties. So she began planning an extended trip to Europe. Tellingly, once she set sail in 1907, she never again set eyes on her father. Within forty-eight hours of her arrival in Paris, she had met Gertrude Stein, with whom she built a life grounded in sensual pleasures, pleasures denied the proper middle- and upper-class American woman.

Stein herself documents the marked improvement in the quality of Toklas' life initiated by travel abroad and completed by the couple's union in "Ada," a word portrait that Stein crafted about Toklas who features as Ada. In it, Stein recounts Toklas' unhappiness taking care of family in San Francisco:

> Her mother died . . . . The daughter then kept house for her father and took care of her brother. There were many relations who lived with them. The daughter did not like them to live with them and she did not like them to die with them. . . . She told her father . . . that she did not like it at all being one being living then. He never said anything. She was afraid then. (15)

The brief sketch ends with a playful, erotic tribute to the physical and emotional intimacy the couple enjoyed together in France: "Trembling was all living, living was all loving some one was then the other one. Certainly this one was loving this Ada then. And certainly Ada all her living then was happier in living than any one else who ever could, who was, who is, who ever will be living" (16). These latter lines of the "Ada" manuscript appear in Toklas' handwriting while the previous ones were clearly written by Stein, a fact that has led one biographer to conclude that they were crafted by Toklas herself (Souhami 96).[11] Regardless of whether or not Toklas authored part of Ada, the sketch undoubtedly articulates Toklas' feelings about her family and for Stein. Thus, in their symbiotic and highly idiosyncratic fashion, the couple document the fact that Toklas' decision to escape the patriarchal confines of home enabled her to build a lesbian identity grounded in pleasures denied by the domestic ideology to which she was heir.

The couple lived together on the Left Bank of Paris from 1910 until Stein's death in 1946; for most of these years, they summered in Brillat-Savarin's home province of Bugey. For Americans living abroad during this time, France allowed, even enabled, a freedom of expression in the literary, visual, and culinary arts. For Toklas, in particular, cookery became a means of constructing her identity as the partner of Gertrude Stein, as an American expatriate living in Paris, and as a regular hostess to the likes of Pablo Picasso and F. Scott Fitzgerald. By creating an expatriate household in which her "husband" was another woman, Toklas queered American domestic ideology, which defined woman's role as nurturing man and, literally as well as metaphorically, reproducing the American nation.[12]

Given Toklas' unconventional life and the radical nature of Stein's own writing, it is hardly surprising that *The Alice B. Toklas Cook Book* blurs the gendered distinctions between men's and women's food writing. It draws as much inspiration from the free form and aesthetic sensibility of gastronomic literature as from the domestic cookbook. Toklas' emphasis on the presentation of self as well as on cooking and on dining as art forms were likewise key concerns of Brillat-Savarin, as they were for other authors of gastronomic literature.

According to Denise Gigante, gastronomic literature traces its roots back to the "eighteenth-century discourse on taste" and identifies "three separate categories of appetite: a basic hunger for food, a desire aroused by the presentation of an appetizing dish, and an appetite stimulated by all the arts of cookery when our hunger has already been satisfied" (*Gusto* xvii). If, as Gigante argues, gastronomers were primarily "concerned with the

---

11. Scholars have long debated Toklas' influence on Stein's oeuvre, with some scholars positing that Toklas herself might have written *The Autobiography of Alice B. Toklas*, Stein's most accessible and popular book. In "A Recipe for Modernism and the Somatic Intellect in *The Alice B. Toklas Cook Book* and Gertrude Stein's *Tender Buttons*," Belinda Bruner names Richard Bridgmen, George Wickes, and Holly Laird as three scholars who argue that Toklas may have authored the *Autobiography*.

12. Although numerous second wave feminist critics describe Toklas and Stein's homosexual relationship as modeled on heteronormativity, with Toklas playing wife and Stein husband, contemporary gender studies scholars have reinterpreted such couplings to draw attention to their gender disruption. In particular, they take into account the playful, subversive, performative nature of such lesbian dynamics to argue that such couples effectively queer (challenge, destabilize, provide a new perspective on) the very dynamic they appear to reproduce.

third, artificial or cultivated type of appetite, at the furthest remove from need," domestic cookbooks might be understood to focus most intently on the first two of these appetites—basic hunger and the presentation of an appetizing dish (xx). Unlike gastronomic literature, nineteenth- and early twentieth-century domestic cookbooks display an ambivalent relationship with the aesthetics of dining, in large part, because American and British Victorian culture worked so hard to elide female sensuality from the dining table in order to repress the erotic component of eating. Toklas' *Cook Book* shows no such indecision. Instead, it focuses on each of the appetites outlined by Gigante, concerning itself equally with the need to put food on the table, particularly during wartime, and with the aesthetics of appetite entirely removed from physical need.

In addition to its emphasis on the aesthetics of appetite, *The Alice B. Toklas Cook Book* also shares with gastronomic literature an attention to the aesthetic quality of its own style. As Priscilla Parkhurst Ferguson notes about Brillat-Savarin's *Physiology of Taste*, the most revered and emulated work of the genre, "the anecdotal mode, the witty tone and the language play ... give this work an almost palpable literary aura" (*Accounting for Taste* 96). Such notable anecdote, wit, and language play likewise saturate the *The Alice B. Toklas Cook Book*. The *Cook Book* also displays an intellectual engagement with the senses and a freedom to travel beyond the home kitchen that moves nimbly beyond the domesticated realm within which most women's cookbooks were contained. In its articulation of such freedom, Toklas' *Cook Book* employs at least six of the key characteristics of the male-authored tradition: 1) an unconventional form that incorporates and crisscrosses between several genres of writing 2) a stress on gastronomic tourism as well as a transnational frame of reference 3) an aesthetic appreciation of the pleasures of the table and of cookery as an art form 4) a reverence for hospitality and the mutual accord and well being that it nourishes 5) a keen sense of humor and a playful attitude toward the deadliness of man's hunger for fish, flesh, and fowl. By incorporating such key tenets of gastronomic literature into a book written for the home cook, Toklas transgresses the private boundaries of domestic food writing in order to articulate an aesthetics of eating pleasure and to establish her credentials as a well-traveled gastronome, conventionally male undertakings.

As much a travelogue as a domestic cookbook, Toklas' memoir is filled with movement, dislocation, relocation, and transgression. This movement works to dissolve the binaries and hierarchies typical of American women's food writing, such as male versus female, native versus foreigner, American versus French, public versus private, and mobility versus stasis.[13] In particular, *The Alice B. Toklas Cook Book* shows the couple wandering the countryside, often during wartime. They refuse to leave France

---

13. As noted in the introduction, the *Cook Book*'s dissolution of boundaries and hierarchies is a common theme in Toklas criticism.

during World War II despite repeated warnings from doctors, friends, and lawyers about the danger of being highly visible Jewish lesbians living in German-occupied territory. Many of Toklas' recipes are literally encased within stories that describe her and Stein's wartime work with the Red Cross, evacuating wounded soldiers, moving supplies, setting up make-shift hospitals, serving as liaison for incoming American troops during World War I, and twice, housing German soldiers under their roof during World War II.

In the chapter "Little-known French Dishes suitable for American and British Kitchens," Toklas reflects that the recipes she includes "are no longer novelties" in France, but rather "a slow evolution in a new direction, which is the way great art is created—that is, everything about is ready for it, and one person having the vision does it, discarding what he finds unnecessary in the past. Even a way of cooking an egg can be arrived at in this way" (139). The notion of art as a "slow evolution in a new direction" with "one person having the vision" to "discard what he finds unnecessary in the past" like-wise stands at the core of Toklas' culinary philosophy and aptly describes the literary form of her own project, which dissolves and reconfigures the rigid format of the cookbook to include the looser structure of gastronomic literature; like *The Physiology of Taste,* which includes personal narrative; a list of aphorisms; reflections on digestion and diet; theories of frying; and gastronomical meditations, Toklas' *Cook Book* comprises a pastiche of style and form, including a collection of dishes for artists; a gastronomic travel-ogue of her and Stein's journeys throughout France, Spain, and the United States; a tribute to her vegetable gardens; reflections on war and conquest; and a collection of recipes from French chefs.

ALICE B. TOKLAS AS A GASTRONOMIC TOUR GUIDE

The Alice B. Toklas Cook Book fashions a new genre of food writing—an idiosyncratic blend of American domestic cookbook, nineteenth-century French gastronomic literature, twentieth-century gastronomic tour guide, war story, and memoir. The genre that Toklas creates owes as much to the aesthetic form pioneered by Brillat-Savarin in the nineteenth century as to its twentieth-century extension—the gastronomic tour guide. In 1923, Toklas and Stein first explored Brillat-Savarin's home province of Bugey with the food guide *La France Gastronomique,* a twenty-eight volume series on French provincial cooking, as their guide. Toklas writes of the series: "As each one appeared I would read it with curiosity. The author [Curnonsky] was paradoxically a professional *gourmet.* Of the places we knew I was not always in agreement with his judgment" (90). Yet, at Curnonsky's recom-mendation, Toklas and Stein traveled to Bourg-en-Bresse, where the "menu at the hotel for dinner was carefully chosen and delicately cooked. We were delighted and toasted the guide book which had led us there and decided to stay for a couple of days" (91). After Bourg-en-Bresse, Curnonsky led the couple to Brillat-Savarin's hometown of Belley.

The mobility that characterizes Toklas' cookbook arises not only from her gastronomic tourism and wartime escapades, but also from her emphasis on the permeability of national boundaries and on the culinary exchanges wrought by wars and conquests. Such permeability is no more apparent than in the chapter "Beautiful Soup." Here Toklas attempts to trace the origins of the "ineffable" Spanish *gazpacho* only to find structural similarities branching geographically outward into countries such as Greece, Turkey, Poland, and even Chile. In the end, Toklas presents seven Mediterranean soups, which she loosely conjectures share a similar origin. She directly attributes such geographic dispersion to war, reflecting that "every nation . . . has its idiosyncrasies in food and drink conditioned by climate, soil, and temperament. . . . Wars and conquests [and their] . . . invading or occupying troops carry their habits with them and so in time [. . .] modify the national kitchen or table" (xvi). Rather than condemning such martial exchanges, Toklas embraces the flavors wrought by transnational culinary contact, refusing to hierarchize French cuisine over that of the French colonies or French cookery over that of the United States.

Although Toklas enjoyed what she calls the less "emasculated" home cookery of the French, she refused the rigid adherence to culinary tradition and, by extension, to national boundaries, which she found typical of the French table. As she explains, "We foreigners living in France respect and appreciate [the link between French culture and French cuisine] but deplore their too strict observance of a tradition which will not admit the slightest deviation in seasoning or the suppression of a single ingredient" (3). Such strict observance excludes the "imaginative" and "exotic" from French cuisine, an exclusion Toklas remedied by incorporating ingredients and cooking techniques imported from colonized lands as well as from the United States into her recipe collection. In fact, she began to seriously learn about the cooking of her home country while preparing meals for Stein in France. As her acumen developed, Toklas felt herself growing "experimental and adventurous" (29). With an appreciation for transnational culinary exchanges as well as a penchant for experimentation, she found what she considered the best foreign cooking in France in the homes of those who had lived "in the colonies" and returned home "not only with the respect of the local cooking [of Indo-China or Africa] but with the materials unobtainable in France and a knowledge of how to prepare them" (21). Not surprisingly, Toklas reflects that three of the finest cooks in her employ came from Indochina and Martinique.

In addition to recalling her culinary adventures in France, Toklas recounts her and Stein's seven-month gastronomic journey to the United States, which took them to the myriad cities and towns where Stein spoke on an extended lecture circuit. In the chapter "Food in the United States," Toklas charts her and Stein's itinerary by describing the regional foods they encountered, providing recipes for such icons of American cookery as wild rice salad, gooseberry jelly, and oysters Rockefeller. Having returned to the United States for the first time in twenty-seven years, Toklas found herself smitten with the flavors of her home country. Stopping in San Francisco, Toklas and Stein "indulged in gastronomic orgies—sand dabs *meunière*, rainbow trout in aspic, grilled soft-shell crabs, *paupiettes* of roast fillets of pork, eggs Rossini, and *tarte Chambord*" (134). In New Orleans, Toklas recalls, "I walked down to the market every morning realizing that I would have to live in the dream of it for the rest of my life" (131). With such recollections, Toklas simultaneously captures the regional bounty and the international flair of American cookery.

Throughout the chapter, Toklas links her final impression of a city with the groups and individuals who hosted the couple, drawing a taut connection between the pleasure of a meal and the social skill of its host. She writes:

> When we were at St. Paul to our surprise and delight there was a telephone message from Sherwood Anderson. He had heard we were in the neighbourhood [sic]. He proposed calling for us and driving us down to meet his wife . . . which he did, through miles of ice and snow-drifts, to sweet people and a festival dinner. It was the happiest of meetings. (128)

Such memories not only link a city with the quality of its hosts but also introduce the private realm into a chapter that charts the couple's publicly oriented, or professional, adventures.

Not surprisingly, Toklas' gastronomic reflections also include commentary on American restaurants. She recalls that

> [i]n Columbus, Ohio, there was a small restaurant that served meals that would have been my pride if they had come to our table from our kitchen. The cooks were women and the owner was a woman and it was managed by women. The cooking was beyond compare, neither fluffy nor emasculated, as women's cooking can be, but succulent and savoury. (128–129)

Like the female restaurant cooks, who skillfully avoid the fluffy and the emasculated in favor of the succulent and savory, Toklas illustrates a remarkable agility in moving between the private and public, the culturally coded feminine and masculine realms, all the while displaying a keen wit and refusing the slightest taint of nostalgia.

CRISSCROSSING THE GENDERED DIVIDE OF FOOD WRITING

Voyaging well beyond the domestic realm not only enabled Toklas to gain a freedom of movement and breadth of perspective accrued through travel, but it likewise enabled her to contextualize cooking and gastronomy in relation to the other arts. Like nineteenth- and early twentieth-century gastronomes, she drew heavily on comparisons to the visual arts, a reliance aided by her intimate knowledge of such painters as Picasso and Matisse; she and Stein not only owned many of their artworks but also hosted the artists regularly. Driven to impart an artistic dimension to her cookbook, Toklas jettisoned the distrust of sensual pleasure that haunted much American home cooking, practicing in its stead an aesthetic approach toward eating and a reverence for the pleasures of good food and wine. She adopted this reverent attitude from the French, who, as she explains, "bring to their consideration of the table the same appreciation, respect, intelligence and lively interest that they have for the other arts, for painting, for literature, and for theatre" (3). Such comparisons of cookery with art are a hallmark of Toklas' cookbook. For example, after encountering a series of "ineffable" *gazpachos* on a tour through Spain, Toklas finds that "the recipes for them had unquestionably become of greater importance than Grecos and Zurbarans, than cathedrals and museums" (49).

Toklas, like authors of gastronomic literature before her, focused on "[e]levating gourmandism to the status of the fine arts and establishing its legitimate link to aesthetic taste" (Gigante, *Taste* 166). Toward this end, she articulates the intellectual and emotional rewards of gastronomy, reflecting that:

> When treasures are recipes they are less clearly, less distinctly remembered than when they are tangible objects. They evoke however quite as vivid a feeling—that is, to some of us who, considering cooking an art, feel that a way of cooking can produce something that approaches an aesthetic emotion. (100)

Here Toklas raises cookery to the level of the less ephemeral arts to argue that an exquisitely wrought dish can affect the diner as profoundly as can a painting by El Greco or, for that matter, one by Matisse or Picasso.

Throughout the cookbook, Toklas documents her many encounters with dishes that produced in her an "aesthetic emotion," elegantly demonstrating a fundamental goal of gastronomy: to nourish aesthetic pleasure so that it may add nuance, depth, and richness to the very way we perceive and interact with the surrounding world. In so doing, she echoes two previous authors of gastronomic literature—Theodore Child and Elizabeth Robins Pennell, each of whom aligned aesthetic emotion with one of the three agents, or artists, involved in the practice of gastronomy—the gourmand, the cook, and the host. Whereas Toklas found that the aesthetic emotion of eating arises from the gourmand's appreciation of the dish itself, Child attributed it to the cook who, as an artist, should approach his work with "a sense of dignity and self respect and a certain emotion" (3); Pennell attributed aesthetic pleasure to the act of hosting "the perfect meal" during which "mind and body alike are satisfied" (12).

In his definition of the French word *Hôte*, André Simon explores why gastronomy relies as heavily on the art of hospitality as it does the art of cookery, explaining that the term is used for both host and guest, and it is as it should be, since there is no differentiation between host and guest, wherever there is true hospitality. . . . *L'Hôte*, the name indicates perfect equality and understanding between two persons entertaining each other. . . . In hospitality as in love, there should be no bargaining: each giveth the best that he hath to give, without any sense of either inferiority or superiority. (29)

Toklas emphasizes just such an undifferentiated rapport between host and guest. As she explains, the most memorable meals to which she has been invited as a guest inevitably "achieve a harmony" and balance (25).

Tellingly, the recipes collected in the chapter "Dishes for Artists" include one from Baronne Pierlot, "an exquisite hostess." Toklas lauds Pierlot as an artist "not only for her wit and charm [and] for her impeccable taste in choosing her guests and her menus, but also for the care with which her old cook, Perrine, prepared the menus" (32). Toklas commends Pierlot as an original and enchanting hostess, including her recipe for "Gigot de la Clinique," or Hospital Leg of Mutton. This latter dish famously requires that the mutton be injected daily with a syringe filled with ½ cup Cognac and ½ cup orange juice and bathed for eight days in a highly spiced and herbed marinade so that it will be "transfused into a strange and exquisite venison" to which "no leg of venison can compare" (33). Toklas closes her commentary on Pierlot's artistry by noting that the hostess' recipe for Gigot de la Clinique was to become so renowned that some years later it appeared in a cookbook:

Everyone thought that the syringe was a whimsy, that Madame Pierlot was making mock of them. Not at all. Years later I found it in that great collection of recipes, Bertrand Geugan's *Le Grand Cuisinier Français*. The Barrone Pierlot's recipe is classified, it has entered into the *Grande Cuisine Française*.

Here Toklas draws attention to one of the primary functions of gastronomic as well as culinary literature—the codification of an aesthetics of taste.

Like Fisher and the founding fathers of gastronomic literature before her, Toklas not only recorded intensely pleasurable meals and dishes, but also memorialized moments of gastronomic harmony and balance in order to capture and convey the essence of hospitality. Toklas' cookbook focuses in particular on those moments of harmony that provided a brief respite from the horrors of everyday existence during the First and Second World Wars. Being able to host the unexpected guest, the usual circle of friends, and any stranger who extended her and Stein hospitality became especially important during wartime, as it provided a means of maintaining dignity. Thus when looking out her window while dressing one morning in 1940 and seeing "German planes firing on French planes, not more than two miles away," Toklas determined to exist *and* be hospitable for as long as possible. Toward that end, she and Stein drove into town to procure

two hams and hundreds of cigarettes and some groceries—the garden
. . . would provide fruit and vegetables. The main road was filled with
refugees, just as it had been in 1914 and in 1917. Everything that was
happening had already been experienced, like a half-awakened from
nightmare. . . . [W]e lived on those two hams during the long lean winter that followed and well into the following spring. (31)

When the Germans forbade fishing, Toklas found a sympathetic butcher
to bring her sacks of crawfish so that she could "give lunch parties." In
return, she recalls, "[o]ur guests brought their own bread or gave me their
coupons" (204).

   One day, while driving around the countryside, Toklas asked a "military
car filled with officers" where to find a bite to eat.

> They said if we followed them we could find something to eat. . . . They
> stopped at a corrugated iron hut and sure enough the man who pre-
> sumably lived there made us an omelette with fried potatoes and a cup
> of real coffee, so rare in those days that at once we realized that the
> officers must have brought their own provisions with them and that we
> were sharing them. And then I remembered the two boxes of cakes the
> *abbé*'s mother had sent to us the day before. So we got them out of [the
> car]. The little Alsatian cakes were of her own baking and delicious.
> We took a few of each kind and gave the rest to the officers whose un-
> witting guests we had been. (70)

Toklas then describes how to make the cakes she gave to the officers, in
effect, providing her readers with a way to materialize the gift she shared
with her hosts. As with each of the recipes Toklas provides, the cakes,
if prepared and eaten, can convey the gustatory pleasures around which
Toklas' memories cohere. Repeatedly within Toklas' wartime stories, the
line between host and guest becomes blurred. By merging the roles of host
and guest, Toklas' stories emphasize hospitality as a mode of exchange in
which, as André Simon defines it, each nourishes the other in such a way
that "there is no differentiation between host and guest."

THE AESTHETIC PLEASURES OF DOMESTICITY

Like Fisher before her, Toklas pushes beyond the more innovative American women food writers by inserting her appetites, her tastes, and her life
story into the narrative flow of her writing. Both Fisher and Toklas craft
gastronomic travelogues of their time in France in which they articulate the
importance of nourishing the self with hospitality and grace during wartime. Both women likewise cultivate a wry sense of humor. Toklas differs
notably from Fisher, however, in her philosophical and practical engagement

with the culinary arts. Fisher explains that in her own work recipes appear "like birds in a tree—if there is a comfortable branch" (*Serve It Forth* 5).[14] Recipes serve a far more foundational role within Toklas' work. In particular, they anchor her memories and offer a way for readers to taste, literally or metaphorically, the gustatory pleasures that enriched her life with Stein. Prepared and eaten, they also enable the reader to literally ingest Toklas' culinary aesthetic.

The importance of domestic cookery to Toklas' project clearly aligns the *Cook Book* with the women's food writing tradition. So too does its emphasis on domestic ritual and household management. Toklas participates in the women's tradition in such a fashion, however, that she not only queers the boundaries between the private and public realms, but also those boundaries traditionally erected between household manager and servant. Nineteenth-century cookbooks often included tips on how to manage domestic workers and notably stereotyped entire nations in so doing. Some authors lumped servants into a subclass of immigrants prone to laziness and insolence. Domestic scientists, in particular, felt it their duty to reform such traits into diligence and alacrity. For example, in a chapter devoted to servants in her *Practical Housekeeper* (1857), Elizabeth Fries Ellet bemoans that fact that

> [h]ousekeepers are mainly dependent on the Irish and German emigrants, who as a rule are utterly ignorant of household service, and have to be taught everything; often receiving wages for months before they begin to make themselves useful. By the time they can be trusted to do the work, they are corrupted by intercourse with other servants, or persons who prompt them to make exaction on your time for visiting their numerous relatives from the old country, as well as to fill your kitchen with strangers, till the annoyance becomes intolerable. A complaint on this front from the employers is followed by an outbreak of insolence. . . . (26–27)

Servants were frequently compared to children, whose willful behavior and ignorance needed a housewife's firm guidance. In *The American Woman's Home* (1869), Catharine Beecher and Harriet Beecher Stowe relate the tale of a housekeeper who "succeeded in procuring a raw Irish maid-of-all-work, a creature of immense bone and muscle, but of heavy, unawakened brain. In one fortnight she established such a reign of Chaos and old Night in the kitchen and through the house that her mistress . . . dismissed her" (230–231).

---

14. *How to Cook a Wolf* is the closest Fisher comes to authoring a cookbook. Even here, however, the recipes ornament, or illustrate, the gastronomic philosophy of the book. Toklas' recipes embody her culinary aesthetic.

In another passage which epitomizes the foundational ideology of nineteenth-century domesticity, the authors reflect on the relationship between housewife and servant:

> It has been shown that the great end for which Jesus Christ came, and for which he instituted the family state, is the training of our whole race to virtue and happiness. . . . In this mission, of which woman is chief minister . . . the distinctive feature is self-sacrifice of the wiser and stronger members to save and to elevate the weaker ones. The children and the servants are these weaker members, who by ignorance and want of habits of self-control are in most danger. (111–112)

Although Beecher and Stowe articulate this message within an etiquette book rather than a cookbook proper, such notions of self-sacrifice and moral duty characterized nineteenth-century women's food writing, which conflated the family's physical nourishment with its moral and spiritual health. A woman who failed to properly feed her family not only risked the physical well-being of its individual members but also jeopardized their spiritual well-being. Certainly, not all domestic cookbook authors adopted such a moralistic tone as Beecher and Stowe or rigorously espoused Christian values. However, the principles of self-sacrifice and moral responsibility would continue to preoccupy much of women's food writing well into the twentieth century.

A comparison of this American domestic ideology with Toklas' discussion of her own household in France illuminates a radical shift in perspective. Tellingly, Toklas does not provide intimate portraits of her dinner guests or even of Stein, who features most commonly as part of the "we" with which Toklas narrates much of her memoir. Rather, she paints intimate portraits that record the idiosyncratic lives and recipes of her "Servants in France." Without a doubt, Toklas writes about these individuals from a position of cultural privilege, which leads her, on occasion, to stereotype her employees according to their nationality. Nonetheless, the fact that she folds their stories into her life writing marks her culinary memoir as a distinctly modern, or modernist, text. Within the chapter, Toklas not only recalls the weaknesses and strengths of her employees, but also relates those instances when servants quit their position, in effect firing Toklas and Stein on moral grounds. One cook quit the couple after seeing their art collection, having been "frightened" by its disturbing content. Another lasted three days before, as Toklas narrates "she looked at me severely and said that we 'lived French,' and that that was not what she had been led to suspect and she was leaving, which she did" (180). Toklas and Stein were not alone in the difficulty they encountered keeping servants. The dawn of the twentieth century brought with it a permanent decline in the number of domestic workers per household, resulting in an increasing shortage of available workers for hire.[15] As a result, cookbooks

---

15. Just as in the United States and England, the disappearance of domestic workers in France was expedited by the First and Second World Wars.

from the 1920s and 1930s illustrate "an increasing emphasis on the problem of getting servants and on their general inadequacies . . . and . . . their willful stupidity in the face of the exotic [such as] mistaking caviare for engine grease" (Humble 51).[16] Like Toklas' cookbook, they also show "the balance of power having shifted to the servants" (Humble 51).

The fact that Toklas and Stein lived together as a lesbian couple, however, meant that they were at a particular disadvantage. As Toklas explains, those servants who stayed "had their weaknesses. . . . Gertrude Stein liked to remind me that if they did not have their faults, they would not be working for us" (173). In this chapter, Toklas comes closest to addressing the downside of living as a lesbian, even in a city such as Paris, which nurtured the Bohemian lifestyle practiced by her and Stein. Toklas addresses the downside in a humorous fashion, however, which inverts the patronizing tone that cookbook authors typically expressed toward domestic workers and destabilizes the hierarchy of master over servant. As Anna Linzie explains:

> Stein's and Tokas's unconventionality, in both sexual and cultural preferences, obviously make them less than ideal employers. The way in which the *Cook Book* openly reveals this to be the case introduces an element of ambiguity in the roles of master and servant as superior and inferior, as dominant and subordinate. (178)

This destabilization extends to Toklas' appreciation of the finest cooks that worked for her and Stein. Hélène, "an invariably perfect cook," hailed from France (171). Tellingly, however, the remaining three hailed from Martinique and Vietnam. Jeanne's "sauces had unknown, delicate and still exotic flavours," (174) Trac's cooking "was delicate, varied and nourishing," (186) Nguyen was "inventive, deft, a wizard" (189). On one level, the fact that three of Toklas' favorite cooks hail from colonized territories speaks to what one critic terms a "colonial inflection" that appears now and again in Toklas' *Cook Book*, one that surfaces in her desire for "exotic" flavors, recipes, and, in this instance, cooks (Garland 46). At the same time, however, in lauding the idiosyncratic skills of such "exotic" cooks and including recipes that showcase their culinary artistry, Toklas pays tribute to their influence on her own culinary aesthetic, which is nourished by domestic workers and professional chefs alike.

The fluid boundaries that characterize Toklas' cookbook extend to the recipes themselves, which eschew the traditional American recipe format. Although Toklas' recipes are visually separated from the narrative as they are in most cookbooks, the beginning and end of the recipes often flow into and out of the "memoir" encasing it. As Traci Marie Kelly notes, "Such interplay makes perfect sense to the reader who understands that Toklas wanted to write a cookbook to be read for enjoyment; she wanted to write the memoirs

---

16. Although Humble makes this commentary about British cookbooks in particular, it also holds true for American cookbooks.

of her years with Stein; and that those two elements (the cookery instructions and the memories) could not be separated" (258). In some cases, such textual flow from recipe into memoir and vice versa so successfully fuses the recipe with the memory of the dish it describes that the two become one. A striking example of this integration appears in the chapter "Food to Which Aunt Pauline and Lady Godiva Led Us," which recounts the couple's adventures roaming the French countryside in search of exquisitely prepared meals. Aunt Pauline, a Model T Ford, took them to a restaurant in Lyon where the owner and chef, Mère Fillioux, awed them with both her cooking and her carving skills, showcased most memorably in the flavor and presentation of her "Steamed Chicken," for which Toklas provides the following recipe:

> The very best quality of chicken was used for steaming, as we use the best steel for gadgets, which is a very smart thing to do. The chicken has very thin slices of truffles slipped with a sharp knife between the skin and the flesh, and before trussing it the cavity is filled with truffles. Place the bird in the steamer over half white wine and half veal broth with salt and pepper and the juice of a lemon. The latter will give a flavour, but above all will keep the chicken white. The chicken was gigantic but so young that less than an hour had sufficed to cook it. This she told me when she came to carve it. She looked at it critically, then proudly. She was an artist. (59)

In this recipe, Toklas interweaves her memory of the dish at the restaurant, directions on how her readers might prepare it, rationale for why only the best ingredients will do, and commentary on the originating chef herself, successfully embedding the recipe within a description of the very "Steamed Chicken" her and Stein ate at the restaurant.

Throughout the chapter in which this recipe appears, "Food to Which Aunt Pauline and Lady Godiva Led Us," Toklas abandons the home kitchen altogether to dine at some of the nation's finest restaurants, ones which often came highly recommended by the *La France Gastronomique*. At the Hôtel de la Côte d'Or the couple dine on a meal created by "one of the great French *chefs*" from whom Toklas remarks that she "learned a great deal." Toklas learned not only by eating the dishes prepared by French chefs, but also by watching them at work in the restaurant kitchen (78). In turn, Toklas includes many of the recipes gathered during the course of such adventures, thereby injecting the professional into the domestic cookbook. She explains how in Chablis, she had the pleasure of watching "Monsieur Bergeran [who] was an intelligent and gifted *chef*. His menus were a history of the French kitchen and he was its encyclopaedia" (90). After Bergeran shows Toklas how to prepare Chicken Sauté aux Ducs de Bourgogne, a recipe for which punctuates the narrative, the couple drive to Dijon, where they dine at the Three Pheasants. Fittingly, Toklas ends this chapter with a tribute to the "perfect cook" Madame Bourgeois, from whom Toklas "learned much of what great French cooking was and had been" (93). That

Toklas awards her highest accolades to a female chef is well in keeping with the gender-bending nature of the *Cook Book*.

Although many female cookbook authors had included recipes from professional chefs by the time Toklas began writing, she stands alone, far surpassing even M. F. K. Fisher, in her macabre sense of humor. Such black humor marks yet one more way that Toklas deviates from the women's tradition in which rare streaks of humor revolve around decidedly more domesticated play, epitomized by the jocular asides that pepper Irma Rombauer's *Joy of Cooking* (1931). Rather than constructing humorous anecdotes about such somber topics as "Murder in the Kitchen," as does Toklas, Rombauer jokes about family crests and apple pies. For example, she puns: "A friend of mine is so fond of Apple Pie that he says his coat of arms bears an apple pie rampant. Every attempt has been made to make this one couchant" (211–212). As Susan Leonardi has astutely detailed in her essay "Recipes for Reading," Rombauer's humor helps create a friendly rapport with the reader. Although Rombauer's *Joy of Cooking* became a bestseller in 1946 and remains immensely popular today, by the time the 1960s rolled around large numbers of American housewives had become disgruntled enough with the daily drudgery of housework that they eagerly imbibed the more cynical humor found in Peg Bracken's *I Hate to Cook Book*. Written for "those of us who want to fold our big dishwater hands around a dry Martini instead of a wet flounder come the end of the day," Bracken's *Cook Book* includes recipes such as "Skid Road Stroganoff" and "Stayabed Stew" (ix). Tellingly, a fiftieth anniversary edition of Bracken's *I Hate to Cook Book* was published in 2010.

Unlike Bracken's book, which appealed to the weary housewife with such cookery instruction as "let it cook for five minutes while you light a cigarette and stare sullenly at the sink," Toklas' humor derives from her reluctant sadism, which is driven by an unapologetic hunger for gustatory pleasures (8). Such humor enables Toklas to lighten heavy subject matter and address the murder of fish, flesh, and fowl required to nourish gourmandize. In one passage in particular, she skillfully treats domestic labor with a dark sense of humor reminiscent of Grimod de la Reynière. The chapter "Murder in the Kitchen" finds Toklas confronted with dispatching the very fish and fowl that she eats, a necessity brought on by war. She reflects on the situation:

> The only way to learn to cook is to cook, and for me, as for so many others, it suddenly and unexpectedly became a disagreeable necessity to have to do it when war came and Occupation followed. . . . It was at this time, then, that murder in the kitchen began. The first victim was a lively carp. . . . A heavy sharp knife came to my mind as the classic, the perfect choice [of weapon]. . . . I carefully, deliberately found the base of its vertebral column and plunged the knife in. I let go my grasp and looked to see what had happened. Horror of horrors. The carp was dead, killed, assassinated, murdered in the first, second and third degree. Limp, I fell into a chair, with my hands still unwashed reached for a cigarette, lighted it, and waited for the police to come and take me into custody. (28)

Here Toklas comments ironically on the fact that the mass slaughter of war brought on her own "horror of horrors"—the necessity of killing for her dinner.

The next murder she commits in the kitchen takes place after a crate of doves arrives, sent by a friend. Toklas recalls that the accompanying note ended with the comment that "as Alice is clever she will make something delicious from them" and reflects:

> It is certainly a mistake to allow a reputation for cleverness to be born and spread by loving friends. . . . I carefully found the spot on poor innocent Dove's throat where I was to press and pressed. The realization had never come to me before that one saw with one's fingertips as well as with one's eyes. It was a most unpleasant experience, though as I laid out one by one the sweet young corpses there was no denying one could become accustomed to murdering. So I plucked the pigeons, emptied them and was ready to cook "Braised Pigeons en Croûtons." (40)

Unlike the easy jocularity of Rombaeur or the flippant disdain of Bracken, Toklas adopts a wry, macabre sense of humor that juxtaposes death with pleasure. Such a tack allows Toklas to illuminate the underside of life, enabling her to safely reveal what would otherwise remain unspeakable within the confines of a cookbook. The chapter "Murder in the Kitchen" explicitly links the murderous nature of war with the murderous nature of cookery and gastronomy—both are predicated on the expendability of life. Packaging such gruesome reflection within a humorous anecdote softens the message into a more palatable form. Such deflective and revealing humor likewise runs throughout *The Physiology of Taste*, which, like Toklas' cookbook, documents a life heavily impacted by war. As Paul Schmidt explains, Brillat-Savarin and Toklas concerned themselves with "the notion . . . that life goes on all around the dining table, and death and destruction are there, waiting, without" (193).[17]

In addition to humor, Toklas relied on food writing itself to help distract from the violent nature of war as well as from the psychological and physical hungers that it unleashed. In the following passage Toklas describes how she coped with rationing at the tail end of the Second World War:

> I betook myself to the passionate reading of elaborate recipes in very large cook-books. Through the long winter evenings close to the inadequate

---

17. Schmidt continues the thought: "We are so taken by the charm of Alice B. Toklas' memories and menus that we forget that the major narrative concerns the way two ladies survived the two greatest wars of history in a foreign country. The context, after all, is clear: For much of the time span of the book people are being starved, tortured, imprisoned, and killed just off its pages—and once or twice right on them. Yet the two imperturbable Americans go on gardening, hoarding, and scrounging rationed foods for what we cannot assume were other than delightful meals. It isn't easy to decide whether to be appalled at such callousness or to admire such sublime detachment. I incline to the latter—it isn't fiction, after all" (193–194).

fire the recipes for food that there was no possibility of realising held me fascinated—forgetful of restrictions, even occasionally of the Occupation, of the black cloud over and about one, of a possible danger one refused to face. The great French chefs and their creations were very real. (214)

Because culinary and gastronomic literature, in the words of Priscilla Parkhurst Ferguson, "transforms the material into the intellectual, the imaginative, the symbolic, and the aesthetic," it provides Toklas with a means of transcending the brutal reality of war (*Accounting for Taste* 105). In turn, as a representation of the material food, culinary literature can evoke taste memory, an evocation powerful enough to provide temporary relief from hunger and fear.

Just as reading about food can provide nourishment, so too can the act of writing about it, a point Toklas underscores in the introduction to her cookbook. Noting that she penned much of the cookbook while suffering from "an attack of pernicious jaundice," she recalls how "remembered health and enjoyment lent special lustre to dishes and menus barred from an invalid table, but hovering dream-like in invalid memory" (xvi). That the act of remembering and recording such dishes provided "an escape from the narrow diet and monotony of illness" attests to the power of gastronomy; a dish, like a painting, can stir an "aesthetic emotion" in the diner that, in turn, leaves an existential trace, or taste memory. Recipe writing itself enabled Toklas to record dishes that stirred in her an aesthetic emotion, thereby evoking the taste memories such dishes left behind.

Toklas' recipe collection conveys her particular aesthetic as well as her approach toward life. As Elspeth Probyn explains, Toklas' "recipes are suggestive of a certain conduct; we glimpse through them the intermingling of bodies, nations, memories, war, and love" (75). Toklas' recipe for fondue exemplifies such intermingling. She introduces the recipe by contextualizing how it came into her life, describing the time "two officers and thirty soldiers of the Italian army were billeted upon" her and Stein (217). The officers thanked the couple by giving them three pounds of parmesan cheese. In reciprocal thanks, Toklas threw a party, inviting the Italians to share the fondue she prepared from their gift. Toklas provides the recipe before dropping the fact that "The Italians stayed until their country accepted the Armistice. . . . There were about six hundred Italian soldiers in the neighborhood and the frontier was only 125 kilometers away. We hoped they would cross it safely. Later we heard that they had all been killed by the Germans" (218). Rather than lingering on the mass slaughter, Toklas includes a recipe for the fondue she made and ate with the Italians. She prefers to memorialize the fondue in a recipe that can, in turn, be transformed into an aesthetic object, a living tribute to the Italians with whom she shared it. In this way, she illustrates that the act of cooking is an attempt "to circumvent decay and death, in the quiet knowledge that the task is impossible" (Schmidt 203). Shortly after the mass slaughter of the Italians, the destructive violence of war once again savages the civilized tone of Toklas' memoir, creating the most unsettling moment of the book. Toklas recalls:

The end was near. So the boys of the *Résistance* came down quietly from their mountain top one morning, drove the seven hundred Germans from Culoz and the neighborhood into the marshes, surrounded them and wiped them out. It was glorious, classical, almost Biblical. We celebrated by taking one of the liberated taxis to Belley. (218–219)

An undomesticated attitude, indeed.

Because of her determination to grasp pleasure amid the horrors of war, Toklas shows little remorse about partaking fully in the black market. On one particular birthday that fell during Occupation, Toklas shared a meal with Stein and a dozen of their friends, dining on: "Aspic de foie gras; Truites en chemise; Braised pigeons—shoestring potatoes; Baron of spring lamb—jardiniere of spring carrots—onions, asparagus tips—string beans *en barquette*; Truffle Salad; Wild-strawberry tart" (208). Hardly a modest, self-denying meal. Toklas herself addresses its extravagance when she writes:

> One remembered the packages of food one was sending to war and political prisoners and felt conscience-stricken at the overabundance of our feast. We did nevertheless recover our high spirits. . . . That lunch was the beginning of the excitement and gratification that came to us gradually from provisions secured on the black market. (209)

With such an unapologetic apology, Toklas underscores her refusal to sacrifice herself or her pleasure even during the worst of times. Although Toklas provided generously for French and American soldiers, she had no qualms about putting her own stomach first.

In conclusion: Toklas may have cooked regularly for Gertrude Stein and taken on other traditional "wifely" duties, but she nevertheless enjoyed a life far outside the bounds of conventional domesticity. For Toklas, as for M. F. K. Fisher before her, leaving the States and setting up home in France enabled her to cohere a set of daily practices that cultivated aesthetic pleasure, to approach cooking *and* eating as art forms. In turn, Toklas' full-fledged participation in the culinary and gastronomic arts nourished an appetite that reconfigured the bounds of American women's food writing. This appetite gave rise to a text that refuses to be neatly contained within men's or women's food writing traditions; the cookbook effectively blends the personal anecdote, wit, aesthetic reflection, and attention to public taste of gastronomic literature with the recipes and attention to domestic ritual of a traditional cookbook.

Like the founding fathers of gastronomic literature and gastronomic tour guides, Toklas charts unexplored territory to create a new genre of food writing. Part domestic cookbook, part gastronomic travelogue, part modernist war story, *The Alice B. Toklas Cook Book* articulates an appetite that queers the heteronormative food writing tradition in its refusal to be bound by convention. By crisscrossing the gendered divide of men's and women's food writing, *The Alice B. Toklas Cook Book* stands out as one of our nation's most innovative contributions to culinary literature. Indeed, hers was a queer appetite, which coalesced in a written form to which many late twentieth- and twenty-first-century food writers have much to be grateful.

4 A Sensual Engagement
Elizabeth David's Gastronomic Cookbooks

Generations of upper- and middle-class English were raised on nursery food—fare variously described by the more literary of its ingesters
as "disgusting," "spiteful," "monstrous," "hateful," "frightening,"
and "repugnant."[1] Nursery food, along with its philosophical twin,
educational food, arose from the widely-held Victorian belief that the
body must be tamed and its desires strictly controlled or, more ideally,
quashed altogether. Consequently, from the mid-1800s up through the
Second World War, children were made to eat dishes that chastened
willfulness and were easily digested.[2] By using children's food as a tool
for "control and subjugation," Victorians not only encouraged fear of

---

1. In *Nursery Cooking*, Molly Keane writes "I was born in 1904, and by 1908 I
had accepted the fact that nursery food was so disgusting that greed, even hunger,
must be allayed elsewhere" (7). David describes the horrors of her own experience
with nursery food as follows:

> Probably some of everyone's most dismal nursery memories are connected with
> food. One might come to accept the stewed prunes, the hateful greens, even the
> tapioca pudding, as part of Nannie's mysterious lore as to what it was necessary
> to eat in order to survive the perils of childhood. The miseries of fish days were
> harder to overcome because the food looked so terrifying even before it was on
> your plate. Egg sauce didn't do much to compensate for the black skin and mon-
> strous head of a boiled cod; fish pudding, a few spiteful bones inevitably lying in
> wait in that viscous mass, and whitings biting their own tails, were frightening
> dishes for children, and often painful too. (*French Provincial* 279)

Writing in 1925, cookbook author Hilda Leyel attributes "the repugnance of many
English children for green vegetables" to "the dishes of stringy, watery, tasteless, tough
green leaves that are sent up for the nursery dinner, a relic of the Victorian days when
grown-up people ate far too much meat, and when butter was regarded as a superfluous luxury for children brought up almost exclusively on starch" (Leyel 31).

2. In *All Manners of Food*, Stephen Mennell describes the philosophy behind
nursery food and its repercussions as follows:

> [T]he notion of food especially suited for children . . . [was] a matter of making
> them eat what was good for them whether they liked it or not. At worst, making
> them eat food to which they actually felt an aversion was seen as a necessary
> part of breaking the child's peevish will. . . . [T]he widespread parental anxiety
> and concern about giving children only very plain, simply cooked, weakly fla-
> voured food must easily have communicated itself to children, and led some of
> them to remain anxious about food as adults. In the most serious cases, it may
> have led to the 'anaesthetising' of the capacity to enjoy eating. (296)

food, but also hampered a child's capacity to enjoy food as an adult.[3] For those English born in the early twentieth century, the capacity to enjoy food also met with more practical limitations; their graduation from educational fare meant propulsion into a national diet of powdered eggs and Spam, thanks to the deprivations exacted by the quick succession of two world wars.

Despite, or perhaps because of, such exposure to bleak food, twentieth-century English gastronomes fought vociferously to aestheticize their nation's palate. One such gastronome was Elizabeth David who, born in 1913, escaped her nation's table at the age of twenty-five, setting sail with her lover for the Mediterranean. Flouting social expectations that she marry and embrace domesticity, David spent six years eating and studying the cuisines of France, Greece, and Egypt. Upon her return to English rations at the tail end of World War II, David began to craft gastronomic cookbooks laden with sensual pleasures. During a ten-year period, David wrote a series of cookbooks on foreign cuisines—*A Book of Mediterranean Food* (1950), *French Country Cooking* (1951), *Italian Food* (1954), *Summer Cooking* (1955), and *French Provincial Cooking* (1960). For the last two books she completed before her death, *Spices, Salt and Aromatics in the English Kitchen* (1970) and *English Bread and Yeast Cookery* (1977), David turned her focus toward English cookery. Over the course of these years David likewise practiced her considerable skill as a magazine writer, authoring articles on foreign cuisines and foreign restaurants as well as English culinary history and its leading figures. Throughout her career, David showcased cookery and food writing as a powerful means of self-expression, crafting a body of writing that transformed domestic ideology into a celebration of the body and the senses.

David first learned to honor food as a source of pleasure and as a medium of artistic expression during her six-year sojourn to the Mediterranean. During her travels, she honed a receptivity to foreign culinary beliefs and practices that nourished the intellectual and sensual pleasures conveyed in her writing. Because David approached food as a medium for self-expression and understood that harnessing food's expressive potential requires intense physical engagement, her written aesthetic conveys an astonishing attunement to sensory impressions. By conveying the culinary aesthetic of cultures that prize and cultivate the relationship between eating and pleasure, David helped to articulate a gastronomically grounded tradition of English female food writing. Her

---

3. In *The Psychology of Food and Eating*, John Smith quotes from V. Mars' "Parsimony Amid Plenty: Views from Victorian Didactic Works on Food for Nursery Children," in G. Mars and V. Mars (eds), *Food Culture and History. Volume I*. London: The London Food Seminar, 1993. The cited quote appears in full as follows: "As the nineteenth century progressed . . . nature [was] increasingly seen as subject to man's control and subjugation. Children's food similarly became the vehicle in its turn for their control and subjugation" (152).

gastronomic cookbooks expel the notion of women's daily cookery as drudgery by unyoking home cooking from family duty and linking it instead with the traditionally male pursuits of pleasure, self-knowledge, and intellectual stimulation. In so doing, David revived and extended the aestheticization of English food writing that had begun during the interwar years, a movement which had been abruptly halted by the onset of World War II.

PAVING THE WAY FOR ELIZABETH DAVID: INTERWAR FOOD WRITING IN ENGLAND

As one of the most illustrious culinary figures of twentieth-century Britain, Elizabeth David has been shrouded in a reputation of mythological proportions; journalists and food writers often describe her as a culinary goddess who single-handedly rescued England from sodden vegetables, nursery school food, and sauces laden with raw flour. Such mythology has come to play a ubiquitous role in David's contemporary portrait within popular culture. Since the 1980s, however, a more nuanced approach has begun to emerge within food studies—one that depicts David as taking part in a cultural shift that began to gather momentum during the 1920s and 1930s before being derailed by the outbreak of World War II. As Arabella Boxer describes, "In the years between the two world wars English food underwent a brief flowering that seems to have gone almost unremarked at the time, and later passed into oblivion" (1).

This interwar revival in the art of cookery and gastronomy was led in part by two French immigrants to England—André Simon and X. Marcel Boulestin, each of whom were prolific writers, authoring memoir, gastronomic literature, and cookbooks that continue to occupy a much revered place in English food culture.[4] A leading figure in the English wine trade for over fifty years and an author of oenophillic, gastronomic, and culinary literature, Simon penned one of the most elegant expressions of twentieth century gastronomy, *The Art of Good Living*. Boulestin worked variously as a music critic for a French weekly, as a ghost writer for Colette's husband, and as an interior decorator in London before becoming England's most influential interwar culinary figure as well as its first television chef.

Boulestin introduced French bourgeois cookery to a select group of English who embraced it as a welcome respite from the staid predictability of English food and the richness and complexity of French *haute cuisine*, especially given that the former had been degraded and the latter made almost unobtainable—at least legally—during years of war rationing. As

---

4. Numerous additional male authors participated in the interwar literary revival of the culinary arts and gastronomy, including Ambrose Heath, P. Morton Shand, Romilly Fedden, and Vicomte de Mauduit.

historian Christopher Driver explains, "Boulestin's enthusiasm, and his identification with the contemporary in music and the visual arts, took him straight to the heart of Bloomsbury and the [Osbert] Sitwell circle, who were delighted to find that they could eat well in London and say boo to Victorian and Edwardian vulgarity at the same stroke" (8).[5] Led by Boulestin and the bohemian lifestyle he represented as well as a general hunger for the sensual pleasures denied during World War I, artists, intelligentsia, and socialites took part in a gastronomic revival that would be curtailed by the onset of the Second World War. Tellingly, at war's end the same sorts of men and women who fed eagerly on Boulestin's culinary philosophy during the interwar years likewise responded enthusiastically to Elizabeth David's *A Book of Mediterranean Food* when it was published in 1950.

An interwar desire for novel recipes and gustatory pleasures nourished innovative forms of domestic food writing, which began to include the sort of gastronomic reflection previously reserved for male authors. As Boxer and literary scholar Nicola Humble have documented in detail, aesthetically grounded domestic food writing positively flourished during the 1920s and 1930s, giving rise to a stable of well-respected authors such as Florence White, Hilda Leyel, Countess Morphy, Agnes Jekyll, and Dorothy Allhusen.[6] White and Leyel are well known among British culinary authorities and scholars for their devotion to English cookery and for their determination to unearth its considerable strengths, buried in part by the rise of the domestic science movement and by the deprivations of World War I. According to White, she compiled *Good Things in England* "in an attempt to capture the charm of England's cookery before it is completely crushed out of existence" (9). Toward that end, she "presented a scholarly, eclectic jumble of recipes dating from the Middle Ages onwards, gleaned from gentlemen's clubs, Oxford and Cambridge colleges, farmhouses, cottages, and the Houses of Parliament" (Humble 72).

Whereas White's work made an invaluable historical contribution to English cookery, Leyel conveyed a finely tuned culinary aesthetic that revived ingredients and recipes considered exotic in interwar English kitchens but that had once played a significant role in medieval cookery (Spencer 309). For example, a chapter on flower recipes includes dishes such as geranium jelly, nasturtium salad, white acacia syrup, and ice cream of roses. The elegance and creativity of Leyel's *Gentle Art of Cookery* would so impress Elizabeth David that she attributed its "imagination-catching" recipes to her own development as a food writer. In

5. The Bloomsbury group, which held regular meetings in the Bloomsbury area of London, drew together many of many of the leading intellectuals and artists of the time, including Virginia Woolf, John Maynard Keynes, E. M. Forester, and Evelyn Waugh.

6. See the introduction to Arabella Boxer's *Book of English Food* and "Fashionable Food and the Invention of the Housewife" in Nicola Humble's *Culinary Pleasures* for more detail on English food writing between the wars.

the 1960s, David would write a series of articles for *The Spectator* in which she paid tribute to several authors of interwar English cookbooks, including Boulestin, Leyel, Morphy, and White.

Unlike these key figures to whom David paid public tribute in writing, Agnes Jekyll and Dorothy Allhusen were not themselves accomplished cooks. Rather, they were English socialites who moved in artistic circles and held more in keeping with gourmands than with culinary artists. As hostesses, they relied on hired cooks to prepare the recipes and meals that appear in their books.[7] Their skills at hosting meals, however, earned them considerable renowned among those whom they entertained—a group composed of the same select English who eagerly followed the Europhilic culinary path forged by Boulestin. Jekyll and Allhusen expanded the bounds of women's English food writing by creating idiosyncratic cookbooks that express their relationship with the culinary and gastronomic arts. Yet despite an affinity for gastronomy and elegant self-expression, each author lauds men as being naturally better hosts than women and strikes a self-demeaning stance in relation to male gourmands.

A collection of cookery columns written for *The Times*, Lady Agnes Jekyll's *Kitchen Essays: With Recipes and Their Occasions* (1922) embeds recipes within gastronomic reflection, aiding her wealthy reader in hosting a variety of meals, ranging from "Shooting-Party Luncheons" and Tuscan-inspired dinners to invalid suppers and vegetarian refreshment. As Nicola Humble succinctly describes, "*Kitchen Essays* is written in a witty and epigrammatic style, with a loose, associative structure lending it a slightly *distrait* charm. . . . [T]he main emphasis is not on detailed directions but on encouraging an attitude that sees food as an interesting, life-affirming element of a rich, cultured existence" (47). Assuming a readership who frequently travels, drawn by "Riviera sunshine, Italian culture, or the lure

---

7. Boxer and Humble both include Ruth Lowinsky and Lady Sysonsby in their list of socialite authors and Humble also adds Alice Martineau. These authors have not been included here as Lowinsky's *Lovely Food*, *Lady Sysonby's Cook Book*, and Martineau's *Caviare to Candy* do not deal as explicitly with food as an aesthetic object and dining as an art form as do Jekyll's *Kitchen Essays* and Allhusen's *Book of Scents and Dishes*. Rather, the former are inventive cookbooks. *Lovely Food* centers around suggested menus, each introduced with a witty description of the occasion on which the menu would be well-suited, such as "A dream party of some of the most celebrated people of the day, whom one can never hope to meet" (54). Otherwise a straightforward recipe collection, *Lady Sysonby's Cook Book* bears an introduction by the novelist Osbert Sitwell and illustrations by the artist and stage designer Oliver Messel. Alice Martineau's *Caviare to Candy* clearly shares the cosmopolitan and authoritative tone of gastronomic literature—"I have tasted the pearl-grey caviare of Roumainia, and the exquisite wild raspberries of Norway. . . . The wayside inns, the palaces of kings, the golden grapes of Tacna, the delicous fruits of Panama—all have helped me write this book" (1). Despite such introductory self-assurance, however, Martineau nevertheless shortchanges women when it comes to gustatory pleasures, suggesting that luncheons for men should begin with caviar while women's should start with sectioned grapefruit.

of Monte Carlo," and who entertains with the help of domestic workers, Jekyll wrote for a well-heeled set as well as for those who enjoyed dining vicariously with the wealthy (177).

Despite her self-presentation as a cosmopolitan, well-traveled gourmand, Jekyll nonetheless depicts women as less adept at hosting than men and as downright foolish when faced with a restaurant menu, noting that

> those who have been privileged to stay in bachelor households or to dine at restaurants with their men friends, will often admit their superlative capability both in running the domestic machinery with noiseless and well-oiled efficiency and in ordering a better dinner from a chef or maitre d'hôtel than most women would be able to achieve.
>
> What female intelligence can decipher rapidly those hieroglyphic sheets when presented in restaurants . . . ? She will vacillate between the super-strange and the ultra-commonplace, or, losing her head, will select the cheapest of the mysteries proffered, or else something recklessly expensive or out of season. (54–55)

Despite her self-styled stance as a gourmand, Jekyll, like Elizabeth Robins Pennell before her, stops short of showcasing women's laurels in the gastronomic arts.[8] Rather, she writes that women must cede first place to men's "superlative capabilities" when it comes to hosting meals within both the private and the public realms.

Jekyll does manage, however, to significantly jostle the housewife's ideological position within the domestic realm. Rather than depicting the ideal woman as an uncomplaining, selfless source of moral and physical nourishment for the family, as did her nineteenth-century predecessors, Jekyll deflates this image with a wry twist:

> If . . . we would have laughter and shining faces at our board—if we would preserve the devotion of our husbands, the enthusiasm of our friends, and the contentment of our domestics—let us as housekeepers give more of our best brains to the work. We must put those thoroughbreds, Imagination, Generosity, Invention, into harness with our jaded hacks, Custom, Thrift, and the Commonplace, as they drag along Time's hurrying chariot to the often depressing sound of the family gong. (12)

Here Jekyll acknowledges that the housewife is still bound by custom and thrift and that she has little choice but to manage the domestic sphere, no matter how "depressing" she might find the chore at times. Since the housewife must perform her duties well in order to nourish "laughter and shining faces," Jekyll urges her readers to invigorate their approach

---

8. For more on Pennell, see pages 51–59.

toward housekeeping with imagination and invention. This same message resounded across the Atlantic in American cookery books, tolling a jaded restlessness among women, a weariness with being tied to the home kitchen. In order to rejuvenate themselves and revamp their place in the kitchen, women began working to transform the drudgery of everyday cookery into a creative endeavor—to lay claim to the culinary artistry and invention long reserved exclusively for men.

A friend of Edith Wharton, Dorothy Allhusen, like Jekyll, sought to incorporate gastronomy into the domestic cookbook. Toward that end, she introduces her *Book of Scents and Dishes* (1926) with a reflection on the culinary and gastronomic arts, leading with a quote by Brillat-Savarin. Like the nineteenth-century gastronome, Allhusen discourses elegantly on food as an aesthetic object and on cookery as an art form, asserting that

> just as a musician has cultivated his ear, so that good combinations of sounds give him the most sincere delight, and irritating, inharmonious noises drive him to distraction, so the man whose sense of taste is highly developed enjoys his meals and derives an artistic satisfaction from a dish that is choice, elegant, and delicately seasoned. For him the chef prepares his choicest viands. Like every artist, he craves the sympathetic reception of the work which he has achieved by his excellent understanding of the laws that govern taste. It is no triumph for him to cook for the ordinary indiscriminating diner or the glutton. He needs one whose palate has not been ruined by coarse and over-seasoned food, who can detect the subtleties of his combinations, and who takes eating as seriously as any other artist regards the art in which he is more than usually proficient. (1–2)

Like her male nineteenth-century predecessors, Allhusen hones a gastronomic philosophy built on the belief that the diner and the cook, if finely tuned toward aesthetic pleasure, each practice a form of artistry. By introducing her domestic cookbook with such gastronomic reflection, Allhusen raises the successful hostess to the status of the artist.

Like male gastronomes, however, Allhusen also places women clearly behind men in terms of gustatory prowess, noting that "the curious part of it all is that men are fonder of food than women, and as a rule have better taste and much more delicate palates" (6). She continues in this vein to conclude her introduction by reflecting on the infancy of her own palate: "Give an infant a toy and he will put it in his mouth. He likes it, it pleases his eye, and he thinks it will please his palate also. He is often disillusioned on that score, but in a sense he has the right instinct . . . . In a measure I have acted like the infant with the toy" (8). Although Allhusen compares herself to an infant in order to underscore the fresh attitude with which she approaches her topic, she nevertheless infantilizes herself, thereby undermining her authority as an artist.

Despite their reluctance to claim women's palate equal to that of men, the more innovative and elegant domestic cookbook writers of this period clearly expressed a devotion to gastronomy, a shift that signaled a growing eagerness to embrace cooking and dining as art forms. As Humble summarizes:

> If one thing unites the many and various cook books of the interwar years, it is that they are the product of a culture that was beginning to talk about what they ate. Food had become something to debate and write about, to consider carefully rather than just consume thoughtlessly. . . . An open enjoyment of food was now in good taste; gusto and even greed were fashionable for women as well as for men. Virtually every cook book of these years includes essays on cooking and eating, on tastes and fashions in food, on skills and techniques, on changes in British eating habits. (72–73)

Even the most gastronomically grounded of these domestic cookbooks written by women, however, still convey a discomfort with claiming a gourmand's palate. A reticence to claim expertise in the field about which they wrote as well as a deferential stance toward male taste differentiated the gastronomically grounded female cookbook writers of the interwar years from their male counterparts.

Fortunately, this reticence failed to make its way into the gastronomic literature written by Gladys Brownwyn Stern, whose essay on gastronomic memoir appears in Edward Bunyard's *The Epicure's Companion*, a work that distills the essence of the gastronomic literary revival of the interwar years. A compilation of essays, the majority of which were written by Bunyard or his wife, Lorna, *The Epicure's Companion* includes contributions by such illustrious figures as André Simon and Marcel Boulestin, the latter of whom wrote on "Gastronomes in French Literature." It ends with an invitation to join the Wine and Food Society, begun by Simon in "1933 to bring together and assist all those who believe that a right understanding and appreciation of good food and wine are essential to contentment and health" (527). Another contributor of particular note, Sir Francis Colchester-Wemyss authored an essay on "Souvenirs Gastronomiques" in which he reflects that "towards the end of a long life any human being, who is not simply bovine or turnip-minded, must have a treasure house of memories and a shelf therein where are to be found his gustatory souvenirs" (447).[9] David found Bunyard's collection alluring enough to carry it along with her to the

---

9. Colchester-Wemyss authored *The Pleasures of the Table* (1931), a cookbook "particularly directed at the vast body of girls, either already housewives or soon to become such, . . . who have, or will have, to run a small house with one to three servants or even with no servant at all" (9).

Mediterranean, where she undertook a voyage that lasted the length of the Second World War.

Without a doubt, Stern's essay on "The Child as Epicure" takes claim as the collection's most innovative contribution to gastronomic literature as a genre. The essay, which appeared in the *Epicure's Companion* the same year that saw the publication of M. F. K. Fisher's *Serve it Forth* (1937), is one of the first to actively address the function and form of gastronomic memoir. In the following passage, Stern reflects on autobiography as a genre:

> Most people when, like Marcel Proust, they sit down to write their remembrances of things past, review their childhood either from the Freudian aspect, the pastoral aspect, or the Little Scholar aspect. . . . But I can hardly remember any autobiography which relates of our early experiences in food and drink; our reactions and discoveries in these; how taste developed, and where the sophisticated palate still clung obstinately to its infantile preferences. So I propose to conduct this examination not in the voluptuous spirit, but meticulously as Proust on French Society. (467–468)

Whereas Fisher would craft gastronomic memoir in the "voluptuous spirit" tempered with a healthy dose of the "Freudian aspect," Stern breezes through her "early experiences in food and drink," wrapping up her study in a few pages.

Fortunately, Stern was far more voluble when she wrote *Bouquet* (1927), possibly the most innovative contribution to women's food writing penned in England during the interwar years. With *Bouquet*, Stern clearly differentiates herself from traditional women's food writing by avoiding the home kitchen altogether. As Colchester-Wemyss so enthusiastically describes in the introduction to his own *Pleasures of the Table*, Stern's *Bouquet* is "a delightful account of a motor tour in France, with special and most interesting reference to the hotels and inns and restaurants encountered along the way" (10). As the title indicates, Stern's book is "mainly devoted to wine" (9). In recounting her journey through France, Stern blends gastronomic tour guide with memoir to create a light, humorous, fast-paced read, which captures road travel through France with the Michelin guide in hand. Stern journeys with her husband and another couple, eating and drinking their way throughout the French provinces, imbibing enough wine and brandy to fuel such "Wellsian" ideas as "the super-car, which, in five hundred years, would be able to manufacture its own road as it went, pushing it ahead, and laying it down, and running over it, and then picking it up again from behind. It seemed to us a brilliant idea as we evolved it" (48). Most remarkable, however, *Bouquet* depicts Stern as an avid wine connoisseur who refuses to be content with the Champagne or sweet wines and garishly colored liqueurs usually poured for women. Instead, she describes a red wine from Hermitage in the Rhone Valley as

> transcendental. The gun-flint backwash was there, and all the other little subtle flavours that run up, one behind the other, elusively blending and disappearing again. For this is the peculiar excitement of a true Hermitage, that you have not yet done with it when you have relished the bouquet, and the rich flavour, and the silky texture, and the sight of its deep clear gold-and-red, shiningly blended. All these are straightforward appeals, but afterwards comes the fascination. You follow up your sensations with the thrill of a hunter after some live creature, with a will and personality of its own, whom he would catch and tame and bring home. But it is no good; you cannot catch the wild charm of Hermitage, though you drink it and drink it again. You can only marvel at it gratefully. (72–73)

Although *Bouquet* does not sustain such refreshing, evocative prose throughout, these occasional gems make Stern's book a remarkable contribution to the literature of gastronomy. Stern's accomplishment is made all the more extraordinary because in choosing "Bacchus [as] the hero of [her] book, and a great love of wine its excuse for being written," she inserts herself into a sub-field of gastronomy especially dismissive of women (9).

Stern was not, however, the first English woman to insert herself into the male realm of wine connoisseurship. In the late nineteenth century, Janet Ross compiled *Italian Sketches* (1887), which includes an essay on a wine harvest from a Tuscan estate as well as an essay on the production of olive oil. Ross lived in a villa near Florence, where she wrote lyrical descriptions of the region's food and wine. David herself found Ross' *Sketches* evocative enough to list it in a select annotated bibliography, which she included for those interested in further reading in *Italian Food*. David likewise lauds Ross' cookbook, *Leaves from Our Tuscan Kitchen* (1900), a fascinating collection of vegetable recipes dictated by Ross' Tuscan cook, Guiseppe Volpi.

Tellingly, many of the aesthetically attuned and innovative domestic cookbooks were authored by women who did relatively little cookery themselves. Like nineteenth-century gastronomes, these amateurs-in-the-kitchen were not bound to the domestic realm. Rather, they enjoyed the wealth and the leisure time to explore the gastronomic arts and to tour the European countryside by foot, horse, or motorcar. Although David drew inspiration from a few such gourmands and amateur cooks, her true compass pointed toward those authors who were elegantly accomplished enough to make a professional career in either the culinary or the literary arts. Boulestin, one of David's all-time favorite mentors, managed to make a career in both fields, becoming a celebrated restaurateur and food writer.

It would not be until David appeared on the literary scene in 1950, however, that an English woman would move so elegantly and authoritatively between the culinary, gastronomic, and literary realms. By uniting a passion for gastronomy with an expertise in the culinary arts, David simultaneously honed a much-revered professional career and helped liberate women's recipe writing from familial duty. Stephen Mennell was perhaps the first scholar to connect David's writing with gastronomic literature. In a passage frequently quoted in David scholarship, Mennell notes that

> there is an ill-defined margin at which the gastronomic essay gradually shades into the cookery book. The more learned sort of cookery book, such as those of Dumas and Ali-Bab, or more recently of Elizabeth David or Jane Grigson might be considered gastronomic literature as much as cookery books. In either case, they seem to be intended to be read as literature. (271)

In "Food Writing and Food Cultures: the Case of Elizabeth David and Jane Grigson," Steve Jones and Ben Taylor follow through on this notion in order to articulate David's connection with gastronomic literature. After recapping Mennell's overview of gastronomic literature, Jones and Taylor surmise that "culinary *joie de vivre* . . . was articulated only in the writing of the male professional cook or gastronome," a statement that this present study works to complicate by flushing out those lesser known women authors who articulated an aesthetics of pleasure (175).

Cultural resistance to women authoring gastronomic literature, however, would remain commonplace enough in the 1960s that David herself fought repeatedly with magazine editors over the restrictive format that women's food writing was expected to follow. As Jones and Taylor astutely point out:

> It was not until David went to work for the *Spectator* in 1961, that she was able to indulge her interests fully, writing pieces on food issues and food histories where the provision of recipes was not necessarily a requirement. It is noticeable, then, that it is a publication with a primarily male readership which allowed her to be "liberated . . . from the straitjacket of the conventional cookery article as decreed by custom" (David, 1986: 9). What this demonstrates is that, even by the early 1960s, the gender divide between cookery writing and gastronomic literature remained institutionalized. (176)

Jones and Taylor push further to conclude that David's drive "to explore the culture of food beyond the confines of domesticity . . . enabled David . . . to gesture towards the myths, histories and memorable meals which lay beyond the home" (178).[10] Jones and Taylor provide several compelling examples of how David's writing verges on gastronomic literature, noting that the

> chapter on pasta in Elizabeth David's *Italian Food*, for example, not only includes an account of the origins of pasta, but also a lengthy discussion of Marinetti's discourse on futurist cooking. . . . David goes on to identify the complicity between futurism and fascism. Meanwhile, in *French Provincial Cooking*, the account of the flavours of each region is heavily indebted to David's personal reminiscences about meals taken and markets visited. (174)

Examples of the aesthetically oriented, learned, and cosmopolitan nature of David's writing especially abound in the essays she contributed to *The Spectator* in the 1960s. Throughout her career as a food writer, David also examined key figures within the culinary realm, articulating each individual's philosophy as well as his or her contribution to the literature of food. The list includes such notable authors of gastronomic and culinary literature as William Verral (*Complete System of Cookery* 1759); Eliza Acton (*Modern Cookery for Private Families* 1845); Isabella Beeton (*Mrs. Beeton's Book of Household Management* 1861); Colonel Arthur Robert Kenney-Herbert (*Culinary Jottings for Madras* 1878); Lieutenant Colonel Nathaniel Newnham-Davis (*Dinners and Diners, Where and How to Dine in London* 1899, *The Gourmet Guide to Europe* 1903); and Edouard de Pomiane (*Cooking with Pomiane* 1930s, *French Cooking in Ten Minutes* 1930). By recreating the lives and writing of such innovative figures, David educated her readers not only about culinary history but also about food scholarship, a field that she helped professionalize in her own writing.

WORLD WAR II INTERVENES

The degree to which interwar cookbooks magnified the aesthetic component of cooking and hosting attests to two overlapping cultural shifts—

---

10. In "Simple, Honest Food: Elizabeth David and the Construction of Nation in Cookery Writing," Janet Floyd also takes up David's relationship with gastronomic literature. Rather than interpreting it as a means of liberation from the "dull compulsion of domestic labour" as do Jones and Taylor, however, Floyd reads it as an elitist stance driven, in part, by nostalgia for a colonialist past. Jones and Taylor likewise briefly touch on David's position of privilege, but rather than interpreting it as leading toward a philosophy that expresses "a last gasp at British colonialism" as does Floyd, they read it as providing her "with a high degree of cultural capital, and access to a diverse range of culinary traditions" (174). My argument extends that of Jones and Taylor and diverges from that of Floyd in its emphasis on gender relations. Rather than focusing on David's position of cultural privilege, this study focuses on her position as a woman who insisted on being taken seriously within a professional food culture traditionally reserved for men.

the disappearance of servants from the home kitchen and a growing appetite for the fresh, stimulating flavors largely eradicated by the First World War. The disappearance of servants from the kitchen meant that middle-class housewives were increasingly forced to take over the laborious task of cooking themselves, a task that they had increasingly distanced themselves from since the late nineteenth century. As a result, the prevalent attitude toward hands-on cookery as a menial chore needed to be entirely revamped. During the same time that servants were disappearing from middle-class home kitchens, England began to yearn for the stimulating, fresh, harmonious flavors virtually eradicated by World War I. Cookbook authors such as Boulestin, Morphy, and Leyel obliged by providing recipes with ingredients that would have been alluring to the more curious palates of 1920s England. As Humble explains: "To cook such exotic, unrestrained and vibrantly flavoured food gave the middle-class housewife an imaginative association with the creative artist, as some compensation for the domestic labour that was now to be her lot" (71).

Before middle-class housewives had adjusted to their new role as family cook and become accustomed to the exotic flavors housed in the gastronomically grounded cookbooks of the interwar years, however, World War II entered the home kitchen forcing them to "depend on more modest resources. They had to go foraging for strange foodstuffs in shops they had never cared to explore, and learnt quickly how to compose and cook meals for their families after their cooks and kitchen maids had vanished into factories" (Driver 14). If this return to the kitchen marked a social decline, the English government's broadening of the housewife's duty from that of nurturing the family to sustaining the English nation provided a patriotic screen behind which middle-class housewives could hide their embarrassment. The Ministry of Food taught women that the best way to help in the war effort was to make "a second front—the Kitchen Front—against Hitler" (Minns 110). Housewives were cautioned to keep dinner conversation off food shortages and to avoid mentioning the ingredients of the meal before their family had already eaten. This last piece of advice would have been indispensable when serving such dishes as Hasty Pudding with its "six tablespoons of oatmeal, three tablespoons of suet, a pint of cold water and one onion *or* parsnip" (91). Other equally bleak dishes printed in cookbooks and pamphlets during this time include a "Mock Fish" made from two ounces ground rice, one-half pint boiling milk, and a teaspoon each of leek, margarine, and powdered egg spread out on a "flat dish" to look like "fish filets" (140). For dessert, the English had such delicacies to relish as "Mock Marzipan," with its one-half pound haricot beans which have been soaked overnight in water, placed "on a tin in a warm oven to get dry and floury," and rubbed through a sieve (128). The cook then added sugar, ground rice, almond essence, and margarine.

As Christina Hardyment writes, by defining the kitchen as a second front and equating food with munitions, "the wartime coalition government had negotiated the challenge of invading the Englishwoman's kitchen without being summarily rapped on the knuckles. . . . This was largely thanks to the organizational flair of Lord Woolton" (19–20). In response to governmental advice, women planted gardens wherever a spare patch of soil could be found. Some even "tended cauliflowers and beans on the local rubbish dump or bomb craters according to the instructions of the latest Growmore bulletin" (Minns 101). Fruit became so scarce that women would willingly wait up to an hour in line for a pound of cooking apples and the Ministry of Food instructed housewives to "use potatoes as the basis of all dishes"—including desserts in which grated potato augmented the shortage of suet and flour. Even the seemingly ubiquitous potato, however, was not immune to shortage. As David pointed out, during post-war rationing "we . . . witnessed the enraged British housewife, . . . deprived of her national birthright, obliged to queue for a pound or two of potatoes" (*French Country Cooking* 156).

The flourish of aesthetically grounded cookbooks during the interwar years could not match the gastronomic consequences of two world wars in quick succession. As a result, early twentieth-century English cooking had a reputation "for being heavy, monotonous and lacking in skill" (Mennell 248). The Second World War, in particular, encouraged several factors that "contributed to a coarsening of the national palate," including the

> forced contraction of choice, . . . the persistent and often lazy-minded substitution of materials in cookery books and newspaper articles, the climate created by years of official advice to 'make do and mend,' and the unpopularity, indeed suspect patriotism until the declining days of the labour Government, of anyone who complained about not obtaining the quality of goods or the courtesy of service that he or she had been brought to expect. The phrase 'Don't you know there's a war on?' lasted several years after the war, only half in jest. (Driver 43–44)

Despite rationing, however, with its requisite lack of fresh foods, the English as a nation ate more nutritionally balanced meals during the 1940s than ever before (17). Taken class by class, though, this meant that while the diet of the lower classes improved, the diet of the middle and upper classes often declined.[11]

---

11. Burnett points to statistics from the Wartime Food Surveys which indicated that "there was now little difference between [the middle class] diet and that of the poorer families, reflecting the general levelling-up of standards" (330). In contrast to the lower and lower-middle-class diets, "the dietary standards of the wealthier classes probably declined somewhat between the wars. This was partly a consequence of choice and partly of necessity. The taste for the solid, endless repasts of Victorian days were changing in favour of shorter, lighter meals more suited to the accelerated pace of life and better adapted to the new knowledge of nutrition which was beginning to influence people's tastes" (296).

Even for the increasing number of individuals whose diet was nutritionally sound, however, these 'healthy' meals did not necessarily nourish psychological satisfaction. Technological advances in the food industry meant that one could ingest balanced meals from jars and tins. However "healthy" these war-rationed portions might have been, they did not always compose well-prepared and tasty dishes, a fact supported by testimonials on the meals eaten during and immediately after World War II. Novelist E. M. Forster found the state of English cuisine so bleak that he wrote the following commentary, which appears in the anthology *We Shall Eat and Drink Again* (1944)[12] edited by Louis Golding and André Simon:

> I was returning to England, my country, by one of her boat trains. . . . We sat in a vacuum waiting, waiting for breakfast. . . . At last . . . the attendants came in crying 'Porridge or Prunes, sir? Porridge or Prunes?'
> . . . That cry still rings in my memory. It is an epitome—not, indeed, of English food, but of the forces which drag it into the dirt. It voices the true spirit of gastronomic joylessness. Porridge fills the Englishman up, prunes clear him out, so their functions are opposed. But their spirit is the same: they eschew pleasure and consider delicacy immoral. That morning they looked as like one another as they could. Everything was grey. The porridge was in pallid grey lumps, the prunes swam in grey juice like the wrinkled skulls of old men, grey mist pressed against the grey windows. (56–57)

The "gastronomic joylessness" that Forster bemoaned would continue well beyond war's end; rationing would become stricter following the war than at any point in its duration. Public dining had descended to such depths by 1949, in fact, that it led Raymond Postgate to write that the bottled sauces appearing on restaurant tables

> were provided on the justified assumption that you would want to hide completely the taste of what you would be offered. Sodden, sour, slimy, sloppy, stale or saccharined—one of these six things (or all) it certainly would be, whether it was fish, flesh, vegetable or sweet. It would also be over-cooked; it might be reheated. (Driver 49)[13]

---

12. The anthology was collected from Simon's *Wine and Food Quarterly*, which began in 1934. As Goldman explains in his preface to the collection: "The present selection from the pages of the 'Quarterly' is made from the issues of ten years, six of peace and four of war. There are some who believe that the continuance of this journal during these war years was the keeping alight of a torch, as gracious a thing as the keeping alive of ballet and music and the other fine arts. I am one of those. Hence this volume" (9).

13. Driver describes Postgate and David as the two figures in the early 1950s who "came to symbolise—much to their own surprise—the richness and variety of what was again permissible to eat" (48).

Postgate, a social historian, was so alarmed by the state of English restaurants that he started collecting reviews of palatable places to dine. Despite the fact that the first edition of his *The Good Food Guide* appeared in 1951, it would be years before he would praise a restaurant with more effusive commentary than "helpings were generous" (Driver 57). David concurred with this assessment when she returned to England in August of 1946 after a seven-year sojourn abroad.

A MEDITERRANEAN ADVENTURE

All the while her compatriots were dining out of tin cans and dehydrated food packets, David had been eagerly imbibing the food cultures of France, Italy, Greece, and Egypt. In rebellion against the social expectation that she marry and embrace the bland and stultifying life she associated with domesticity, David set sail for the Mediterranean with her married lover, Charles Gibson Cowan, in July of 1939. Taking along a trunk filled with travel literature and cookbooks, David began, at the age of twenty-five, to gather the intellectual capital needed to claim authority within a professional field almost exclusively dominated by men.[14] Over the next thirty years, she devoured an estimable library's worth of fiction, travel writing, culinary and gastronomic memoir, cookbooks, gastronomic literature, and history, all of which saturate her prose. Among the list of authors whose writing most profoundly influenced David's own can be found women who effectively joined elegance of expression, aesthetic sensibility, and practical knowledge—namely Countess Morphy and Hilda Leyel, both of whom accompanied her in book form to the Mediterranean. In addition to these authors, Marcel Boulestin and Norman Douglas would profoundly effect David's trajectory as a writer and as a scholar.

Although David had been versed in Boulestin's culinary aesthetic well before she first landed in France, having set sail from England with three of his books in hand, Norman Douglas would first enter David's life in

---

14. Biographer Lisa Chaney provides a partial list of the cookbooks David took on her voyage to the Mediterranean. The list was drawn from a letter David wrote to her sister Priscilla asking her to send replacements for books that had been confiscated by the Italian government when she and Cowan were placed under arrest; soon after David and Cowan left Norman Douglas in Antibes, Great Britain declared war against Italy, and the couple were arrested off the coast of Sicily under suspicion that they were spying for the British government. On June 10, 1940, they began a nineteen-day internment, which ended when an American consul helped the couple out of Italy and across the Yugoslav border. David asked Priscilla to try and find replacement copies of Boulestin's *The Finer Cooking, 100 Ways of Cooking Eggs*, and *Hors d'Oeuvres and Savouries* along with Bunyard's *The Epicure's Companion*, Morphy's *Recipes of All Nations*, and Leyel's *Gentle Art of Cookery*.

Antibes. The travel writer and gourmand would prove an impressive mentor, helping to form David's budding gastronomic philosophy along with her writing career. David describes Douglas as

> a great epicure in matters gastronomical . . . in an uncommon way; in a way few mortals can ever hope to become. . . . He himself preferred the study of the original sources of his food and wine. . . . Cause and effect were eminently his concerns, and in their application he taught me some unforgettable lessons. (*Omelette* 123)

Douglas taught David about the symbiosis of flavor, place, and the people who nourish, gather, and produce what grows on a given stretch of land.

David payed homage to Douglas in an article that she wrote for *Gourmet* in 1969. In addition to relating stories that capture his eccentric sense of humor, impeccable palate, keen aesthetic sensibility, and power as a writer, David conveys his methods as a mentor:

> Once during the last summer of his life, on Capri, I took him a basket of figs from the market in the piazza. He asked me from which stall I had bought them. "That one down nearest to the steps." "Not bad, my dear, not bad. Next time, you could try Graziella. I fancy you'll find her figs are sweeter; just wait a few days, if you can."
>
> He knew, who better, from which garden those figs came; he was familiar with the history of the trees, he knew their age and in what type of soil they grew; he knew by which tempests, blights, invasions, and plagues that particular property had or had not been affected during the past three hundred years; how many times it had changed hands, . . . that the son now grown up was a man less grasping than his neighbours and was consequently in less of a hurry to pick and sell his fruit before it ripened. (*Omelette* 123)

Like her mentor, David colors her cookbooks and journalism with just such particulars of place, but her focus lies less in the details of the growing process than it does in the flavors imparted by the topography, soil, climate, and culture of a given place, or its *terroir*. Thus, when David describes the most exquisite fruits, vegetables, or prepared dishes she has encountered, the places where she ate them and where they were produced feature prominently; these locations are virtually one and the same because the foods she finds most memorable are eaten either where they are grown or in close proximity to their place of origin. She writes in *Italian Food*:

> No two figs are alike. That is one of the joys of figs, for it makes the perfect one far to seek. For me, the best figs are not Sicilian, nor the flavoury little figs of the Abruzzi. They are the figs from one particular tree in a garden on the Greek island of Euboea—figs with fine skins of

a most brilliant green, the fruit itself of a deep rich purple, with more body, less honey sweet, but with a more intense flavour than figs anywhere else in the world. (261)

David's ability to enjoy the flavor of the Euboean fig and to capture such enjoyment in prose stemmed from her attunement to *terroir*. By memorializing the beauty of the figs grown on one particular tree on the Grecian island of Euboea, David not only emphasizes the relationship between the flavor of food and the region in which it is grown, but she also encourages her readers to taste more carefully and to learn about the origins of their food. She also foregrounds the importance of sensory engagement to eating pleasures.

Alongside Douglas, Boulestin would prove one of David's favorite authors of all time as well as a keen influence on her focus as a writer. Boulestin, a native of Perigord, had become so enamored with England on his first visit to London in 1907 that he soon made it his permanent home. Upon returning to England after a five-year stint in the French Army during World War I, Boulestin launched his career as a cookbook author. Recalling this first endeavor, he observes:

> I had eaten well all my life and, like all French men from the South-West of France, I instinctively knew how to cook. So my idea was to produce a book which, ignoring the rules and the jargon of cookery books, could be understood by anybody just gifted with a little common sense—a book written as simply as possible, containing not only simple and genuine recipes of French *cuisine bourgeoise*, but recipes of remarkable local dishes, handed down, like Homer's verses, from generation to generation. (*Myself, My Two Countries* 287)

Although almost three decades would pass between the publication of Boulestin's first book, *Simple French Cooking for English Homes* (1923), and David's first book on *French Country Cooking* (1951), Boulestin's idea of producing "a book which, ignoring the rules and the jargon of cookery books, could be understood by anybody just gifted with a little common sense" forms the core of David's first four books. In turn, the six months she spent in France in the company of Norman Douglas served to reinforce her growing appreciation for fresh ingredients, simply prepared to enhance their natural flavors. The recipes David began to collect on her journey through France and that would eventually become *Mediterranean Food* not only included the "simple and genuine recipes of the French *cuisine bourgeoise*" but also the "simple and genuine" recipes from each of the countries she visited—including Italy, Greece, and Egypt.

As she began to collect recipes, David augmented her natural eye for the most alluring and magical traits of Mediterranean cuisine with the wit and wisdom of her favorite authors, including Hilda Leyel and

Countess Morphy from whom she had first taught herself to cook. Looking back on this time in her later years, David recalled that the lure of Leyel's book arose from its portrayal of "food as unlike as could be to any produced by the conventional English cook of the time" and in its "appeal to the imagination of the young," who "will usually prefer a book which provides stimulus to one which goes into technical details" (*Spices* 17). In describing the appeal of Leyel's sparse instruction, David underscores the connection between appetite and imagination. She also explains the appeal of her first two cookbooks, *Mediterranean Food* and *French Country Cooking,* which are themselves remarkably spare in technical detail.

Like the typical English gastronome, Leyel urged her compatriots to counteract England's heavy hand with vegetables by turning to France for inspiration, a message David heard loud and clear. More than the gentle treatment of vegetables, a cause taken up by many cookery writers of the interwar years, however, Leyel's evocation of "Dishes from the Arabian Nights" fueled David's passion for cookery and inspired her first recipe collection. In large part, David attributed her ready embrace of Middle Eastern cookery to Leyel's *Gentle Art of Cookery. Mediterranean Food* includes not only David's favorite dishes gathered from her travels with Cowan to France, Italy, and the Greek island Syros but also those collected from 1941 to 1945, when she worked for the English war effort in Alexandria and Cairo.[15] Just as Boulestin had prepared David to appreciate and later to write about the cooking of provincial France, Hilda Leyel stirred David's passion for the flavors and ingredients of Middle Eastern cookery to which she would devote generous portions of *Mediterranean Food.*

David pays tribute to Leyel's influence on her own taste and, in turn, her profession, when she writes:

> I fell under the spell of the beautiful food of the Levant—the warm flat bread, the freshly pressed tomato juice, the charcoal-grilled lamb, the oniony salads, the mint and yogurt sauces, the sesame seed paste, the pistachios and the pomegranates and the apricots, the rosewater and the scented sweetmeats, and everywhere the warm spicy smell of cumin. Because I had so often pored over Mrs Leyel's cookery book without quite realizing what she was putting into my head, the food of the Levant appeared more attractive than perhaps I should have found it without the background of that book. Come to that, I

---

15. After having escaped internment by the Italian government, Cowan and David settled in Syros, Greece for six months. When the Germans began bombing Crete, they fled Greece for Alexandria, where they parted ways. In addition to enjoying an active romantic life, David held a job for the Ministry of War in Alexandria and ran the reference library for the Ministry of Information in Cairo.

wonder if I would have ever learned to cook at all had I been given a routine Mrs. Beeton to learn from instead of the romantic Mrs Leyel, with her rather wild and imagination-catching recipes. (*Spices, Salt and Aromatics* 15)

David's *Mediterranean Food* not only captures the sensual pleasures of dining in the Levant but also conveys the same "wild and imagination-catching" quality of Leyel's writing, a trait that allowed David to convey flavors so evocatively that her readers could imagine tasting the dishes she describes. Leyel's *Gentle Art of Cookery* not only prepared David for the Egyptian delicacies she encountered and helped her translate them into recipes for *Mediterranean Food*, but it also inspired *Spices, Salt and Aromatics in the English Kitchen*, David's first book devoted to a study of English cuisine and a work that shares more in keeping with gastronomic literature than with the domestic cookbook. In *Spices* David displays an encyclopedic knowledge of culinary and gastronomic history alongside a remarkable capacity to render poetic dishes from a handful of ingredients, a skill she honed during her stay in the Middle East (20).

Leyel's *Gentle Art of Cookery* was not the only interwar cookbook with which David taught herself how to cook; she also relied heavily on Morphy's *Recipes of all Nations*, a book that she found indispensable enough to carry along when she set sail for the Mediterranean.[16] Morphy conveys an aesthetic sensibility, a cosmopolitan approach toward cookery, and a capacity to synthesize vast amounts of culinary information, traits that would characterize David's own oeuvre. Morphy divides her book into chapters, each of which are devoted to a particular nation and are introduced with a brief overview of its cookery. In these introductory remarks, Morphy repeatedly links cookery with the visual and literary arts. About France, she reflects:

Just as the art of Watteau, Fragonard, Boucher, and Lancret is typically French, so is the art of blending edible ingredients. The same indefinable quality of mind we find in Ronsard, Clement Marot, Montaigne and, in modern times, Anatole France, we also find in the great French culinary innovators of the past and present. There is the same *finesse*, the same subtle delicacy of touch, the same unfailing sense of balance

---

16. An American and an English edition of Morphy's book were published, both of which appeared in 1935. The main difference between the two editions is that the English edition includes a section on the cookery of the "United States of America" while the American edition replaces this section with one on the cookery of "England." Only those comments on English cookery are taken from the American edition. All other citations in this chapter are taken from the English edition.

and proportion—all of which are essentially and typically French. (23–24)

A native of New Orleans, Morphy, like Boulestin, immigrated to England, where her previous exposure to Creole cooking and its blend of Spanish, French, and African cuisines inspired her to introduce the English housewife to a wide range of foreign cookery. In order to do so Morphy frequently relied on professional male chefs to select and authenticate recipes, thanking chefs from such diverse countries as Spain, France, India, Sweden, Portugal, and China among numerous others. Whereas Morphy relied on professional male chefs to authorize her book, David felt no such compulsion, nor did she devote her book as Morphy did to the "ordinary woman" and the "housewife." Writing after World War II, David would address her book to "people," that is, anyone—male or female, home cook or professional—who takes an interest in cooking. Another key difference distinguishes David's professed goal in writing from that of her mentor. Morphy hoped that her readers would prepare the "exciting and delicious foreign dishes" she reproduced in her cookbook. In writing *Mediterranean Food*, David could only hope that her readers on strict ration would find solace in her words. In the preface to the revised 1958 edition of *Mediterranean Food*, David explains that she wrote to stir the imagination of the English public, to nourish them with words.

A SENSUAL ENGAGEMENT

The power of David's prose stems from its portrayal of a gastronomic philosophy that focuses on food as an art and on the palate's education as integral to the attainment of pleasure and self-knowledge. David's aesthetic and its transgression of the domestic food writing tradition was inspired in large part by her prolonged exposure to cultures such as France, Italy, Greece, Egypt, and Spain. She began to articulate the sensual and intellectual pleasures of her Mediterranean adventures upon returning to England in 1946. Once home, David faced the stringent rationing and dearth of fresh ingredients with which her compatriots had been making due for years. She devoted her first six months in London struggling to gather foods for palatable meals before venturing to Ross-on-Wye for a respite. Instead of relief, however, she found herself trapped by floods and forced to eat meal after meal of "flour and water soup," "bread and gristle rissoles," and "dehydrated onions and carrots" (*Omelette* 21). Returning to her hotel room after one of these meals, David found that

> Hardly knowing what I was doing, I who had scarcely ever put pen to paper except to write memos to the heads of departments in the

Ministry which employed me during the war, I sat down and . . . started to work out an agonizing craving for the sun and a furious revolt against the terrible, cheerless, heartless food by writing down descriptions of Mediterranean and Middle Eastern cooking. Even to write words like apricots, olives and butter, rice and lemons, oil and almonds, produced assuagement. (*Omelette* 21)

Unable to eat Mediterranean and Middle Eastern foods in post-war England or to enjoy the sun-baked countryside and pleasant setting of her travels, David reconstituted these experiences in language. She did so by harnessing food's symbolic resonance to create a sense of well-being from memory, thereby assuaging her "agonizing craving" for another land and time.

David's self-proclaimed project in *A Book of Mediterranean Food* was to convey "some idea of the lovely cookery of [Mediterranean] regions to people who do not already know them, and to stir the memories of those who have eaten this food on its native shores, and who would like sometimes to bring a flavour of those blessed lands of sun and sea and olive trees into their English kitchens" (6). To encourage her readers' connection with the Mediterranean, David saturated her work with sensory images, which—aside from being a natural component of food writing—enabled her to capture a former psychological integrity experienced in "those blessed lands," to bring the past into the present. By using language to recreate a previous sensory engagement, David incorporated her Mediterranean experience into her present life, reliving emotional and material plenitude in a time of scarcity. Writing about the foods of foreign lands eased David's anxiety and cohered a life which seemed fragmented in post-war England. By recreating a particular time, place and flavor through language rather than the material food itself, David used the writing process, or language, as a substitute for food.

Mediterranean Food not only "assuaged" David's post-war anxiety, but it did wonders for its select readership as well, who responded enthusiastically when the book was published in 1950. Historian Christopher Driver helps to illuminate the enthusiasm of David's readers. In his analysis of effective food writing, Driver points out that the food writer's success depends upon his or her ability to write using language

accurate and imaginative enough to jog people's memories back to similar tastes and occasions that they can recognise and remember for themselves. Without this sharing of sensory experience, most communication about food fails altogether, although every now and then food writers appear—in our own time notably Elizabeth David and M. F. K. Fisher—whose descriptive and reminiscent powers are more nearly self-sufficient. At their best, one reads under the illusion that one is simultaneously tasting. (130)

The power of David's writing and the essence that allows her readers to feel that they are "simultaneously tasting" lie in the sensory impressions that saturate her prose. A particular tree on the Italian island Anacapri grows figs with skin that "cracks gently as it is picked, disclosing a rose madder flesh which is sweet with a dry aftertaste" (*Italian Food* 261). The candied walnuts of Turin resemble "nuggets of onyx, sugar dusted" (200). They are "soft as fresh plums or damsons would be, sweet of course, a little crunchy with their dusting of sugar, and with that haunting scent and taste of cloves" (292). By describing precisely how a given food tastes, smells, and looks, as well as her own physiological response to it, David feeds her readers language filled with sensory impressions.

The eating pleasures that saturate much of David's best food writing hold an undeniably erotic appeal, as illustrated by the following passage, which appears in *Mediterranean Food*:

> The cassoulet is . . . the genuine, abundant, earthy, richly flavoured and patiently simmered dish of the ideal farmhouse kitchen. Hidden beneath a layer of creamy, golden-crusted haricot beans in a deep, wide, earthen pot, the cassoulet contains garlicky pork sausage, smoked bacon, salt pork . . . perhaps a piece of mutton . . . or half a duck. . . . The beans are tender, juicy, moist[, and] . . . aromatic smells of garlic and herbs escape from the pot as the cassoulet is brought smoking hot from the oven to the table. (107)

David's description largely centers around the consistency of the dish. The cassoulet is "creamy," "tender, juicy, moist," and "smoking hot," adjectives that convey an erotic engagement. Like its texture, the appearance of the cassoulet is vividly depicted as "golden-crusted" in a "deep, wide, earthen pot" which "is brought smoking hot from the oven to the table."

While adjectives abound in David's description of the cassoulet's texture and appearance, she devotes noticeably less attention to its smell, which is simply characterized by the "aromatic scent of garlic and herbs," or to its taste, which is "richly-flavoured." In *Remembrance of Repasts*, anthropologist David Sutton offers one possible explanation for David's more cursory description of the aroma and flavor of the cassoulet—aroma and flavor are far more difficult to convey through language than appearance. Whereas aroma and flavor tend to evoke memories laden with emotion, sight is closely linked to cognitive memories. As Sutton explains: "smells more easily connect with 'episodic' than 'semantic' memories (i.e., life-history memories as opposed to 'recognition of a phenomenon' memories)" (89). As a result, smell evokes memories that are less cognitive, and thus less easy to capture semantically, than those triggered by sight. Because of the difficulty in describing smell and aroma and the resulting paucity of language with which to do so, David often evokes aroma using what might be described as "self-reflexive" terms. For example, David writes of the enchantment of a "*soufflé omelette aux liqueurs*, brought to table frothing and spilling over the dish, an aroma of fresh eggs, sizzling butter and mellow liqueur sharpening your senses" (*French Provincial Cooking* 449). David captures her sensory impression of the dish with such terms as "frothing and spilling" and "sizzling," which convey both texture and sound. To evoke the aroma, however, David relies on more self-reflexive terms—"mellow" and "fresh." The adjective "mellow" conveys that the aromatic burn of the liqueur's alcohol has been cooked off, requiring that the reader know the difference between the smell of a heated liqueur with alcohol still present versus one in which the alcohol has been cooked off. David's language becomes even more self-reflexive when she describes the omelette as smelling of "fresh eggs." When David describes the aroma of a dish as like that of one or more of its ingredients, she relies on the reader's familiarity with the food about which she is writing. In the case of the cassoulet, the reader must be familiar with the "aromatic scent of garlic and herbs." To imagine the omelette, the reader must know the smell of "fresh eggs." This self-reflexivity allows David, as Driver observes, to "jog people's memories back to similar tastes and occasions."

Although such descriptions can trigger memories in the reader who has eaten a similar dish, David circumvents this self-reflexivity at times by relying on the erotic nature of a food's aroma and flavor. The following passage, which captures an October day in Spain, depicts aroma in a way that underscores the pleasure that results from the intermingling of eater and eaten, self and other:

> Now there are signs of autumn on the leaves of some of the almond trees. They have turned a frail, transparent auburn, and this morning when I awoke I devoured two of the very first tangerines of the season. In the dawn their scent was piercing and their taste was sharp. . . . At midday we picked small figs, dusty purple and pale jade green. On the skins is a bloom not to be seen on midsummer figs. The taste, too, is quite different. The flesh is clear garnet red, less rich and more subtle than that of the main-crop fruit, which is of the *vernal* variety, brilliant green. In the north we can never taste fruit like this, fruit midway between fresh and dried. It has the same poignancy as the black Valencia grapes still hanging in heavy bunches on the vines. . . . To start our midday meal we have, invariably, a tomato and onion salad, a few slices of fresh white cheese, and a dish of olives. The tomatoes are the Mediterranean ridged variety of which I never tire. They are huge, sweet, fleshy, richly red. (*Omelette* 94)

This scene is typical of David's writing in its emphasis on the visual. However, it varies markedly from the passages mentioned earlier in that David does not rely on self-reflexive terms to describe the aroma and flavor of the tangerine. Rather, David describes her physiological response to the fruit, depicting the tangerine as an agent that acts on her body. She describes her response using terms that denote penetration, showing that even if scent itself may be difficult to translate into language, its effect on the body is not. Any term that denotes an intermingling—the crossing of thresholds, blending, ingestion, introjection—will work to describe the effect of the tangerine because an aroma, like a flavor, literally enters the body, crossing the threshold between self and other. The tangerine is "sharp" and "piercing" as it enters through the mouth and nose. In turn, the 'sharp' and 'piercing' scent sediments the memory of the autumn dawn in David's body; the Spanish flavors form a memory whose erotic pleasure David expressed years later in prose.

By focusing on the precise moment when the self and other merge—on the threshold of incorporation—David captures the aroma and flavor by describing their effect on the boundaries of her body. In so doing, she avoids the self-reflexive terminology that requires the familiarity of her reader with given ingredients. Her description of the cassoulet as "richly-flavoured" and "aromatic" may be "accurate and imaginative enough to jog people's memories back to similar tastes and occasions that they can recognise and remember for themselves" (Driver 130). However, her depiction of the tangerine as sharp and piercing conveys the process of incorporation, thus encouraging her reader to "feel that they are simultaneously tasting" (Driver 130). David "feeds" her readers by translating her own physical pleasure into language, a capacity derived from an aesthetic firmly grounded in the body.

FOOD AS A MEANS OF SELF-EXPRESSION

After David returned to England at the tail end of World War II, she began to write *A Book of Mediterranean Food*, which helped to reintroduce stimulating and flavorful food to her compatriots worn down by years of rationing. Her next four projects, *French Country Cooking* (1951), *Italian Food* (1954), *Summer Cooking* (1955), and *French Provincial Cooking* (1960), would articulate a culinary philosophy that showcases food as a means of engaging with foreign beliefs and practices and of nourishing aesthetic pleasure—a philosophy in keeping with the gastronomic tradition. In turn, David fashioned the sensual pleasures of gastronomy into language, showcasing how food nourishes creativity. In so doing, David educated her readers to approach food as more than just an end in itself, to understand eating and cooking as means of self-construction as well as self-expression. This, in fact, was to become one of the fundamental goals of her journalistic and cookbook writing.

In *French Country Cooking* and *French Provincial Cooking*, David explores the difference between French and English attitudes toward the table. Such inquiry clearly participates in the tradition of gastronomic literature, which was likewise preoccupied with defining the French culinary aesthetic in relation to that of the English. Like the more Francophilic gastronomes before her, David also incorporated key tenets of the French approach toward food and cookery into her own gastronomic philosophy. In particular, the same emphasis on composition and appreciation of food as a means of self-expression that David lauds in the French are foundational components of her own food writing.

David's first exposure to French culture came at the age of sixteen, when she spent a year and a half in Paris studying at the Sorbonne. During this time, she stayed with a French family, enjoying her first taste of French cuisine. David recalls the impact of her stay in Paris:

> It was only later, after I had come home to England, that I realized in what way the family had fulfilled their task of instilling French culture into at least one of their English charges. Forgotten were the Sorbonne professors and the yards of Racine learnt by heart, the plans of cathedrals I had never seen, and the saga of Napoleon's last days on St. Helena. What had stuck was the taste for a kind of food quite ideally unlike anything I had known before. Ever since, I have been trying to catch up with those lost days when perhaps I should have been more profitably employed watching [the cook] in her kitchen rather than trudging conscientiously round every museum and picture gallery in Paris. (*French Provincial Cooking* 240)

That the kitchens of a country are more memorable for David than its museums and picture galleries might be explained, in part, by the fact that cooking encourages a relationship based on participation as opposed to galleries and museums, which are based on observation. Whereas sightseeing encourages an objective distance, cooking and eating entail what philosopher Lisa Heldke terms "bodily knowledge," which is acquired while performing activities that conjoin mind and body as well as self and other. David's description of her first exposure to French culture at the age of sixteen underscores the difference between knowledge gained through less embodied experiences such as sightseeing and that gained through a physical engagement that involves all the senses.

Because of her gastronomical studies, David was keenly aware of the connection between sensual pleasure and intellectual growth. Thus she adopted the French belief that pleasure in food should be a daily occurrence and that, toward this end, one should procure "excellent ingredients" for everyday dishes as well as for special occasions. As a result, she was fascinated by French food markets, which she declared "as good a way as any to the beginnings of an understanding and appreciation of any French province, to see the local markets in action, to watch the produce unloaded from the carts and vans, to hear the talk of the farmers and buyers in the cafés after the main business has been transacted" (*Omelette* 261).

The time David spent observing and shopping at French markets not only taught her about the centrality of fresh food to the everyday French diet, but it also allowed her to see how the French gather and procure the freshest local ingredients available. The markets also showcase the French emphasis on the composition, or presentation, of food, one of the most important influences on David's culinary aesthetic. David would become so attuned to the beauty of markets—what she terms "the stomach of a city"—that she asks how the

Montpellier fishwife so mastered the art of composition that with her basket of fish for the *bouillabaisse* she is presenting a picture of such splendour that instead of going to look at the famous collection of paintings in the Musée Fabre you drive off as fast as possible to the coast to order a dish cooked with just such fish? (*Omelette* 266)

Here David foregrounds food as a medium through which the self can be constructed in relation to other nations, other cultures, and other individuals. This self-construction is based on the expansion and reconfiguration of her own culinary beliefs, practices, and attitudes through an active engagement with those of foreign cultures. It also underscores gastronomy as a means of attaining knowledge about the self and the self in relation to others. Like the male gastronome, David encouraged her compatriots to embrace sensual pleasure as a fundamental goal of cookery and of eating. She did so by demonstrating that food treated as an artistic medium, as a means of conveying aesthetic pleasure, stimulates the mind as well as the body.

Incorporating the French emphasis on composition into her culinary philosophy as well as her written aesthetic enabled David to demonstrate the role that presentation plays in the stimulation of appetite. It also enabled her to forge an engaging, evocative aesthetic. The power of visual presentation comes into particular play in David's many depictions of European markets, such as the following one in Venice:

The light of the Venetian dawn in early summer . . . is so limpid and so still that it makes every separate vegetable and fruit and fish luminous with a life of its own, with unnaturally heightened colors and clear stenciled outlines. Here the cabbages are cobalt blue, the beetroots deep rose, the lettuces clear pure green, sharp as glass. Bunches of gaudy gold marrow flowers show off the elegance of pink-and-white marbled bean pods, primrose potatoes, green plums, green peas. The color of the peaches, cherries and apricots, packed in boxes lined with blue paper matching the blue canvas trousers worn by the men unloading the gondolas, are reflected in the rose-red mullet and the orange vongole and cannestrelle, which have been pried out of their shells and heaped in baskets. (*Italian Food* 109)

This portrait of the Venetian market is typical of David's best food writing in that it displays the same "genius for presentation" for which she lauds the French. Much of David's most celebrated writing translates the visual impact of European markets into language, thereby demonstrating the importance of balance and contrast, color and proportion to the stimulation of appetite.

David's sensual engagement with her environment was honed in large part during her extended travels throughout the Mediterranean during World War II as well as during regular trips she took to France and Italy in the 1950s. During these latter sojourns, David set up house for extended periods of time in order to collect the knowledge and skill articulated in *French Country Cooking, Italian Food*, and *French Provincial Cooking*. Returning home after each of her journeys, David spent hours every day in the kitchen working to recreate the dishes she encountered on her travels. Such cooking clarified her memory. She describes the effect:

> Here in London it is an effort of will to believe in the existence of such a place [as Provence]. But now and again the vision of golden tiles on a round southern roof, or of some warm, stony, herb-scented hillside will rise out of my kitchen pot with the smell of a piece of orange peel scenting a beef stew. (18–19)

That the "smell of orange peel scenting a beef stew" could trigger the delightful vision of a Provençal afternoon attests to the fact that David successfully integrated "the French attitude of mind towards" food into her own culinary philosophy. She attained a knowledge of French regional dishes as a cultural expression of a bond between a land and its people. This knowledge was housed in her body, so to speak, and traveled back with her to England, where it could be accessed each time she prepared a dish that brought to mind her travels through France.

LOST LOVE AND LATER WORKS

David connects her drive to write about food with erotic intimacy in her personal correspondence, consciously linking food, romance, and creativity in a way that foregrounds intimacy as a powerful source of inspiration. During mid-life, however, David temporarily lost her inspiration to write cookbooks. She did not write a book for seven years after losing a lover and suffering a stroke, events that left her physically and emotionally numb. With her romantic inspiration gone, David sought and found another creative muse, learning to savor pleasure in the incorporation and expression of language; reading and writing about food enabled her to access and recreate former pleasures, thereby nourishing creativity from within. An examination of the aesthetic shift between her earlier and later writing demonstrates how language that stimulates the memory of embodied pleasure nourishes creativity.

David dedicated *French Provincial Cooking* to Peter Higgins, a man with whom she first became sexually involved in 1949, the year before *Mediterranean Food* was published. The couple carried on a tumultuous, sporadic affair that lasted fourteen years. Although each of them took many other lovers during this period, David developed a strong attachment to Higgins over the course of their affair. David's feelings had grown intense enough by 1960 that she dedicated *French Provincial*

Cooking "To P. H. With Love." Within three years, however, Higgins had become seriously involved with another woman, whom he would eventually marry. Upon learning of their relationship, David went into what her biographer Artemis Cooper describes as a "rage, flinging herself about and hurling things across the room" (Cooper 225). David's fury over what she considered Higgins' betrayal, compounded by long working hours and a weakness for brandy, contributed to a mild stroke. David recovered quickly, but her ability to taste was permanently damaged.[17] Although she returned to work almost immediately writing magazine articles, she did not write another cookbook for seven years.

David confessed in anger to Higgins:

> I dedicated [*French Provincial Cooking*] to you because it was you who provided the conflict and stress which, for such as I, alone make writing possible. For that matter, for better or worse, it was you who were responsible for all my books, right from the beginning. . . . It is not, you know, my illness which has stopped me writing. It is the ending of a . . . prolonged torment (Cooper 234).

Although David's passion for Higgins could hardly have been the sole source of inspiration for all her books—she began writing *Mediterranean Food,* for example, years before she became seriously involved with Higgins—the letter indicates how strongly David relied heavily on romantic inspiration for her creativity. Linking her passion for Higgins (whether love, lust, or fury) to her drive to write, David connects romantic inspiration with creativity.

The dual blow struck by the hemorrhage and Higgins' withdrawal led to David's physical and psychological disengagement; she could no longer immerse herself in another culture to the extent required to write a cookbook on foreign cuisine. She did, however, open a cookery store, Elizabeth David, Ltd. Through the store, David resuscitated her passion for foreign cuisines and channeled it into procuring the best of European cookery equipment; she also continued to write engaging magazine articles. Increasingly, however, she turned to books rather than to travel for her "tasting" knowledge and to inspire the many articles she wrote during this time. She also relied heavily on memory to sample the flavors her tongue could no longer taste. David's eventual return to cookbook writing was inspired, in large part, by her love of language, a passion that replaced Higgins as her muse. Just as M. F. K. Fisher had before her, David, having lost her lover, found inspiration in the words of her favorite food writers.

---

17. Although both of David's biographers, Cooper and Chaney, mention her loss of taste, specifically citing her inability to taste salt, the extent to which this impairment extended to the other taste receptors remains vague in their accounting.

From 1950 to 1960, David authored four books on foreign cuisines. Her next book *Spices, Salt and Aromatics in the English Kitchen* did not appear until 1970. This cookbook marked a shift in her focus from foreign to English cuisine and signaled David's immersion into her nation's culinary history as well as its literature. *Spices* is so heavily laden with the gems David unearthed in her study of English cuisine that it might be defined most accurately as gastronomic literature of a scholarly bent. Like the learned gastronome, David embeds an array of literary, culinary, and gastronomic sources into her project in order to contextualize her topic historically. She likewise draws heavily on the favorite works of her youth, those authors who most inspired her own professional career. Referring to her stroke in 1963, David states: "House-bound after a temporarily incapacitating illness during the early nineteen-sixties, I enjoyed my compulsory leisure re-reading old favourites in my cookery library. . . . Among the authors who came out as sturdy survivors were, predictably, Marcel Boulestin and more surprisingly, Mrs Leyel of Culpeper House fame" (15). This rereading triggered a "moment of comprehension which sparked off a train of thought, an idea. The train of thought has crystallized in [*Spices*], still incomplete, still not more than a glance into the English preoccupation with the spices and scents, the fruit, the flavourings, the sauces and condiments of the orient, near and far" (20).

David pays tribute to Leyel's influence on her own career by recalling her initial response to the "imagination catching" quality of her *Gentle Art of Cookery*, musing that Leyel's "'Arabian way of cooking red mullet' sounded irresistible, so much so that even if you barely knew whether a red mullet was a bird, a flower or a fish you very quickly set about finding out" (19). David also drew creative inspiration from Eliza Acton, who wrote *Modern Cookery for Private Families* before English sauces became "the laughing stock of Europe" (75). Explaining the need to return to earlier authors, David states: "Somewhere along the line we began to confuse good plain cooking with plain bad cooking. At this stage our English melted-butter sauce became . . . billstickers' paste, and on this basis . . . perfectly respectable sauces fell toppling to their ruin. To restore them, we need to go back, far back . . . (76). David takes her readers back to 1845 to reclaim the elegant sauces of Acton's *Modern Cookery*.

The English kitchen, which David had spurned furiously in her youth, became a logical focus for her considerable energy. With her capacity to taste compromised, she could no longer depend on her body to register the unfamiliar flavors encountered during travel. Instead, she needed to rely on her memory of flavors previously tasted as well as on those authors she found most evocative and inspiring; Leyel's writing evoked the heady spices that flavored the "magical" dishes David had imbibed so readily in Egypt thirty years earlier. In *Spices*, David also drew on recipes from cookbooks ranging from Robert May's *Accomplisht Cook*

(1660) to Sir Harry Luke's *Tenth Muse* (1954), relying more heavily on outside sources than she had for any of her previous endeavors. David incorporates centuries of English culinary history and literature in order to examine her nation's "preoccupation with the spices and scents" of the Middle East (20). In both its content and form, *Spices* embodies several key characteristics of gastronomic literature: a reverence for the pleasures of the table and for cookery as an art form; an unconventional form that incorporates and crisscrosses between several styles of writing; a cosmopolitan flair and a transnational frame of reference; and an appreciation of gustatory pleasure as a means of attaining wisdom. Perhaps most important of all, however, *Spices* works to educate the English palate about the flavors of its nation's past and to nourish its capacity to draw pleasure from the unfamiliar.

David devoted her next seven years to researching *English Bread and Yeast Cookery* (1977), the last cookbook she completed before her death. This work departs markedly from her previous books in its girth and its weight in scholarship. David had conducted painstaking research for *Italian Food*, *French Provincial Cooking*, and *Spices, Salt and Aromatics*, ending each of these projects with an exhaustive bibliography. Never before, however, had she devoted herself completely to such a narrow focus. *Mediterranean Food* provided a captivating sketch of a vast region; *English Bread and Yeast Cookery* offered an exhaustive, unsurpassable reference. No longer writing about exotic ingredients tasted on distant shores, David dove increasingly into the past for her material. She did so with passion and skill. David also relied increasingly on intellectual, rather than physical, stimulation to nourish her drive to write. Strikingly, her final book project, the posthumously published *Harvest of Cold Months: The Social History of Ice and Ices*, returns to the Middle East, inspired as it was by David's research into "early ice-cream recipes and the links between Levantine sherbets and the sorbets and ices of Europe" (*Harvest* vii).

David restored her creative inspiration by channeling her passion for Peter Higgins into a passion for culinary history. In so doing, David began to nourish herself with language, a feat that illustrates the power of eating and language to mutually construct one another. As scholar Elspeth Probyn writes, while we may be 'articulated' subjects in that we are "the products of the integration of past practices and structures," we are also 'articulating' subjects as "through our enactment of practices we reforge new meanings, new identities for ourselves" (17). This capacity for transformation was central to David's own food writing process. In the end, David's rebellion against the "gastronomic joylessness" of England sparked an adventure that gave her the imagination and hands-on practice needed to merge the gastronomic and the culinary arts. It also enabled her to become a professional author unhindered by the ideological boundaries that had so long kept women's food writing firmly tethered to the home kitchen.

5 From "Aesthetic Choice" to a "Diasporic Aesthetic"
Patience Gray, Vertamae Smart Grosvenor, and Monique Truong

If modernization is understood as a process by which "places are disembedded from their locale, and brought into contact with other distant and disparate places," the founding fathers of gastronomic literature were strong proponents of modernity (Jones and Taylor 178). Grimod de la Reynière and Brillat-Savarin both lauded international culinary exchange and celebrated Paris as a locale where foods from around the world could readily be found. They likewise venerated the well-traveled, cosmopolitan palate honed from such culinary and gastronomic exchange. Two centuries and two world wars later, the globalization of the food supply has continued at such an exponential pace that the cosmopolitan palate, which the early gastronome worked to define, has been democratized to an extent unimaginable in the nineteenth century. At the same time, the industrialization of the food supply has transformed food's relationship to space and time and increasingly divorced food from nature. Such widespread transformation of the food supply has given rise to a backlash against globalization, one that has worked its way forcefully into contemporary culture.

By the mid-twentieth century a decided ambivalence begins to surface within food writing, one that embodies the tension between the local and the global that atomizes contemporary culture at large. Writing during a time that witnessed the post-World War II boom in commercialism, Fisher and David expressed ambivalence about the effects that increased trade and industrialization had on the food supply. On one hand, Fisher and David celebrated and took part in cultural globalization, introducing their readers to foreign culinary beliefs and practices. The increase in global trade likewise enabled them to prepare a reputable facsimile of many of the dishes encountered on their travels once returned to their homelands. Each author likewise felt a key number of tinned and jarred ingredients were acceptable, or even welcome, substitutes for fresh. Fisher's list far exceeded David's in this regard. On the other hand, both authors feared the palate-deadening industrialization of their nations' food supplies, which, if taken to the Twinkie extreme, becomes entirely divorced from time, place, and nature. As a result, Fisher and David each expressed a strong conviction that the flavors imparted by the topography, soil, climate, and culture of a given place, its *terroir*, play an essential role in gastronomically sound cookery.

Toklas' *Cook Book* too shows a reverence for the French attention to *terroir*, yet the mobility of her writing, which moves fluidly between disparate culinary, gastronomic, and national realms, marks it as an unabashed celebration of cultural exchange. Toklas' aesthetic might be classified as gastronomic globalism—an embrace of transnational flavors and culinary crosspollination that can be traced back to the founding fathers of gastronomic literature. Whereas Brillat-Savarin wrote at the dawn of the modern era, however, Toklas, writing in the 1950s, was clearly perched on the transitional edge between a modern and a postmodern worldview. On one hand, despite being prescient and avant-garde for 1954, Toklas' *Cook Book* clearly belongs to a bygone era, one during which a chapter on "Servants in France" would not appear entirely out of place. On the other hand, Toklas' discussion of her "Servants in France" repeatedly eddies around situations in which the balance of power between master and servant has been reversed—Toklas and Stein are fired by cooks, Toklas takes on the more menial chores one of her cooks refuses to perform. Toklas' playful insistence on upending hierarchies as well as destabilizing ideological and national boundaries imbues her text with a postmodern sense of humor about the disruption and disorder of tradition effected by two world wars.

The globalism and disruption of tradition playfully showcased in Toklas' cookbook, and approached with a mild degree of caution by Fisher and to a greater degree of caution by David, play a central role in contemporary food writing, which often revolves around the political, economic, and social ramifications of daily food choices. In particular, the tension between the local and the global has been sharply manifest within women's food writing. Some works that revere the local exhibit a deeply embedded sense of place, one that evokes nostalgia for an era that predates modernity, or what might be called a premodern way of life. In turn, some works that embrace globalism look back on the premodern way of life as one that relied heavily on the laboring bodies of immigrant and colonial workers.

This chapter explores three contemporary authors who work through the tension between the local and global in distinct ways. In particular, it examines the English author Patience Gray, whose *Honey From a Weed* (1986) champions a premodern aesthetic, which disavows disembedded culinary practices along with the commercialism and globalism that enable them. Gray was so passionate in her embrace of premodern existence, in fact, that she refused to install electricity in her farmhouse in rural Italy, where she settled permanently in 1970. In so doing, she exercised a privileged choice. Whereas Gray, just like Fisher, Toklas, and David, exercised choice in undertaking a voyage of rebellion, myriad contemporary authors examine journeys of forced dislocation, eloquently showcasing food as a form of communication and self-nourishment with the power to mediate the cultural dissonance of colonization, immigration, and exile. Thus, the second half of this chapter explores what the scholar Doris Witt terms a "diasporic aesthetic" that arises from a desire to cohere a hybrid identity from seemingly dissonant cultural heritages. In particular, this chapter examines the influence of Toklas' global aesthetic on Vertamae Smart Grosvenor and Monique Truong. Inspired by the geographic and cultural fluidity of Toklas' cookbook, Grosvenor's *Vibration Cooking* (1970) and Truong's *The Book of Salt* (2003) each fashion a transnational culinary aesthetic, one that blends and moves between different culinary realms and cultures. If the traditional nineteenth-century cookbook defined the domestic boundaries within which white middle-class women were expected to remain, Grosvenor and Truong fashioned forms of writing that showcase a diasporic culinary aesthetic that articulates and works to combat a history of marginalization and servitude. This aesthetic figures a postcolonial palate not bound by geography or nationality, one that defines itself through mobility and cultural exchange. The diasporic aesthetic articulated by Grosvenor and Truong refracts the elitist, colonial inflection of the nineteenth-century gastronome, reconfiguring it into a postcolonial critique of the Western appetite as defined and codified within nineteenth-century gastronomic literature. By giving voice to the laboring body and its appetites, Grosvenor and Truong not only destabilize the Western appetite as defined by male-authored gastronomic literature but also deconstruct and destabilize the ideology of female domesticity and self-sacrifice cohered by nineteenth- and early twentieth-century cookbooks. They do so by claiming the embodied desires that remained eerily absent in women's food writing well into the twentieth century.

THE MINIMALIST AESTHETIC OF PATIENCE GRAY'S *HONEY FROM A WEED*

Like Fisher, Toklas, and David, Patience Gray refused to be demure or apologetic about being a woman, projecting an authorial persona as self-assured, eloquent, and learned as the male gastronome. Like David, Gray shared with male gastronomes a heavy reliance on food scholarship, travel writing, and aesthetic reflection in order to capture and convey the way of life that flavored the recipes housed in her books. Gray co-authored her first cookbook, *Plats du Jour* (1957), with Primrose Boyd. Gray was largely in charge of the discursive parts of the book, which contextualize the cooking practices, techniques, and dining habits of France, Italy, and, to a lesser extent, Spain within a broader cultural framework; Boyd focused largely on the recipes themselves. Like David's first two cookbooks, *Mediterranean Food* (1950) and *French Country Cooking* (1951), *Plats du Jour* showcases an elegant style and a learned familiarity with an expanse of literature. Sales of *Plats du Jour* reached over 50,000 the first year after it was published, far outpacing the sales of David's earlier works, *Mediterranean Food*, *French Country Cooking*, and *Italian Food* (1954).[1] Until the surge of David's influence in the mid-1960s, *Plats du Jour* enjoyed a primary role in introducing everyday southern European cookery to the English.

In the early 1960s, Gray met and fell in love with the Flemish sculptor Norman Mommens. Soon after, the couple departed for the Mediterranean, living where marble and sedimentary rock could be quarried for Mommens' sculptures. After writing *The Centaur's Kitchen* (1964), a recipe book commissioned for use on Blue Funnel Line steamships that helped fund her journey to southern Europe with Mommens, Gray spent over twenty years fashioning her next book, *Honey From a Weed* (1986), a project that revolves around her and Mommens' adventures living on the Greek island of Naxos, and in Catalonia, Tuscany, and lastly Apulia, the boot heel of Italy, where they settled permanently in 1970. Whereas *Plats du Jour* might be described as occupying that same "ill-defined margin at which the gastronomic essay gradually shades into the cookery book" where the bulk of David's work resides, *Honey From a Weed* stands out as one of the most fiercely unconventional and imaginatively conceived works of culinary literature written in the English language.[2] A blend of memoir, cookbook, philosophic musing, gastronomic reflection, and mystical quest, *Honey From a Weed* embodies a detailed study of existence "among the vestiges of neolithic and bronze age life," a place "where one can confront the imagination and pretensions of another age" (59, 227).

Whereas Toklas and Stein flourished in a community of artists, enjoying accolades for Stein's genius, Gray and Mommens lived in the wild, imbibing a premodern existence. The couple vigorously embraced life within communities outside the bounds of modern civilization—living without electricity or, often, running water, gathering weeds in spring to nourish health, harvesting grapes to fashion wine, gathering olives for the oil essential to daily meals, bartering for food staples, following long fasts with communal feasts, and learning to thank nature for the little it provided for the table. The juxtaposition of the couple's cosmopolitan background with their wild environs fueled creative expression that embodies an intoxicating blend of Apollinian and Dionysian forces. Gray's written and culinary aesthetic captures an attunement to the wilderness and to a

---

1. In the obituary he wrote for Patience Gray in *The Guardian* (March 18, 2005), Tom Jaine of Prospect Books wrote of *Plats du Jour* "It was almost the earliest international cookery book aimed at the mass market, and sold more than 50,000 copies in its first year, dwarfing the impact of such early prophets as Elizabeth David." Prospect Books, then run by Alan Davidson, first published Gray's *Honey from a Weed*.

2. Mennell, 271. See the Introduction for an extended discussion of the "ill-defined" margin between gastronomic essay and cookbook, an area first tentatively mapped by Stephen Mennell in his *All Manners of Food* and which recent food writing scholars have begun to explore in more detail.

people who struggled to exact the pleasures of communion from the land's meager provisions. Gray's rough-hewn life was channeled through a keen aesthetic sensibility, giving rise to a style that her publisher Tom Jaine so aptly describes as "muscular" and "sinewy" and that none other than the literary genius Angela Carter pronounces "usually ravishing, sometimes breathtaking" (103).

That *Honey From a Weed* includes a bibliography listing Peter Kropotkin's *Memoirs of a Revolutionist* alongside works by authors ranging from Apicius and Bartolomeo Scappi to Harold McGee and Jane Grigson, from Archestratus and Rabelais to Antonin Artaud and Gertrude Stein reflects much about its author, indicating a voracious appetite for historical cookbooks, experimental writing, and radical thought. The innovative style, anarchistic message, and finely crafted aesthetic of *Honey From a Weed* clearly affirms this correlation. Whereas authors such as Fisher, Toklas, and David defiantly transgressed the domesticated boundaries of women's food writing to articulate an undomesticated appetite for life, Gray embraced a lifestyle and gastronomic philosophy that extended beyond the territory staked out by her predecessors.

In particular, Gray figures an appetite surfeited by the very same commercialism and globalization celebrated by Grimod and Brillat-Savarin. Such surfeit leads her toward a minimalist aesthetic that eschews the cosmopolitan sensibility honed by earlier gastronomes. Gray celebrates in its stead the local, the regional, and the provincial. Absent from Gray's work are the fine restaurants, emphasis on etiquette, urban sophistication, costly ingredients, and elaborate meals that characterize much gastronomic literature. In their place Gray inserts recollections of impromptu gatherings; advice on identifying, gathering, and cooking weeds; reflections on fasting; and a strong conviction in Antonin Artaud's words: "every step forward, every convenience acquired through the mastery of a purely physical civilization, also implies a loss, a regression" (quoted in *Honey* 30).

Such nostalgia for premodern authenticity likewise marks David's ouevre. Unlike Gray, however, who aggressively championed and philosophically aligned herself with a premodern way of life, David remained simultaneously drawn toward and anxious about modernity. As Ben Taylor and Steve Jones convincingly demonstrate, David's "work embraces some of the novel benefits of certain modernized food processes, while at the same time acknowledging the impact of modernity upon the authenticity of food in time and space" (180). For example, David, if given the time, would prefer to whisk mayonnaise by hand. However, she relied on the food processor in a pinch and expected that her readers would rely on modern conveniences even when faced with ample time to craft mayonnaise from hand. David likewise lauded the spike in importation of foreign ingredients into England that began in the late 1950s and readily listed specialty food purveyors where her readers might track down hard-to-find ingredients. Within *Honey From a Weed*, Gray disavows all such modern convenience. For example, when coming across a male hare at the poulterers, she reflects: "It was a beautiful creature. . . . There was no question of roasting the saddle, because there wasn't an oven. The absence of alternatives is often a great relief in cooking. You use what you've got, you do what you can" (241–42). Gray embraced a premodern lifestyle so passionately, in fact, that once permanently settled in Apulia in 1970 she chose to live without electricity; she did so until after Mommens died in 1986 and then only acquired it at the insistence of her son, who moved to Gray's farmhouse to care for his mother during the last years of her life.

Unlike the nineteenth- and early twentieth-century gastronome, who distanced himself from the home kitchen and cookery by declaring himself an amateur, Gray celebrated the knowledge gained from everyday food preparation and the flavors of the rustic table. Whereas Grimod critiqued Parisian food purveyors and their goods and created a code of behavior for the gourmand, Gray recorded "the skill and knowledge required in food gathering" and learned from the peasants how to read "the landscape and its flora" (189). In so doing, she gathered knowledge from the land and its people, recording a way of cookery fast disappearing from modern life. Unlike Grimod, Gray does not critique commercial products. Rather she records the cookery traditions being eroded by the globalization and commercialization of the food supply. So too did David.

Gray, like David, also brings gastronomy to bear on practical cookery instruction. In particular, Gray connects practical hands-on culinary knowledge with gourmandism to note: "In my experience it is the countryman who is the real gourmet and for good reason; it is he who has cultivated, raised, hunted, or fished the raw materials and has made the wine himself" (13). Gray herself imbues everyday cookery with gastronomic knowledge cultivated by intensive research, aesthetic pleasure, and philosophical reflection. By marrying the erudite curiosity of the gastronome with the hands-on skills needed for everyday cooking, Gray created a form of food writing that blends gastronomy with the practicality of the domestic cookbook. Just as David did, Gray also immersed herself in the travel writing, historical cookbooks, botanical treatises, and the literature born of a given region, gathering the details needed to contextualize the cultural and social meaning of the cookery she describes. As Gray herself explains in the introduction to the extensive bibliography that concludes *Honey From a Weed*: "The weed from which I have drawn the honey is the traditional knowledge of Mediterranean people; the books cited can be regarded as the distillation of this knowledge" (349). Unlike her female predecessors, however, Gray eschewed the urbane inflection of the gastronomic tradition as passed down by Grimod and Brillat-Savarin, a tradition skillfully adapted by Fisher, Toklas, and David in order to articulate a twentieth-century female appetite. Rather, Gray configures a minimalist gastronomic philosophy, one that gives voice to the landscape and articulates aesthetic emotions forged as much from the pangs of hunger as from the feasts of plenty. In so doing, she posits an alternative aesthetic that fuses the domestic tradition's attention to frugality and necessity with gastronomy's attunement to pleasure, conviviality, and elegance of self-expression.

Gray herself illuminates the relationship between the austerity of her environs and the piquancy of her prose when she reflects on the reason why certain wild herbs are more flavorful than their domesticated version:

> The reason is that, thriving on limestone, these herbs alter their nature in richer damper soils; in the droughty limestone wilderness, resort of bees and butterflies, they grow out of the rock and produce a higher concentration of their essential oil, contained in minute sacs in their leaves. (34)

The same might be said of Gray's prose. *Honey From a Weed* attains its "muscular" and "sinewy" and "usually ravishing" style, in part, because it has been concentrated, refined, and strengthened by the austerity of Gray's existence. For example, she offers the following reflection on the power of herbs in cookery:

> The secret of cooking is the release of fragrance and the art of imparting it. Fragrance: the bay laurel, *Laurus nobilis*, a sacred tree, how brightly, how fiercely it burns. . . . Sweet the influence of rosemary, its ungainly shrubby stems bursting with pale lilac flowers. Pungent the mint trodden underfoot on the way to the orchard. . . . Savour the strange sweet taste of juniper berries, blueblack, picked in September on a chalk down where nothing much else will grow. Wander through the maquis in spring when shrubby sages, thyme, rosemary, cistus, lentisk and myrtle are in flower. Inhale the fragrance of the wilderness. (94)

This passage evocatively captures the aromatic nature of the roughhewn landscape in which Gray lived as well as the pungency arising from the herbs' hard-won survival in rock, dry soil, and fierce sun.

Life in the wilderness not only nourished the power of Gray's prose, but it also helped her fashion a remarkable gastronomic philosophy—one as influenced by the experience of pronounced hunger as by the southern European flavors she learned to savor. Hence, the subtitle of her work *Honey From A Weed: Fasting and Feasting in Tuscany, Catalonia, the Cyclades and Apulia*. Like Fisher before her, Gray explores the nuances of hunger. Whereas Fisher used food as a metaphor through which to explore psychological hunger, however, Gray captures the effect that physical hunger has on the psyche as well as on the hospitality so central to the cultures within which she resides. The difficulty of provisioning for life in the wilderness led to what Gray describes as "the solidarity and improvisation—the hard core of anarchism" that characterized the Catalan spirit. In turn, she notes that

> frugality, mysteriously combined with liberality epitomized the old Catalan way of life, so that—exposed to the rigours of a climate with its extremes of heat and cold—the provision of food took on the quality of life-restoring, rather than the satisfaction of appetite. . . . Wherever a spirit of independence flowers, austerity and fellowship combine. (83)

As Gray ascertains, austerity itself deepens the meaning of food, transforming its function from the satisfaction of a need into a life-restoring gift. In turn, a culture of fellowship leads to hospitality, which plays a crucial role in the daily life of each of the hardscrabble cultures that Gray describes. Hospitality transforms the act of eating from a purely physical need into an act of communal exchange and conviviality. Thus frugal means become life-affirming, thereby nourishing a dignified way of life.

Reliance on nature to provide the bare means of existence not only nourishes a life-affirming form of hospitality but it also binds people to the land. Gray reflects on the providential attitude of the Greeks on Naxos "whose solemn four week Advent fast and six week Lenten one, in fact, corresponded with moments when on Naxos there was hardly anything to eat. Fasting is therefore in the nature of things and feasting punctuates it with a joyful excess" (229). Because the Naxians among whom Gray and Mommens lived during the 1960s gathered their food directly from the land, barren months corresponded by necessity to fasts. Such dependence, Gray observes, infuses the land's meager offerings with tremendous significance, a meaning lost to cultures surfeited by the overabundance of modern life. Gray reflects on the loss that occurs when a culture dissociates itself from times of scarcity:

> Once we lose touch with the spendthrift aspect of nature's provisions epitomized in the raising of a crop, we are in danger of losing touch with life itself. When Providence supplies the means, the preparation and sharing of food takes on a sacred aspect. (11)

For Gray, the pleasures of gastronomy are, in large part, derived from a strong dependency on the land—growing, harvesting, hunting, gathering, and preparing each meal. Such a philosophy is redolent with nostalgia for a way of life lost to much of the modern world. Yet it also explains Gray's commitment to living on the margins of civilization.

Gray's passion and eccentricity infuses *Honey From a Weed*, transforming it into one of the most original works of gastronomic literature authored in the English language. Gray herself describes eccentricity as "living according to priorities established by one's own experience" (111). Gray's determination to embrace just such an eccentric life for herself gave rise to what Angela Carter describes as Gray's "aesthetic choice" to live on the edges of civilization. Whereas Gray and Mommens chose to embrace a meager existence, however, choice did not fall to most of those with whom they socialized. Such disparity between choice and necessity led to some terrifying moments, many of which Gray reveals in her memoir *Ringdoves and Snakes* (1989). The memoir revolves around the year that she and Mommens lived in the village of Apóllona on the Greek island of Naxos, where the couple felt themselves welcome participants in village life for a full three seasons until a series of events led them to realize that they had overstayed their welcome. Several of Mommens sculptures were stolen, their wine was drugged, and they felt simultaneously guarded and spied on at all times of day and night.

After reporting the theft of the sculptures to the police, Gray and Mommen's idyllic life began to unravel. The couple felt resented by those villagers whom the police questioned. The police report, in turn, tarnished the entire village's reputation for hospitality. The couple likewise began to feel resentment for their position as outsiders as well as for their generosity, which illuminated their privilege relative to the villagers. Mommens had a lorry in which he could cart the occasional Apollonian for free, infuriating the two locals who made a living charging for such a service. Mommens' sculptures embodied the fact that he chose rather than needed to labor. As Gray reflects: "Norman, Belgian artist in Apollo, looks from a distance like an escapist. Or he's a free man who went off to chip at marble from a convenient quarry. Neither is true. He is an anomaly. A sculptor he is not a working man" (*Ringdoves* 47). His liberty begins to wear on the Apollonians, who, if they did not steal his sculptures, likely knew who did, as well as how, why, and when.

Unlike *Honey from a Weed*, *Ringdoves and Snakes* does not posit an aesthetic philosophy. Rather it takes shape in a startling journal, which captures the psychological nuances of a year living with the Apollonians. It also captures the raw reality of hunger:

> Looking for food in Apóllona is sampling the taste of nothing. Nothing is as dry as tamarisk twigs in August, shapeless as a cloud of dust rising from the lorry. If nothing has no feel, form, shape, it sometimes smells a little rancid. Nothing is a natural condition. It's the hollow flank of a cream-coloured cow waiting for rain. It's the pale sunken cheek of a quarryman after a day spent swinging a sledgehammer. Nothing can't afford a word, it has become a reitierated stylized gesture. (*Ringdoves* 23)

Though *Ringdoves* would not be published until 1987, Gray wrote much of it during the year she lived on Apóllona in the early 1960s. As a result, the raw experience had yet to be transformed through reflection. On the other hand, she authors *Honey From a Weed* as a gastronome—albeit one ideologically opposed to elitist, ultra-civilized, and self-indulgent gastronomy. Unlike *Ringdoves*, which captures the psychological immediacy of life among the Apollonians, *Honey From a Weed* conveys an aesthetic philosophy honed from over a quarter century living in the southern Mediterranean, a period during which Gray distills scarcity into a minimalist aesthetic. Gray fashions this aesthetic into a gastronomic cookbook in which the recipes serve as one of many elements that materialize a vanishing way of life.

In order to convey the experience of life in Apulia, for example, Gray describes harvesting olives for the year's supply of cooking oil. To capture the experience, she details the event on several levels, noting the camaraderie fueled by the communal effort, the physical discomfort of gathering olives from the ground for days in a row, and the mental release that the rhythms of intense physical labor provide. In the following passage, Gray muses on the effect such labor has on her own sense of embodiment and connection to the landscape:

> Because the work is endless, there is a strange feeling of timelessness among the trees. When you are most exhausted you suddenly find that your fingers have acquired eyes and are gathering olives on their own. The phenomenon of the second, third, and fourth wind appears. Your mind is free to listen to a bird's song or the ceaseless conversation in the trees. (313)

Reflecting on the body's physical engagement and the mental relaxation this effects, Gray details the connection between the body and the mind, a connection omnipresent in gastronomic writing yet oddly absent from the domestic cookbook. Gray brings this connection to the foreground. Unlike gastronomic literature, however, which features a consuming body that ingests food, literature, and culture and that works for pleasure, Gray brings gastronomic reflection to bear on the laboring body, which gathers pleasure from the daily work of cookery.

By illuminating the pleasures of food preparation Gray, like Toklas and David, helped to restore the body so oddly absent from women's cookery writing, the body omnipresent in Gray's *Honey From a Weed*. Each of these women showcase how cookery, like gastronomy, gives rise to sensual pleasure, which, in turn, nourishes a sense of well-being, or emotional satiety. Unlike the nineteenth-century gourmand who positioned himself as, above all, a consumer, Toklas, David, and Gray positioned themselves as producers *and* consumers of the gastronomic *and* the culinary arts.

Gray directly addresses the well being derived from the physical act of cookery when she reflects:

> Pounding fragrant things—particularly garlic, basil, parsley—is a tremendous antidote to depression. But it applies also to juniper berries, coriander seeds and the grilled fruits of the chilli pepper. Pounding these things produces an alteration in one's being—sighing with fatigue to inhaling with pleasure. The cheering effects of herbs and alliums cannot be too often reiterated. (34)

Here Gray not only articulates the sensual pleasures of food preparation and the effect these pleasures have on her psyche, but also expresses the core of both her culinary and gastronomic philosophies; whether inhaling the fragrant aromas of freshly ground spices, achieving the "time-out-of-mind" that accompanies an olive harvest, or imbibing the conviviality and refreshment of an afternoon *merenda* shared with friends, Gray approached food with an unwavering belief in its transformative potential, its capacity "to produce an alteration in one's being."

Gray shared her belief in the transformative potential of food with her mentor Irving Davis, to whom she pays tribute in *Honey From a Weed*. According to Gray, Davis approached food with "an unquenchable belief in the possibility of unprecedented experience, all part of a search for perfection" (112). An antiquarian book dealer who spoke five languages, Davis not only encouraged Gray to embrace the transformative potential of food, but also showcased the elegant rapport between gastronomy and literature, a rapport celebrated by the nineteenth-century gastronome as well as by his twentieth-century male and female heirs. As Gray describes, Davis

> was sufficiently eccentric to arrange his book-buying forays to coincide with the season of new peas in Florence and young asparagus. . . . The purchase of old manuscripts in Italy was dovetailed with the acquisition of virgin olive oil from some book collector whose cellar was as well stocked as his library, which conjunction shows that bibliophiles are inveterate gastronomes. (111)

Here Gray touches on the same link between literature and gastronomy (or reading, eating, and writing) that abounds in gastronomic essays, a link that she forges powerfully in *Honey From a Weed*. Like Elizabeth David, Gray demonstrates that the union of literature with gastronomy can be elegantly merged yet again with practical cookery to fashion the gastronomic cookbook, a genre exemplified by *Honey From a Weed* as by David's numerous recipe collections.

As is fitting of its nature, *Honey From a Weed* follows an idiosyncratic pattern. Interspersed between chapters on "Fasting," "Feasting," and "Furred and Feathered Holocausts," come chapters on "Beans, Peas, and Rustic Soups," "Edible Weeds," and "Boar, Hare, Fox, Pheasant, Partridge, Pigeon." Some chapters feature an illustrative first-person narrative, others are loosely segmented according to featured ingredients and accompanying recipes. Taken as a whole, the text produces a striking blend of literature, gastronomy, memoir, cultural history, practical cookery advice, and recipes. In other words, *Honey From a Weed* blends several key traits of gastronomic literature (first person narrative and anecdote, literary allusion, immersion in cultural history and historical texts) with the practical advice and recipe instruction of a cookbook. The learned nature of Gray's text blended with first person reflection, personal anecdote, and practical cookery instruction creates a narrative flow meant to be read from cover to cover, as with any work of literature.

While the majority of the book's recipes can be readily reproduced, several are included for illustrative purposes; they capture the vanishing way of life that *Honey From a Weed* so powerfully evokes. A fox recipe, for example, given to Gray "by an old anarchist in Carrara" begins "'A male fox shot in January or February. Skin it, and keep the carcase in running water for 3 days, or, otherwise, hang it outside in the frost'" (241). Other recipes, such as the one for braised wild boar, evocatively showcase the "recipe narrative" Gray wove together for informative, literary, and practical purposes:

> Driving through Provence late one November, we saw hanging outside a butcher's shop in Vidauban three wild boars, suspended from their hind-legs, their huge snouts jutting forward with ivory crescent tusks. These shaggy beasts, as dark as Cerberus, were the only presences in the deserted streets.
>
> The boar is sacred to the horned moon goddess; she is the patron of poets and metalworkers. The thought of the wild boars, their immense size, the mountain wilderness from which they came, haunted us for a long time.
>
> The best boar, however, that we encountered was in a back street tavern in Volterra, to which we had been directed by a reassuringly portly gentleman after visiting the Etruscan museum. In this museum the Boar Hunt is portrayed as an emblem of death on funerary urns, with other themes: the Wheel of Fortune, the Combat outside the House of Death, the Flower of Immortality, the Chariot, the Embarcation.
>
> *CINGHIALE ARROSTO* • braised wild boar
>
> To return to the tavern: *arrosto* means roast, but it is often employed to indicate a braise. First eat your wild boar, and then hasten into the kitchen, if you dare, to enquire how it has been prepared. This is what I gathered from Giovanna Benedetta, the skilful cook:
>
> Hang the boar for 7 or 8 days . . . (240–241).

In the book, the preceding passage is followed by a page of detailed instruction. Reminiscent of the recipes in Toklas' *Cook Book*, Gray's boar recipe is embedded within the narrative flow in such a manner that it cannot easily be extracted. In this case, Gray encases the recipe within a narrative that contextualizes the wild boar, explaining its spiritual and historical meaning within the cultures where it is hunted, hung, braised, and eaten.

The mythological and spiritual importance of food courses throughout *Honey From a Weed*. Gray tells the reader that "The octopus, 'Old No-bones the Polyp' as Hesiod called it, was a powerful fertility symbol in Mycenaean times" and that "It was in the hollow pith of the giant fennel, *Ferula communis*, that Prometheus concealed a lump of live charcoal broken from the torch he lit at the fiery chariot of the sun, defying Zeus, and brought fire to mankind: a sacred plant, the fire bearer" (47, 159). In addition to food's symbolic meaning, Gray also includes its medicinal uses; its taxonomy; where and in what form it grows; its role in the cookery of a given region; and the ways in which it is typically prepared. For example, after exploring fennel as the fire-bearing plant, Gray continues:

> The wild form of *F vulgare* (till recently classified separately as *F officinalis,* to indicate its use by apothecaries and its health-giving properties)

grows vigorously, with the giant fennel, in droughty calcareous situations all round the Mediterranean and can be sown from seed. It is these seeds which are used in cooking and conserving, being far more fragrant than the cultivated kind. The fronds are used in delicate fish stuffings, in soups, and—along with thistles, dandelions, etc—in a Tuscan dish of boiled weeds in spring.

Finocchio, the bulbous fennel, whose aromatic swollen stem is a winter vegetable, is a valuable and easily cultivated plant; it is earthed up to blanch it. It is often served whole and without dressing to conclude a meal; it clears the palate. It can be finely sliced and dressed with oil and vinegar and served as salad. As a vegetable it is boiled, fried, braised. In the 19th century in Italy this aromatic vegetable, along with aubergines, was only eaten by Jews, says [Pelligrino] Artusi, thus proving their gastronomic perception. (159)

The entry ends with a recipe for braised fennel. Encasing recipes within such informative, historically contextualized, and culturally nuanced prose enabled Gray, like David before her, to forge a cookbook that captures and conveys an approach toward cookery and the way of life that gave rise to it. As Gray explains: "my ambition in drawing in the background to what is being cooked is to restore the meaning. I also celebrate the limestone wilderness" (12). Restoring the cultural, historical, and mythological meaning to a given ingredient or method of cookery enriches and enlivens the kitchen as well as the dinner table. The breadth of vision and knowledge needed for such an undertaking requires the passion for reading, eating, cooking, and eloquent self-expression that Gray so admired in her mentor Irving Davis. Blending the practical instruction of a cookbook with the passion for aesthetic pleasure of gastronomy enabled Gray, like Toklas and David before her, to fashion a form of gastronomic cookbook that pays fitting and equitable tribute to both the women's and the men's food writing traditions.

TOWARD A POSTMODERN PALATE: VERTAMAE SMART GROSVENOR'S *VIBRATION COOKING* AND MONIQUE TRUONG'S *THE BOOK OF SALT*

Filled with movement, dislocation, relocation, wars, and conquests, *The Alice B. Toklas Cook Book* inspired books by Vertamae Smart Grosvenor and Monique Truong that explore the effects of culinary colonialism, dealing respectively with the slave diaspora and with the French colonization of Vietnam. Impressed by the unconventional nature of Toklas' *Cook Book*, Grosvenor crafted her own autobiographical cookbook in order to challenge the racist stereotypes that haunt the African American woman in the kitchen, articulating what scholar Doris Witt describes as a "diasporic aesthetic." In so doing, she parodies the cookbook as a genre and deconstructs its configuration of white middle-class domesticity. After reading Toklas' recollection of two Vietnamese cooks who worked for her in France, Monique Truong found herself drawn to write a novel narrated by a Vietnamese exile who works for Toklas and Gertrude Stein. In so doing, Truong deconstructs parts of Toklas' cookbook and reconfigures them within a twenty-first-century novel in order to refract their meaning through a postcolonial lens. The novel, *The Book of Salt*, not only illuminates the dynamics of culinary colonialism but also foregrounds cooking as a means of articulating a postcolonial identity, one that interrogates and reconfigures the very notion of home and the domesticated heterosexual female around which it has traditionally revolved.

THE POLITICIZATION OF THE CULINARY AUTOBIOGRAPHY: VERTAMAE SMART GROSVENOR'S *VIBRATION COOKING*

Like Toklas' *Cook Book*, which employs a genre and gender-blending form that challenges and reconfigures the domestic bounds of women's food writing, Grosvenor's *Vibration Cooking* "stands out from many contemporaneous African American cookbooks in its attempt to disrupt normative categories of racial identity and textual genre alike" (Witt, "*My Kitchen*" 229). Just as Elizabeth Robins Pennell's *Feasts of Autolycus* simultaneously parodies and participates in the male-authored genre of gastronomic literature, Grosvenor's culinary memoir parodies, mocks, and yet adopts the cookbook as a genre in order to flout and to reconfigure its conventions. As Witt explains: "Part autobiography, part travelogue, part culinary anthropology, part social history, part political commentary, *Vibration Cooking* undertook the paradoxical task of attempting to parody the genre of the standard cookbook even as it emulated Toklas's famous text" (231). Both Pennell and Grosvenor used parody to undermine the ideological foundation of the genre that they simultaneously adopted. Pennell did so in order to challenge the misogyny and egocentrism that denied women access to the gastronomic realm and its literature. Grosvenor did so in order to write against the white cookbooks that elided African Americans and to confront an openly racist society. She did so by mobilizing the culinary memoir toward political engagement. The use of food writing as a means to effect political change can be traced all the way back to the founding work of gastronomic literature. Thus, ironically given Grosvenor's anti-elitist stance, her politicization of food writing harkens back to Grimod's invention and deployment of gastronomic literature to critique the post-Revolutionary French state and its censorship of his political expression.

As Witt has documented, Grosvenor paid tribute to *The Alice B. Toklas Cook Book* in an interview published in *Ebony* shortly after *Vibration Cooking* was first published in 1970. In the interview, Grosvenor explains:

While reading the *Alice B. Toklas Cook Book*, I'd been impressed with the way she had captured the feeling of her times in Paris during the 20s and people she had known, of Gertrude Stein, the salon and Picasso. So I thought I'd do a little cookbook for the people *I* knew in Paris, New York, and even back home in South Carolina and Philadelphia. (quoted in Witt 231)

Whereas the mobility in Toklas' *Cook Book* stems, in large part, from her gastronomic adventures with Gertrude Stein, the mobility in Grosvenor's cookbook is largely reflective of the African diaspora. Thus, although Grosvenor recounts her travels to Paris, Rome, Venice, and London as well as her struggles as an artist, her primary goal in writing the cookbook is inarguably political. She works to construct an identity that simultaneously celebrates the culturally rich foods of the African diaspora and confronts racism head on. Just as Toklas refused to separate the recipes housed in her gastronomic cookbook from the memories that surround them, Grosvenor refused to separate the recipes housed in *Vibration Cooking* from the friends and family that nourish them *or* from the racism she and her loved ones face on a daily basis.

In place of the travelogue of French provincial restaurants housed in Toklas' memoir, Grosvenor recounts the racist responses that she has met with during her travels. Grosvenor recalls that "[t]he Venetian women were the worst. They just out and out laughed. It was funny to them to see something in the shape of a woman with black skin. You know how people laugh (uncomfortably most of the time) at chimpanzees" (140). Grosvenor likewise recalls the countless New York City taxis that refused her a ride and the particular driver who called her a "nigger bitch" (97). She recounts the story of a man who, seeing her dressed in "African clothes" asked her if she spoke English. When she said, "I sho do honey," he responded "Well, why are you wearing those African clothes, you are a Negro." I said, "I am who I think I am. I am free and free to define myself" (128). In *Vibration Cooking*, Grosvenor defines herself, or her literary persona, with gusto.

In keeping with the fierce confrontation and brazen humor that infuses her project, Grosvenor begins *Vibration Cooking* with the following reflection:

In reading lots and lots of cookbooks written by white folks it occurred to me that people very casually say Spanish rice, French fries, Italian spaghetti, Chinese cabbage, Mexican beans, Swedish meatballs, Danish pastry, English muffins and Swiss cheese. And with the exception of black bottom pie and niggertoes, there is no reference to black people's contribution to the culinary arts. (3)

Here Grosvenor simultaneously announces her drive to challenge the silence on "black people's contribution to the culinary arts," to rewrite the recorded history that omits African Americans, and to mock the language that perpetuates racism.[3]

Vibration Cooking took part in a larger movement to "recontextualize the foods most commonly associated with slavery" by configuring "soul food" in relation to the "culinary history of colored peoples around the world" (Witt, *Black Hunger* 15, 161). Tellingly, as Witt recounts, in the 1986 edition of her memoir Grosvenor

> disavowed the influence of Toklas on her initial conceptualization of *Vibration Cooking*, asserting in the new introduction: "The only thing I have in common with Alice B. Toklas is that we lived on the same street in Paris." . . . She repeated this disclaimer in the 1992 edition. ("My Kitchen" 232)

Scholar Rafia Zafar addresses Grosvenor's turnabout, surmising that her "reluctance to admit kinship with Toklas stems not from an inability to admit a connection with a white predecessor—she does refer to her after all—but from her much greater desire to form of chain of Black women forebears" (253). The turnabout also expresses Grosvenor's intent to write an autobiographical cookbook that details a decidedly African American heritage as well as an African American palate.

Whereas Toklas played with the cookbook genre, Grosvenor aggressively parodied those conventions of the cookbook through which it defines the properly contained and domesticated white, middle-class female. She dismisses exact measurements as the fallback for cooks who have no soul, who can't cook by "vibration." Grosvenor tells her readers: "It don't matter if it's Dakar or Savannah, you can cook exotic food any time you want. Just turn on the imagination, be willing to change your style and let a little soul food in" (4). With imagination, she suggests, foods can be transformed to express the cook's own tastes and cultural identity. Grosvenor figures cooking by vibration as a form of self-expression and self-construction. For example, she reflects that "Salade Niçoise is a French name but just like with anything else when soul folks get it they take it out into another thing" (66).

---

3. See Doris Witt's *Black Hunger: Soul Food and America* for an extensive bibliography of African American cookbooks, which were not as few and far between as Grosvenor may have believed at the time she first wrote *Vibration Cooking*. Although the number of African American cookbooks published during the nineteenth-century may number as few as four, the twentieth-century saw a steady rise in these figures. After World War II these numbers boomed exponentially, in large part, due to the increasing interest in and commitment to documenting, celebrating, and recovering African American history and culture. *Vibration Cooking* reflects the growing post-war tendency of African American women food writers "to combine autobiography and creative writing with political and cultural history—as exemplified by Aldeen Davis's commentary about black history in *Soul—Food for Thought* (1984) and the short tales included in Alice McGill, Mary Carter Smith, and Elmira Washington's *The Griots' Cookbook* (1985)" (*Black Hunger* 219).

Throughout her cookbook, Grosvenor juxtaposes the imagination, flavor, and cultural richness of soul food with the artificiality and sterility of white cooking. For example, she explains that her friend

> Dorothy was the one who hipped me on how to prepare myself before eating at white folks' houses. They invite you to dinner and when you get there at 8 p.m. (which is already much too late to eat) they act surprised to see you and start giving you a bunch of whisky. I think it is so you can act the fool (everybody knows about niggers and Indians and firewater). Around 10: 00 they start asking in a weird voice, "Anybody hungry?" So Dorothy says before you leave home on such an occasion eat some collards and rice. (117)

Here, as she does in several other places in her book, Grosvenor foregrounds the lack of sustenance found at the white table, suggesting that the only way for an African American to meet such an encounter and return home unscathed, unhumiliated, and unfamished is to arrive pre-fortified by soul food. In this configuration, soul food provides the nourishment needed to combat a racist dynamic.

Grosvenor likewise mocks the artificiality of etiquette and formality along with the racism that often undergirds it, observing:

> Europeans can really be unnatural. Like one thing that used to gas me is in European restaurants people ate fruit with a knife and fork. It didn't take me long to adapt. . . . [B]eing the granddaughter of a slave who adapted to the unnatural ways of his master, I, too, soon caught on and there I was eating fruit with a fork. How unnatural can you get! (72–73)

By figuring white culture as sterile and artificial, Grosvenor underscores that it lacks the sustenance needed to nourish the African American identity. Such sustenance can be readily drawn from soul food. In order to celebrate the soul of African American cookery and to reclaim the souls and soulful self-expression maimed by racism and slavery, Grosvenor challenges her oppressors, both their actions and the language which misnames her "nigger bitch" and "Negro." For example, she gives a recipe for "So-Called Okra," following it with the explanation:

> If you are wondering how come I say so-called okra it is because the African name of okra is gombo. Just like so-called Negroes. We are Africans. Negroes only started when they got here. I am a black woman. I am tired of people calling me out of my name. Okra must be sick of that mess too. So from now on call it like it is. Okra will be referred to in this book as gombo. Corn will be called maize and Negroes will be referred to as black people. (82–83)

Inspired by the unconventional nature of Toklas' *Cook Book*, Grosvenor crafted her own cookbook in order to challenge culinary racism. She did so by reconfiguring and parodying a genre that traditionally elided the African American voice and the African American contribution to American cookery. She also combats the racist stereotypes that haunt the African American woman in the kitchen. As Zafar notes, Grosvenor "regards modern Black cookery as an agent of change" (259). Toward that end, the recipes Grosvenor includes not only record the dishes prepared by her own family and friends as well as those acquired during her travels, but they also claim a distinctly African American identity and bear witness to the diaspora. Alongside recipes for "Cornmeal Mush," "Steak with Beautiful Black Sauce" and "Stuffed Heart Honkey Style," Grosvenor includes "Bamya from Egypt," "Boeuf aux Gombos from Cameroons," and "Northern Labajabaja, an adaptation of a Senegalese dish."

The history of women's food writing clearly explains Grosvenor's choice of an unconventional form to challenge prejudice against African American agency and self-expression; each of the authors examined here challenged the traditional role of women and the limits on women's self-expression by venturing into uncharted territory. In so doing, they fashioned innovative forms of food writing, which enabled them to celebrate their considerable appetites for knowledge and for a means of self-expression. Grosvenor's diasporic aesthetic, in turn, inspired Ntozake Shange's *If I Can Cook/You Know God Can* (1998), a blend of "history, literature, vernacular, culture, and philosophy, 'long with absolutely fabulous receipts . . . meant to open our hearts and minds to what it means for black folks in the Western Hemisphere to be full" (Shange 3). Because Grosvenor adopted the innovative form of Toklas, deconstructed it, and reconfigured it to suit her political self-expression and "diasporic aesthetic," Shange had an African American lineage to inspire her own project. *If I Can Cook/You Know God Can* begins fittingly with a Foreword written by Grosvenor herself, in which she reflects on the changes that occurred during the twenty-eight years between the publication of her own book and Shange's:

> For my generation, it was a mark of shame to be like an African. But all praises to the food goddess. Now we have *If I Can Cook/You Know God Can*, a creative culinary celebration that compels us to hear the words, taste the spices, and feel the rhythms of Africa in the new world. (xii)

FROM CULINARY COLONIALISM TO CULINARY COMMUNICATION IN MONIQUE TRUONG'S *THE BOOK OF SALT*

When Alice B. Toklas wrote her *Cook Book* in which she records the flavors and aromas of her life in Paris with Gertrude Stein, she paid tribute to the Vietnamese cooks who fed her and her lover. On first encountering Toklas' *Cook Book* and reading about the Vietnamese cooks, Monique Troung found that

By this point in the book, I had already fallen for these two women and for their ability to create an idiosyncratic, idyllic life. When I got to the pages about these cooks, I was, to say the least, surprised and touched to see a Vietnamese presence and such an intimate one at that in the lives of these two women. These cooks must have seen everything, I thought. But in the official history of the Lost Generation, the Paris of Gertrude Stein and Alice B. Toklas, these "Indo-Chinese" cooks were just a minor footnote. There could be a personal epic embedded in that footnote.[4]

Thus, Truong fashioned the novel, *The Book of Salt* (2003), which is narrated from the perspective of Bình, a composite of the two Vietnamese cooks whom Toklas recalls in her memoir. Although a fictional creation of Truong, the contours of Bình's life are given flesh in part from Toklas' recollection of her time in France. The dishes Bình serves and that sustain some of his most poignant memories are created from the recipes Toklas records in her memoir. By giving fictional life to a Vietnamese cook inspired by Toklas' memoir and fashioning his voice in order to explore and articulate the complex relations between Vietnam and France as well as Vietnam and the United States, Truong skillfully interweaves and fulfills tasks that function on a variety of levels. On the political and cultural levels, she gives voice to the colonized Other as well as sheds light on the dynamics of colonialism and the longing of exile. On the linguistic and imaginative levels, Truong engages playfully with *The Alice B. Toklas Cook Book*, filling in textual and cultural gaps in Toklas' memoir. Such intertextuality allows Truong to carry bits and pieces of Toklas' mid-twentieth-century text into a twenty-first-century novel, refracting them through a postcolonial lens.

One particular passage from Toklas' *Cook Book* undoubtedly informed Truong's novel. In the passage, Toklas describes the cookery of Nguyen, a Vietnamese man who had worked for the French Governor General of Indochina before taking up residence with her and Stein. Toklas recounts:

Nguyen cooked [Vietnamese][5] dishes and French dishes and to perfection, but objected to preparing a menu with both. It was his correct sense of balance that influenced him. Both our French and American friends disagreed with him, they considered a whole [Vietnamese] menu excessive. Finally he compromised. The first course—soup, fish or shellfish with noodles or rice—would be [Vietnamese]. What followed would be French. It was suspiciously a plot to enhance the quality of [Vietnamese] cooking. In the course of time Nguyen confessed

---

4. This quote appears in an interview with Truong conducted with Houghton Mifflin, which can be found at the following website: http://www.houghtonmifflinbooks.com/readers_guides/truong_salt.shtml.

5. In her memoir, Toklas uses the term Vietnamese to describe Trac and Nguyen yet the term Chinese (referencing Indochina) to describe their cooking. For consistency's sake and to avoid confusion, the term Vietnamese has been substituted throughout the quote.

that by its delicacy and unblended flavour [Vietnamese] cooking could
be remembered, and French cooking following it could not. (188)

Here Toklas explores cooking as a means of subverting authority. Whereas
Toklas' American and French friends felt that an entire meal of Vietnamese
dishes was "excessive," Toklas acknowledges that it was Nguyen's "sense
of balance" that led him to keep French and Vietnamese cuisines separated.
Nguyen's belief that the two cuisines should not mingle likewise suggests
his resistance to the French colonization of Vietnam. Challenged to blend
the two cultures, or to create a hybrid meal, Nguyen serves a Vietnamese dish that will overpower the French flavors that follow, symbolically
restoring the balance of power to the Vietnamese. Toklas' own playful and
subversive sense of humor, which infuses the entirety of her *Cook Book*,
strongly suggests that she not only approved of, but even relished Nguyen's
anti-imperialist gesture.

Nguyen imported his mastery of French culinary techniques from his
native land. As Vietnam scholar Erica Peters explains, because "The French
community in Vietnam wanted to make sure it was easy to differentiate colonizer from colonized," they were troubled "when Vietnamese people incorporated French practices into their own lives" (23). Thus mastering French
culinary techniques provided "one way for the Vietnamese to delegitimize
colonial authority" (30). Wealthy Vietnamese who served flawlessly prepared
French meals to colonial administrators demonstrated a cultural fluidity that
"challenged rigid colonial hierarchies of cultural practices and identities"
(24). As Toklas points out, Nguyen gained his cultural fluidity by working
for the French Governor General of Indochina. He, in turn, exported this
mastery of French cuisine onto French soil, where it provided him with a
means of economic survival in his colonizer's homeland. Such mastery likewise enabled Vietnamese cooks living in France to subtly reconfigure the
power dynamics of everyday practices. If you are what you eat, then the
French who dined with Toklas and Stein on Nguyen's hybrid meals had their
palates challenged by the flavors of Vietnam, which lingered on their tongues
and overpowered the French dishes subsequently served.

Toklas' discussion of Nguyen's subversive culinary techniques undoubtedly
influenced Truong's exploration of culinary colonialism in *The Book of Salt*.
Like Nguyen, the novel's protagonist, Bình, worked for the French Governor General of Indochina. Through Bình's first-person narrative, we learn
that he was fired from a position as *garde manger* in the French Governor-
General's kitchen for sleeping with the French head chef and was subsequently
disowned by his father for his homosexual desires. The dismissal jettisons
the young lover out to sea—both literally and metaphorically. Bình reflects:
"[T]o take one's body and willingly set it upon the open sea, this for me is
not an act brought about by desire but a consequence of it" (56). The French
culinary skills Bình acquired under his lover's watch eventually lead him to
France, where he is hired by a succession of Parisian couples, many of whom,

as Bình describes, "insist on stripping [him] with questions" in order to find out how he came to land on their "hallowed shores" (16). Sometimes these couples hire Bình, yet their questions continue unabated until one day Bình finds: "This [French] language that I dip into like a dry inkwell has failed me. It has made me take flight with weak wings and watched me plummet into silence" (17). Bình's only means of communicating verbally with these collectors is through the colonizer's language, a language that denies and negates his self-expression. Such silence inevitably ends with his dismissal.

Bình works for yet another type of employer, whom he describes as collectors who crave the "sea-salt sadness of the outcast" (19). Each time he is taken in by such collectors, Bình finds that entering their kitchens

> is a homecoming, a respite, where I am the village elder, sage and revered. . . . During these intervals I am no longer the mute who begs at this city's steps. Three times a day, I orchestrate, and they sit with slackened jaws, silenced. Mouths preoccupied with the taste of foods so familiar and yet with every bite even the most parochial of palates detects redolent notes of something that they have no words to describe. They are, by the end, overwhelmed by an emotion they have never felt, a nostalgia for places they have never been. (19)

Truong suggests here that Bình's emotions are imparted by his embodied practices. In other words, the ingredients Bình chooses, the way in which he handles them, and the techniques he uses to combine them convey flavors and aromas that capture his nostalgia for Vietnam. Even though many of the ingredients Bình uses in the dishes he prepares hail from French soil, the embodied practices he uses to combine them speak of the climate, soil, and way of life of the land he left behind. The dishes these collectors taste embody Bình's Vietnamese heritage and attest to his apprenticeship in a French colonial kitchen. They also communicate Bình's nostalgia for his homeland.

Each time Bình is taken in by such collectors he inevitably finds himself "driven out by [his] own willful hands. . . . I forget how long to braise the ribs of beef . . . where to buy the sweetest trout. I neglect the pinch of cumin, the sprinkling of lovage, the scent of lime. And in these ways, I compulsively write, page by page, the letters of my resignation" (20). Bình wanders from kitchen to kitchen, collector to collector until he happens on the following advertisement in a newspaper, the first two lines of which come straight from Toklas' *Cook Book*:

> *Two American ladies wish*
> *to retain a cook—27 rue de*
> *Fleurus. See the concierge.*

On reading the advertisement, Bình reflects, with his usual ironic wit, "Two American ladies 'wish'? Sounds more like a proclamation than a help-wanted ad. Of course, two American ladies in Paris these days would only 'wish' because to wish is to receive. To want, well, to want is just not American" (11). With this one passage, Truong playfully delineates the economic, social, and political power dynamics between Bình and his American employers. Throughout her novel, Truong interrogates the dynamic between Bình and his American masters as well as between the American masters themselves. In order to do so, she often fills gaps in Toklas' memoir. For example, Truong fills the gap in Toklas' text that might detail Nguyen's and Trac's departure from Vietnam as well as their lives before and outside of 27 rue de Fleurus. Truong fills the gap by giving us Bình's life story narrated in his own words. Truong also interrogates the complex dynamic that exists between Toklas, Trac, and Nguyen by exploring colonized life in Vietnam as well as the life of the Vietnamese exile in France. In so doing, Truong responds to the "colonial inflection" in Toklas' cookbook, one that figures Trac's and Nguyen's cookery as exotically Other.[6] She does so by familiarizing what remains exotic in Toklas' text. Toward that end, Truong submerges her reader into Bình's thoughts, his detailed memories of cooking in Vietnam, his time in the French colonial kitchen, even his reasons for marrying key flavors in the dishes he prepares. On an intertextual level, Truong interrogates and partially fills the gaps that might provide emotional details of Toklas' rapport with her lover Gertrude Stein, a gap around which Toklas' text eddies but intentionally declines to enter. Truong fills the gap with Bình's intimate knowledge of the couple's lives and the ways in which they nourish and sustain one another. She also fills it with Bình's nuanced interpretation of their rapport.

Once employed by the two American lesbians in Paris, Bình finds a place of safety and comfort for the first time in his life. He reflects on his relationship with the famous couple:

> My Madame and Madame sustain me. They pay my wage, house my body, and I feed them. . . . The day to day is what I share with them. . . . These two, unlike all the others [I have worked for] extend to me the right to eat what they eat, a right that is . . . really a privilege when it is I who am doing the cooking. (209)

Bình not only reflects on what his Mesdames have offered him, but also on what they offer one another. Toward that end, Bìhn describes the apartment where he resides with Toklas and Stein as a temple, not a home, reflecting:

---

6. Critic Sarah Garland uses the term "colonial inflection" in her analysis of Toklas' cookbook, "'A cook book to be read. What about it?' Alice Toklas, Gertrude Stein, and the Language of the Kitchen." In particular, she states: "When Toklas revels in recipes that are 'romantic' and 'seducing' the force of potential ravishment is translated into objects that are Other, and there is certainly a colonial inflection to this—to borrow bell hooks's phrasing, 'ethnicity becomes a spice' just as historically desire has been given a material measure in the long and arduous trade routes behind sugar, coffee, sesame, and cocoa (hooks, 1999: 197)" (46).

"My Mesdames live in a state of grace. . . . Gertrude Stein feeds on affection, and Miss Toklas assures that she never hungers. . . . No man's god can tell me that *that* is wrong" (71). In return for a room of his own, Bình feeds Toklas and Stein, who empathize with and take pleasure in his limited access to the French language.

Unlike the French, who "never tired of debating why the Indochinese of a certain class are never able to master the difficulties, the subtleties, the winged eloquence, of the French language," Stein finds inspiration from Bình's French voice and so, too, does Bình in Stein's (13). He reflects on the exchange:

> her French, like mine, has its limits. It denies her. It forces her to be short if not precise. In French, GertrudeStein finds herself wholly dependent on simple sentences. She compensates with the tone of her voice and the warmth of her eyes. She handles it with stunning grace. When I hear her speak it, I am filled with something close to joy. I admire its roughness, its unapologetic swagger. I think it a companion to my own. . . . She is a co-conspirator. (34)

In Truong's tale, Bình's French words prove inspirational enough to Stein that she begins "wrapping them around her tongue" and eventually writes a book about Bình.[7]

Although Bình finds Stein a co-conspirator, his Madame has the time and wealth to play with language, fashioning her own native tongue into forms and structures that earn her tremendous acclaim. Bình enjoys no such luxurious relationship to the Vietnamese language; nobody in Bình's daily life understands the words he speaks fluently. Whereas Stein nourishes a large reading public with her fresh approach toward language, Bình has only his colonizer's language with which to articulate himself in France. As a result, language repeatedly fails Bình. It erects distance and barriers, denying him intimacy and connection. Throughout the novel, Truong underscores the failure of the colonizer's language to capture and convey the needs, desires, and wishes of the colonized body. Food, however, enables Bình an outlet for self-expression, a way to blend two seemingly disparate cultures, neither of which provides him a welcome home.

Bình may not be able to fashion his desires into French words, but he can fashion them from the ingredients at hand, communicating in a medium that speaks eloquently to Vietnamese, French, and American palates alike.

---

7. For a provocative analysis of intertexuality and collaborative autobiography in *The Book of Salt*, see Y-Dang Troeung's "'A Gift or a Theft Depends on Who is Holding the Pen': Postcolonial Collaborative Autobiography and Monique Truong's *The Book of Salt*." Troeung's essay addresses the intertexuality of Truong's novel with Toklas' *Cook Book* and Stein's *Autobiography of Alice B. Toklas* in order to examine "how Truong uses the parameters of the historical Stein-Toklas controversy in *The Book of Salt* to extend a political project about postcolonial collaborative autobiography and Vietnamese American identity" (114).

In particular, his culinary mastery pleases Toklas and, by extension, nourishes Stein. Toklas recognizes and respects Bình's expertise in the kitchen, being herself a woman, as Bình describes, who "can reach far beyond the foods of her childhood. She is a cook who puts absinthe in her salad dressing and rose petals in her vinegar. Her menus can map the world" (27). Trained in a professional kitchen, Bình respects Toklas' educated palate as one that appreciates the cultural nuances contained in each of the dishes he prepares. He understands that Toklas' innate skill and training as a gourmand enable her to understand the artistry of his cooking and to register the nuanced stories that his dishes contain.

Bình explains the power of the culinary skills he gained in the colonial kitchen and the "aesthetic emotion" his dishes evoke in the temple he now calls home when he reflects:

> Every day, my Mesdames and I dine, if not together, then back-to-back. Of course there is always a wall between us, but when they dine on *filet de boeuf Adrienne*, I dine on *filet de boeuf Adrienne*. When they partake of *salade cancalaise*, I partake of *salade cancalaise*. . . . When I place that first bite of *boeuf Adrienne* in my mouth and am brought to my knees—figuratively speaking, of course. . . . I know that my Mesdames are on their knees as well. *Salade cancalaise*. . . . A shaving of black truffle covers all. The potatoes are there for heft and texture, but the truffle, ah, the truffle is a gift for the nose. Pleasure refined into a singular scent, almost addictive, a lover's body coming toward yours on a moonless night. Even this my Mesdames have shared with me. (209–210)

Here Bình underscores the pleasure his culinary mastery enables him to give and receive, a pleasure forbidden him in the colonial kitchen where he could never become *chef de cuisine*. Truong explores the potential of this mastery to communicate the nuances of desire in a way that disrupts existing hierarchies. Bình's mastery enables him to communicate with Toklas and Stein, to speak eloquently about physical desire and to convey aesthetic pleasures in a way not possible with words. Although a wall might separate the famous pair from their cook, thereby materializing the hierarchy of master over servant, America over Vietnam, the flavors, in effect, permeate the barrier, enabling Toklas and Stein to share the erotic pleasures conveyed by Bình's cookery. The French dishes Bình prepares enable him to achieve an intimacy with his Mesdames by speaking a language that momentarily dissolves the cultural barriers that separate their lives. In turn, Toklas' and Stein's ability to read the meaning of Bình's dishes and to experience the sensual pleasure they communicate enables Bình to find a temporary room of his own. Truong suggests, on one level, that finding Toklas, a gourmand attuned to his cookery and the nuances it conveys, enables Bình to feel momentarily at home. The dishes Bình creates, in effect, contain the meaning that he cannot express in the French language and enable him to articulate a hybrid identity, fashioned in part from the colonization of his homeland as well as by his subsequent exile from it. In turn, finding two women who understand the language of his cookery, its elegant, at times playful, blend of Vietnamese and French flavors and techniques as well as the desire, longing, and nostalgia it conveys, provides Bình with a temporary respite.

In *The Book of Salt*, Truong sheds light on precisely why the French were so concerned with maintaining their own foodways in Vietnam, often disdaining Vietnamese cookery and discouraging the Vietnamese from eating French food (Peters 23). Eating the same dish as another is an intimate act—to taste the same flavors, to smell the same aromas, to ingest the same flesh allows for what might be termed an "existential equality." How each eater experiences a particular food may vary, yet the stimulus does not. Thus partaking of the same dish unites the diners in an innately sensual act, one during which the hierarchies between self and other are momentarily dissolved and reconfigured.

By creating a novel narrated by a colonized other, albeit a fictional one, who articulates himself by blending French and Vietnamese culinary techniques and practices, Truong underscores the subversive power of food and showcases cooking as a medium though which rigid hierarchies can be challenged and reconfigured. She also illuminates eating as an intimate act through which we ingest flavors, textures, and aromas that, in turn, communicate lived experiences and the nuanced emotions these experiences inspire. *The Book of Salt* not only pays tribute to the Vietnamese cooks who worked for Toklas and Stein by fashioning Bình from the few printed words that record their lives, but likewise pays tribute to Toklas and Stein by portraying their ability to taste the meaning of his dishes. By creating such a fictional dynamic, Truong interweaves cultures and cultural values into a poignant tale about the power of cooking to forge transnational identities and to express universal desires.

Bibliography

Abramson, Julia. "Grimod's Debt to Mercier and the Emergence of Gastronomic Writing Reconsidered." *Rethinking Cultural Studies.* Edited by David Lee Rubin. Charlottesville: Rookwood Press, 2001.

Acton, Eliza. *Modern Cookery for Private Families.* 1845. Lewes, East Sussex: Southover, 1993.

Allhusen, Dorothy. *A Book of Scents and Dishes.* 1926. London: Williams and Norgate, 1927.

Andrews, Julia C. *Breakfast, Dinner, and Tea: Viewed Classically, Poetically, and Practically.* Facsimile of the 1860 edition. Charleston: BiblioLife, 2009.

Aresty, Esther. *The Delectable Past.* Indianapolis: Bobs-Merrill, 1978.

Armitage, Merle. *"Fit for a King": The Merle Armitage Book of Food.* 1939. Edited by Ramiel McGehee. New York: Duell, Sloan and Pearce, 1949.

Arndt, Alice. *Culinary Biographies.* Houston: Yes, 2006.

Ashley, Bob, Joanne Hollows, Steve Jones, and Ben Taylor. *Food and Cultural Studies.* Routledge: London, 2004.

Bailey, Paul. "The Glorious Pages of Patience." *Financial Times.* 4 September 2005, p. 5.

Barber, Joseph. *Crumbs from the Round Table: A Feast for Epicures.* New York: Leypoldt & Holt, 1866. http://books.google.com.

Beard, James. *Cook it Outdoors.* New York: M. Barrows & Co., 1941.

———. *The Fireside Cook Book.* New York: Simon & Schuster, 1949.

———. *Fowl and Game Cookery.* New York: M. Barrows & Company Inc., 1944.

———. 1940. *Hors d'Oeuvre and Canapes.* Philadelphia: Running Press, 1999.

Beck, Leonard N. *Two "Loaf-Givers" or A Tour through the Gastronomic Libraries of Katherine Golden Bitting and Elizabeth Robins Pennell.* Washington: Library of Congress, 1984.

Beecher, Catharine and Harriet Beecher Stowe. *The American Woman's Home.* 1869. Piscataway, NJ: Rutgers University Press, 2002.

Beetham, Margaret. "Of Recipe Books and Reading in the Nineteenth Century: Mrs. Beeton and Her Cultural Consequences." *The Recipe Reader.* Edited by Janet Floyd and Laurel Forster. Burlington: Ashgate, 2003.

Beeton, Isabella. *Mrs. Beeton's Book of Household Management.* Abridged from the first volume edition, 1861. Oxford: Oxford University Press, 2000.

Bellows, A. J. *The Philosophy of Eating.* New York: Hurd and Houghton, 1867. http://www.googlebooks.com.

Bentley, Amy. *Eating for Victory: Food Rationing and the Politics of Domesticity.* Chicago: University of Illinois Press, 1988.

Benstock, Shari. *Women of the Left Bank.* Austin: University of Texas Press, 1986.

Betterton, Rosemary. "'A Perfect Woman': The Political Body of Suffrage," *An Intimate Distance: Women, Artists and the Body*. London: Routledge, 1996.

Bird, Elizabeth. "'High Class Cookery': Gender, Status and Domestic Subjects." *Gender and Education* 10 (June 1998): 117–135.

Bordo, Susan. *Unbearable Weight*. Berkeley: California University Press, 1993.

Boulestin, X. Marcel. *Myself, My Two Countries*. London: Cassell, 1936.

———. *Simple French Cooking for English Homes*. 1923. London: Heinemann, 1938.

Bowler, Arthur R. Introduction to *A New System of Domestic Cookery* by Maria Eliza Rundell. Reprint of the Fort Niagra edition of original 1806 printing. Youngstown, NY: Old Fort Niagra Association, 1998.

Boxer, Arabella. *Arabella Boxer's Book of British Food: A Rediscovery of British Food from Before the War*. London: Hodder and Stoughton, 1991.

Bracken, Peg. *The I Hate to Cook Book*. New York: Harcourt, Brace and Company, 1960.

Brillat-Savarin, Jean Anthelme. *The Physiology of Taste*. Trans. Anne Drayton. London: Penguin, 1994.

———. *The Physiology of Taste: Or, Meditations on Transcendental Gastronomy*. Trans. M. F. K. Fisher. New York: Heritage Press, 1949.

Brumberg, Joan Jacobs. "The Appetite as Voice." *Food and Culture: A Reader*. Edited by Carole Counihan and Penny Van Esterik. New York: Routledge, 1997.

Bruner, Belinda. "A Recipe for Modernism and the Somatic Intellect in *The Alice B. Toklas Cook Book* and Gertrude Stein's *Tender Buttons*." *Papers on Language and Literature* 45.4 (Fall 2009): 411.

Bryan, Lettice. *The Kentucky Housewife*. Facsimile of the 1839 edition. Paducah, KY: Collector Books, n.d.

Bunyard, Edward and Lorna. *The Epicure's Companion*. London: J. M. Dent, 1937.

Burnett, John. *Plenty & Want: A Social History of the Diet in England from 1815 to Present Day*. Rev. ed. London: Scolar, 1979.

Campbell, Julie D. "M.F.K. Fisher and the Embodiment of Desire: A Study in Autobiography and Food as Metaphor." *Biography* 20.2 (1997): 181–202.

Carruth, Allison. "War Rations and the Food Politics of Late Modernism." *Modernism/Modernity* 16.4 (November 2009): 767–795.

Carter, Angela. Review of "Patience Gray: *Honey From a Weed*." *Shaking a Leg: Collected Writings*. Edited by Jenny Uglow. New York: Penguin, 1998.

Chamberlain, Samuel. *Bouquet de France*. New York: Gourmet Distributing Company, 1952.

———. *Italian Bouquet*. New York: Gourmet Distributing Company, 1963.

Chaney, Lisa. *Elizabeth David*. London: Macmillan, 1998.

Chaudhuri, Nupur. "Shawls, Jewlery, Curry, and Rice in Victorian Britain." *Western Women and Imperialism: Complicity and Resistance*. Edited by Chaudhuri and Margaret Strobel. Bloomington: Indiana University Press, 1992.

Child, Lydia Maria. *The Frugal Housewife*. Second edition. Boston: Carter and Hendee, 1930.

Child, Theodore. *Delicate Feasting*. New York: Harper and Brothers, 1890.

Clarke, Meaghan. "'Bribery with Sherry' and 'The Influence of Weak Tea': Women Critics as Arbiters of Taste in the Late-Victorian and Edwardian Press." *Visual Culture in Britain* 6.2 (Winter, 2005): 139–155.

Colchester-Wemyss, Sir Francis. *The Pleasures of the Table*. London: James Nisbet, 1931.

Collation of Authorities. *The Oyster Epicure*. New York: White, Stokes, and Allen, 1883. http://books.google.com

Colman, Louis. Editor's Introduction to Alexander Dumas' *Dictionary of Cuisine*. Edited, abridged, and translated by Louis Colman. New York: Simon and Schuster, 1958.

Cooper, Artemis. *Writing at the Kitchen Table: The Authorized Biography of Elizabeth David*. New York: Ecco. 1999.

Curnonsky. *The Traditional Recipes of the Provinces of France*. Edited and translated by Edwin Lavin. Garden City: Doubleday, 1961.

Curtin, Deane W., and Lisa M. Heldke. *Cooking, Eating, Thinking*. Bloomington: Indiana University Press, 1992.

Dallas, E. S. *Kettner's Book of the Table*. 1877. London: Centaur Press, 1968.

David, Elizabeth. *Elizabeth David Classics: Mediterranean Food, French Country Cooking, Summer Cooking*. New York: Knopf, 1980.

———. *English Bread and Yeast Cookery*. London: Penguin, 1977.

———. *French Country Cooking*. 1951. *Elizabeth David Classics*. New York: Knopf, 1980.

———. *French Provincial Cooking*. 1960. New York: Penguin, 1999.

———. *Harvest of the Cold Months: The Social History of Ice and Ices*. Ed. Jill Norman. 1994. New York: Viking, 1995.

———. *Is There a Nutmeg in the House?* London: Michael Joseph, 2000.

———. *Italian Food*. 1954. New York: Smithmark, 1996.

———. *Mediterranean Food*. 1950. *Elizabeth David Classics*. New York: Knopf, 1980.

———. *An Omelette and a Glass of Wine*. 1984. New York: Lyon's, 1997.

———. *South Wind through the Kitchen*. New York: North Point, 1998.

———. *Spices, Salt and Aromatics in the English Kitchen*. 1970. Rev. ed. Harmondsworth: Penguin, 1979.

———. *Summer Cooking*. 1955. *Elizabeth David Classics*. New York: Knopf, 1980.

Davidson, Alan. *The Oxford Companion to Food*. Oxford: Oxford University Press, 1999.

Davis, Irving. *A Catalan Cookery Book*. Edited by Patience Gray. 1969. Devon: Prospect Books, 1999.

Dawson, Lawrence R. Introduction to *The Country Kitchen*. Detroit: Wayne State University Press, 1992.

D'Emilio, John and Estelle Freedman. *Intimate Matters: A History of Sexuality in America*. Chicago: University of Chicago Press, 1997.

Denisoff, Dennis. *Aestheticism and Sexual Parody, 1840–1940*. Cambridge: Cambridge University Press, 2001.

De Mauduit, Vicomte. *The Vicomte in the Kitchen: The Art of Cooking, Preserving, Eating, and Drinking; Also a Selection of Recipes from Many Countries*. New York: Covici Friede Publishers, 1934.

Derwin, Susan. "The Poetics of M. F. K. Fisher." *Style* 37.3 (Fall 2003): 266–278.

Dolby, Richard. *The Cook's Dictionary, and Housekeeper's Directory*. Facsimile of the 1833 edition. Charleston: Bibliobazaar, 2009.

Driver, Christopher. *The British at Table: 1940–1980*. London: Hogarth, 1983.

Dumas, Alexandre. *Dictionary of Cuisine*. 1873. Edited, abridged, and translated by Louis Colman. New York: Simon and Schuster, 1958.

Ellet, Elizabeth Fries. *The Practical Housekeeper; A Cyclopaedia of Domestic Economy*. New York: Stringer and Townsend, 1857.

Ellwanger, George H. *The Pleasures of the Table: An Account of Gastronomy from Ancient Days to Present Times*. 1902. Detroit: Singing Tree, 1969.

Eng, David L. "The End(s) of Race." *PMLA: Publications of the Modern Language Association of America* 123 (2008): 1479–1493.

Farmer, Fannie Merritt. *The Original Boston Cooking-School Cook Book*. Facsimile of the first edition, 1896. Westport: Hugh Lauter Levin Assoc., 1996.

Fedden, Romilly. *Food and Other Frailties*. London: Seeley, n.d.

Ferguson, Priscilla Parkhurst. *Accounting for Taste: The Triumph of French Cuisine*. Chicago: University of Chicago Press, 2004.

———. "A Cultural Field in the Making: Gastronomy in 19th-Century France," *The American Journal of Sociology* 104.3 (November 1998): 587–641.

Ferrary, Jeannette. *M. F. K. Fisher and Me: A Memoir of Food and Friendship*. New York: St. Martin's, 1998.

Finck, Henry Theophilus. *Food and Flavor, A Gastronomic Guide to Health and Good Living*. Facsimile of the 1913 edition. LaVergne, TN: General Books, 2009.

Fink, Beatrice. "Enlightened Eating in Non-Fictional Context and the First Stirrings of *Écriture Gourmande*." *Dalhousie French Studies* 11 (1986): 9–20.

Fisher, M. F. K. *Among Friends*. 1971. New York: North Point, 1998.

———. "An Alphabet for Gourmets." 1949. *The Art of Eating*. New York: Macmillan, 1990.

———. *As They Were*. 1982. New York: Vintage, 1983.

———. *The Art of Eating*. 1954. New York: Macmillan, 1990.

———. *To Begin Again: Stories and Memoirs 1908–1929*. New York: Pantheon, 1992.

———. *Consider the Oyster*. 1941. *The Art of Eating*. New York: Macmillan, 1990.

———. *The Cooking of Provincial France*. New York: Time-Life, 1968.

———. *A Cordiall Water*. 1961. San Francisco: North Point, 1981.

———. *Dubious Honors*. San Francisco: North Point, 1988.

———. *The Gastronomical Me*. 1943. New York: North Point, 1998.

———. *Here Let Us Feast: A Book of Banquets*. 1946. San Francisco. North Point, 1986.

———. *How to Cook a Wolf*. 1942. *The Art of Eating*. New York: Macmillan, 1990.

———. *Last House*. 1995. New York: Random House, 1997.

———. *A Life in Letters*. Washington D.C.: Counterpoint, 1997.

———. *Long Ago in France*. New York: Touchstone, 1992.

———. *Map of Another Town*. 1964. *Two Towns in Provence: Map of Another Town and A Considerable Town*. New York: Vintage, 1983.

———. *The Measure of Her Powers: An M. F. K. Fisher Reader*. Edited by Dominique Gioia. Washington D.C.: Counterpoint, 1999.

———. *Serve It Forth*. 1937. *The Art of Eating*. New York: Macmillan, 1990.

———. *Sister Age*. 1983. New York: Vintage, 1984.

———. *Stay Me, Oh Comfort Me: Journals and Stories, 1933–1941*. New York: Pantheon, 1993.

———. *Two Towns in Provence: Map of Another Town and A Considerable Town*. New York: Vintage, 1983.

———. *With Bold Knife and Fork*. New York: Paragon Books, 1969.

Floyd, Janet. "Simple, Honest Food: Elizabeth David and the Construction of Nation in Cookery Writing." *The Recipe Reader*. Edited by Janet Floyd and Laurel Foster. Aldershot: Ashgate, 2003.

Forster, E. M. 'Porridge or Prunes, Sir?' *We Shall Eat and Drink Again*, edited by Louis Golding and André L. Simon. Plymouth: Mayflower Press, 1944.

Fougner, G. Selmer. *Gourmet Dinners*. New York: M. Barrows & Co., 1941.

Francatelli, Charles Elmé. *The Modern Cook: A Practical Guide to the Culinary Art in All its Branches*. 1845. London: Richard Bentley, 1871.

———. *A Plain Cookery Book for the Working Classes*. 1861. Whitstable: Pryor, 1993.

Frawley, Maria H. *A Wider Range: Travel Writing by Women in Victorian England*. Madison, NJ: Farleigh Dickinson University Press, 1994.

Fussell, Betty. *Masters of American Cookery: The American Food Revolution and the Chefs Who Shaped It*. New York: Times Books, 1983.

Garland, Sarah. "'A cook book to be read. What about it?' Alice Toklas, Gertrude Stein and the Language of the Kitchen." *Comparative American Studies* 7.1 (March, 2009): 34–56.

Garval, Michael. "Grimod de la Reynière's *Almanach des Gourmands*: Exploring the Gastronomic New World of Postrevolutionary France." *French Food on the Table, on the Page, and in French Culture*. Edited by Lawrence R. Schehr and Allan S. Weiss. Routledge: New York, 2001.

Gigante, Denise. *Gusto: Essential Writings in Nineteenth-Century Gastronomy*. New York: Routledge, 2005.

———. *Taste: A Literary History*. New Haven: Yale University Press, 2005.

Gioia, Dominique. *A Welcoming Life: The M. F. K. Fisher Scrapbook*. Washington D.C.: Counterpoint, 1997.

Glasse, Hannah. *The Art of Cookery Made Plain and Easy*. Facsimile of the 1805 edition. Bedford: Applewood Books, 1997.

Glave, Thomas. *Words to Our Now*. Minneapolis: University of Minnesota Press, 2005.

Gray, Patience. *The Centaur's Kitchen: A Book of French, Italian, Greek and Catalan Dishes for Ships' Cooks on the Blue Funnel Line*. Dover: Prospect, 2009.

———. *Honey from a Weed: Fasting and Feasting in Tuscany, Catalonia, The Cyclades and Apulia*. 1986. North Point Press: San Francisco, 1990.

———. *Ringdoves and Snakes*. London: Macmillan, 1989.

Gray, Patience and Primrose Boyd. 1957. *Plats du Jour*. London: Persephone Books, 2008.

Grimod de la Reynière, Alexandre Balthazar Laurent. From *The Gourmand's Almanac* and *The Host's Manual*. Translated by Michael Garval. *Gusto: Essential Writings in Nineteenth-Century Gastronomy*. Edited by Denise Gigante. New York: Routledge, 2005.

Grosvenor, Vertamae Smart. *Vibration Cooking: Or the Travel Notes of a Geechee Girl*. Ballantine: New York, 1970.

Haber, Barbara. *From Hardtack to Home Fries: An Uncommon History of American Cooks and Meals*. New York: Free Press, 2002.

Hardyment, Christina. *Slice of Life: The British Way of Eating Since 1945*. London: BBC Books, 1995.

Harland, Marion. *Common Sense in the Household*. Birmingham, Alabama: Antique American Cookbooks, 1985.

Hayward, Abraham. *The Art of Dining; or on Gastronomy and Gastronomers*. London: John Murray, 1852. http://books.google.com.

Heath, Ambrose. *Good Food Again*. London: Faber and Faber, 1945.

Heldke, Lisa. *Exotic Appetites: Ruminations of a Food Adventurer*. New York: Routledge, 2003.

Heller, Tamar and Patricia Moran. *Scenes of the Apple: Food and the Female Body in Nineteenth- and Twentieth-Century Women's Writing*. Albany: State University of New York Press, 2003.

Hess, John and Karen Hess. *The Taste of America*. Chicago: Illinois University Press, 2000.

Hess, Karen. Historical Notes. *The Art of Cookery Made Plain and Easy*, by Hannah Glasse. Bedford: Applewood Books, 1997.

Hibben, Sheila. *The National Cookbook: A Kitchen Americana*. New York: Harper & Brothers Publishers, 1932.

———. *American Regional Cookery*. New York: Gramercy Publishing Company, 1946.

Hill, Janet Mackenzie. *Salads, Sandwiches and Chafing-Dish Dainties*. Facsimile of the 1903 edition. Charleston: BiblioLife, 2008.

Hines, Duncan. *Adventures in Good Eating*. Bowling Green: Adventures in Good Eating, Inc., 1943.

———. *Duncan Hines' Food Odyssey*. New York: Thomas Y. Crowell, 1955.

hooks, bell. 'Eating the Other: Desire and Resistance' in *Feminist Approaches to Theory and Methodology: An Interdisciplinary Reader*, eds. S. Hesse-Biber, C. Gilmartin, & R. Lydenberg. New York: Oxford University Press, 1999.

Horner, Jennifer R. "*Betty Crocker's Picture Book*: A Gendered Ritual Response to Social Crises of the Post war Era." *Journal of Communication Inquiry*. 24.3 (2000): 332–345.

Horowitz, Helen Lefkowitz. "The Body in the Library." *The 'Women Question' and Higher Education*. Edited by Ann Mari May. Northampton: Edward Elgan, 2008.

Horrocks, Jamie. "Camping in the Kitchen: Locating Culinary Authority in Elizabeth Robins Pennell's *Delights of Delicate Eating*." *Nineteenth-Century Gender Studies* 3.2 (Summer 2007): http://www.ncgsjournal.com.

Howlett, Caroline J. "Writing on the Body? Representation and Resistance in British Suffragette Accounts of Force Feeding." *Genders* 23 (June 30, 1996): 3–49.

Humble, Nicola. *Culinary Pleasures: Cookbooks and the Transformation of British Food*. London: Faber and Faber, 2005.

Jaine, Tom. "Patience Gray." *The Guardian*. 18 March 2005. http://www.guardian.co.uk/news/2005/mar/18/guardianobituaries.food.

Jeaffreson, John Cordy. *A Book About the Table*. London: Hurst and Blackett, 1875. http://books.google.com.

Jekyll, Agnes. *Kitchen Essays*. 1922. London: Persephone Books, 2001.

Jerrold, William Blanchard. *The Epicure's Year Book for 1869*. London: Bradbury, Evans, & Co., 1869. http://books.google.com.

Jones, Steve and Ben Taylor. "Food Writing and Food Cultures: The Case of Elizabeth David and Jane Grigson." *European Journal of Cultural Studies* 4.2 (2001): 171–188.

Kander, Lizzie Black. *The Settlement Cook Book*. Facsimile of the 1903 edition. Bedford: Applewood Books, 1996.

Keane, Molly. *Molly Keane's Nursery Cooking*. London: Macdonald, 1985.

Kelly, Traci Marie. "'If I Were a Voodoo Priestess': Women's Culinary Autobiographies." *Kitchen Culture*. Edited by Sherrie A. Inness. Philadelphia: University of Pennsylvania Press, 2001.

Kilgour, Maggie. *From Communion to Cannibalism*. Princeton: Princeton University Press, 1990.

Kirwan, A. V. *Host and Guest: A Book About Dinners, Dinner-Giving, Wines, and Desserts*. London: Bell and Daldy, 1864. http://googlebooks.com.

Kitchiner, William. *The Cook's Oracle and House Keeper's Manual*. Facsimile of the 1830 edition. Bedford: Applewood Books, n. d.

Korsmeyer, Carolyn. *Making Sense of Taste*. Ithaca: Cornell University Press, 1999.

Lady, A. *Domestic Economy and Cookery for Rich and Poor; Containing an Account of the Best English, Scotch, French, Oriental and Other Foreign Dishes; Preparations of Broths and Milks for Consumption; Receipts for Sea-Faring Men, Travellers, and Children's Food*. Facsimile of the 1827 edition. LaVergne, TN: General Books, 2009.

Lamb, Charles. 1823. "A Dissertation Upon Roast Pig." *Essays of Elia*. London: J. M. Dent, 1915.

Laubreaux, Alin. *The Happy Glutton,* translated by Naomi Walford. London: Ivor Nicholson and Watson, 1931.

Lazar, David, ed. *Conversations with M. F. K. Fisher.* Jackson: Mississippi University Press, 1992.

Leed, Eric J. *The Mind of the Traveler: From Gilgamesh to Global Tourism.* New York: Basic Books, 1991.

Leonardi, Susan J. "Recipes for Reading: Summer Pasta, Lobster à la Riseholme, and Key Lime Pie." *PMLA* 104.3 (1989): 340–347.

Leslie, Eliza. *Miss Leslie's Directions for Cookery: An Unabridged Reprint of the 1851 Classic.* Mineola: Dover, 1999.

Levenstein, Harvey. *Paradox of Plenty: A Social History of Eating in America.* New York: Oxford University Press, 1993.

Levy, Anita. *Other Women: The Writing of Class, Race, and Gender, 1832–1898.* Princeton: Princeton University Press, 1991.

Levy, Esther. *Jewish Cookery Book.* Facsimile of the 1871 edition. Bedford, MA: Applewood Books, n.d.

Leyel, Hilda and Olga Hartley. 1925. *The Gentle Art of Cookery.* London: Hogarth Press, 1983.

Linzie, Anna. *The True Story of Alice B. Toklas: A Study of Three Autobiographies.* Iowa City: University of Iowa, 2006.

Loeb, Robert. *Wolf in Chef's Clothing.* 1950. New York: Wilcox & Follett Company, 1954.

Long, Lucy. "Culinary Tourism: A Folkloristic Perspective on Eating and Otherness." *Southern Folklore* 55.3 (1998): 181–204.

Longone, Jan. Introduction to *Miss Leslie's Directions for Cookery* by Eliza Leslie. Reprint of 1851 edition, New York: Mineola, 1999.

Lowinsky, Ruth. *Lovely Food.* London: Nonesuch Press, 1931.

Lukanuski, Mary. "A Place at the Counter: The Onus of Oneness." *Eating Culture.* Edited by Ron Scapp and Brian Seitz. Albany: State University of New York, 1998.

Lupton, Deborah. *Food, the Body and the Self.* London: Sage, 1996.

Lutes, Della. 1936. *The Country Kitchen.* Detroit: Wayne State University Press, 1992.

MacDonogh, Giles. *A Palate in Revolution: Grimod de La Reynière and the Almanach des Gourmands.* London: Robin Clark, 1987.

MacPherson, John. *The Mystery Chef's Own Cook Book.* 1934. New York: Longman's Green and Co., 1935.

Malcolm, Janet. "As the French Do," *The New Yorker,* August 19, 2002.

Marano, Salvatore. "'Consider the Menu Carefully': The Dining Room Tales of Alice B. Toklas." *Prospero* 11 (2004): 173–187.

Martineau, Alice. *Caviare to Candy: Recipes for Small Households from All Parts of the World.* London: Rachard Cobden-Sanderson, 1927.

McFeely, Mary Drake. *Can She Bake a Cherry Pie? American Women and the Kitchen.* Amherst: University of Massachusetts Press, 2000.

McCannell, Dean. *The Tourist: A New Theory of the Leisure Class.* New York: Schocken Books, 1976.

Mennell, Stephen. *All Manners of Food: Eating and Taste in England and France from the Middle Ages to the Present.* Chicago: University of Illinois Press, 1996.

Michie, Helena. *The Flesh Made Word.* New York: Oxford University Press, 1987.

Minns, Raynes. *Bombers and Mash: The Domestic Front 1939–45.* 1980. London: Virago, 1999.

Moody, Harriet C. *Mrs. William Vaughn Moody's Cook-Book.* New York: Scribner's, 1931.

Morphy, Countess. *Recipes of All Nations*. London: Herbert Joseph, 1935.
———. *Recipes of All Nations*. New York: William H. Wise, 1936.
Neuhaus, Jessamyn. *Manly Meals and Mom's Home Cooking: Cookbooks and Gender in Modern America*. Baltimore: Johns Hopkins University Press, 2003.
Newnham-Davis, Lieutenant-Colonel Nathaniel. *Dinners and Diners: Where and How to Eat in London*. 1899. LaVergne, TN: Dodo Press, 2009.
Nicholson, Mervyn. "Eat—or Be Eaten: An Interdisciplinary Metaphor." *Mosaic* 24.3–4 (1991): 191–210.
Orioli, Gino. *Moving Along*. London: Chatto and Windus, 1934.
Owen, Catherine. *Culture and Cooking; or, Art in the Kitchen*. LaVergne, TN: Dodo Press, 2009.
Pennell, Elizabeth Robins. *Feasts of Autolycus: The Diary of a Greedy Woman*. Chicago: Saalfield Publishing, 1900.
Perreault, Jeanne. "Autography/Transformation/Asymmetry." *Women, Autobiography, Theory: A Reader*. Edited by Sidonie Smith and Julia Watson. Madison: University of Wisconsin Press, 1998.
Peters, Erica. "Culinary Crossings and Disruptive Identities: Contesting Colonial Categories in Everyday Life." *Of Vietnam: Identities in Dialogue*. Edited by Jane Winston. New York: Saint Martin's Press, 2001.
Probyn, Elspeth. *Carnal Appetites: FoodSexIdentities*. New York: Routledge, 2000.
Randolph, Mary. *The Virginia Housewife or, Methodical Cook*. Facsimile of the 1824 edition. New York: Dover, 1993.
Rawlings, Marjorie Kinnan. *Cross Creek Cookery*. New York: Charles Scribner's Sons, 1942.
Reardon, Joan. *M. F. K. Fisher, Julia Child, & Alice Waters: Celebrating the Pleasures of the Table*. New York: Harmony, 1994.
———. *Poet of the Appetites: The Lives and Loves of M. F. K. Fisher*. New York: North Point Press, 2004.
Reboux, Paul. *Food for the Rich*. Translated from *Plats Nouveaux* by Margaret Costa. London: Anthony Blond, 1958.
Rhode, William. *Of Cabbages and Kings*. New York: Stackpole Sons, 1938.
Rombauer, Irma S., *The Joy of Cooking, A Facsimile of the First Edition*. 1931. New York: Scribner, 1998.
Ross, Janet. *Italian Sketches*. Facsimile of the 1887 edition. La Vergne TN: General Books, 2010.
———. *Leaves from Our Tuscan Kitchen: Or How to Cook Vegetables*. Facsimile of the 1900 edition. La Vergne TN: Kessinger, 2010.
Rudin, Max. "M. F. K. Fisher and the Consolations of Food." *Raritan Quarterly Review* 21.2 (Fall 2001): 127–138.
Rundell, Maria Eliza. *A New System of Domestic Cookery*. Reprint of the Fort Niagra edition of original 1806 printing. Youngstown NY: Old Fort Niagra Association, 1998.
Rupp, Leila J. *A Desired Past: A Short History of Same-Sex Love in America*. Chicago: University of Chicago Press, 1999.
Rutledge, Sarah. *The Carolina Housewife*. Facsimile of the 1847 edition with an Introduction by Anna Wells Rutledge. Columbia: University of South Carolina Press, 1979.
Sala, George Augustus. *The Thorough Good Cook: A Series of Chats on the Culinary Art, and Nine Hundred Recipes*. 1896. La Vergne, TN: Kessinger, 2009.
Sceats, Sarah. *Food, Consumption and the Body in Contemporary Women's Fiction*. Cambridge: Cambridge University Press, 2000.
Schaffer, Talia. "The Importance of Being Greedy: Connoisseurship and Domesticity in the Writings of Elizabeth Robins Pennell." *The Recipe Reader*. Edited by Janet Floyd and Laurel Forster. Burlington: Ashgate, 2003.

Schenone, Laura. *A Thousand Years Over a Hot Stove: A History of American Women Told Through Food, Recipes, and Remembrances.* New York: W. W. Norton & Company, 2003.

Schlossberg, Linda. "Consuming Images: Women, Hunger, and the Vote." *Scenes of the Apple: Food and the Female Body in Nineteenth- and Twentieth-Century Women's Writing.* Edited by Tamar Heller and Patricia Moran. Albany: State University of New York, 2003.

Schmidt, Paul. "As If a Cookbook Had Anything to Do with Writing." *Prose* 8 (1974): 179–203.

Schofield, Mary Anne. *Cooking by the Book: Food in Literature and Culture.* Bowling Green: Bowling Green State University Press, 1989.

Schriber, Mary Suzanne. *Writing Home: American Women Abroad 1830–1920.* Charlottesville: University Press of Virginia, 1997.

Schwartz, Hillel. *Never Satisfied: A Cultural History of Diets, Fantasies and Fat.* New York: Free, 1986.

Shand, P. Morton. *A Book of Food.* New York: Knopf, 1928.

Shange, Ntozake. *If I Can Cook/You Know God Can.* Boston: Beacon Press, 1998.

Shapiro, Laura. *Perfection Salad: Women and Cooking at the Turn of the Century.* New York: North Point. 1995.

Shaw, Nancy. *Food for the Greedy.* London: Kegan Paul, 2005.

Shay, Frank. *The Best Men are Cooks.* New York: Coward-McCann Inc., 1941.

Silver, Anna Krugovoy. *Victorian Literature and the Anorexic Body.* Cambridge: Cambridge University Press, 2002.

Simmons, Christina. "Companionate Marriage and the Lesbian Threat," *Frontiers: A Journal of Women's Studies* 4.3 (Autumn, 1979): 54–59.

Simon, André. *The Art of Good Living.* 1929. London: Michael Joseph, 1951.

Simon, Linda. *The Biography of Alice B. Toklas.* Lincoln: University of Nebraska Press, 1991.

Smith, Andrew. *The Oxford Encyclopedia of Food and Drink.* Oxford: Oxford University Press, 2004.

Smith, John. *Psychology of Food and Eating.* New York: Palgrave, 2002.

Smith, Grace and Beverly and Charles Morrow Wilson. *Through the Kitchen Door: A Cook's Tour to the Best Kitchens of America.* New York: Stackpole Sons, 1938.

Smith, Sidonie. *Moving Lives: 20th-Century Women's Travel Writing.* Minneapolis: University of Minnesota Press, 2001.

Souhami, Diana. *Gertrude and Alice.* London: Phoenix Press, 1991.

Soyer, Alexis. *The Modern Housewife.* Facsimile of the 1st American edition. Bedford: Applewood Books, 2009.

———. *A Shilling Cookery Book for the People.* Facsimile of the 1860 edition. Kent: Pryor Publications, 1999.

Spencer, Colin. *British Food: An Extraordinary Thousand Years of History.* New York: Columbia, 2002.

Spry, Constance. *Come Into the Garden, Cook.* 1942. London: J. M. Dent and Sons, 1952.

Stein, Gertrude. *Geography and Plays.* Boston: Four Seas, 1922.

Stern, Gladys Brownwyn. *Bouquet.* London: Chapman and Hall, 1927.

Strauss, Gustave Louis M. *Dishes and Drinks; or, Philosophy in the Kitchen.* London: Ward and Downey, 1887.

Sturgeon, Launcelot. *Essays Moral, Philosophical, and Stomachical, on the Important Science of Good Living.* Facsimile of the second edition, 1823. BiblioLife: La Vergne, TN, 2010.

Sutton, David. *Remembrance of Repasts.* Oxford: Berg, 2001.

Sysonby, Ria. *Lady Sysonby's Cook Book.* 1935. London: Putnam, 1948.

Tickner, Lisa. *The Spectacle of Women: Imagery of the Suffrage Campaign 1907–1914.* Chicago: University of Chicago Press, 1988.

Toklas, Alice B. *The Alice B. Toklas Cook Book.* 1954. New York: Lyons Press, 1984.

———. *What is Remembered.* New York: Holt, Rinehart and Winston, 1963.

Troeung, Y-Dang. "'A Gift or a Theft Depends on Who Is Holding the Pen': Postcolonial Collaborative Autobiography and Monique Truong's *The Book of Salt. Modern Fiction Studies* 56.1 (Spring 2010): 113–135.

Truong, Monique. *The Book of Salt.* Boston: Houghton Mifflin, 2003.

Ude, Louis Eustache. *The French Cook.* London: John Ebers and Co., 1829. http://books.google.com.

Upton, Lee. "Eating Our Way Toward Wisdom: M. F. K. Fisher's Oysters." *Cooking by the Book: Food in Literature and Culture.* Edited by Mary Anne Schofield. Bowling Green: Bowling Green University Press, 1989.

Van Den Abbeele, Georges. *Travel As Metaphor: From Montaigne to Rousseau.* Minneapolis: University of Minnesota Press, 1992.

Walker, Thomas. Selections from *Aristology; or the Art of Dining.* 1836. In *Gusto: Essential Writings in Nineteenth-Century Gastronomy.* Edited by Denise Gigante. New York: Routledge, 2005.

White, Florence. *Good Things in England.* 1932. London: Futura, 1974.

Williams, Jacqueline Block. Introduction to *The Delights of Delicate Eating* by Elizabeth Robins Pennell. Urbana: University of Illinois Press, 2000.

Wilson, Edward. *The Downright Epicure: Essays on Edward Bunyard.* Devon: Prospect Books, 2007.

Winn-Smith, Alice. *Thrifty Cooking for Wartime.* New York: Macmillan, 1942.

Witt, Doris. "'My Kitchen Was the World' Vertamae Smart Grosvernor's Geechee Diaspora." *Kitchen Culture in America.* Edited by Sherrie A. Inness. Philadelphia: University of Pennsylvania Press, 2001.

———. *Black Hunger: Soul Food and America.* Minneapolis: University of Minnesota Press, 2004.

Wood, Roy C. *Sociology of the Meal.* Edinburgh: Edinburgh University Press, 1995.

Yaeger, Patricia. *Honey-Mad Women: Emancipatory Strategies in Women's Writing.* New York: Columbia University Press, 1988.

Yagoda, Ben. *Memoir: A History.* New York: Riverhead Books, 2009.

Zafar, Rafia. "The Signifying Dish: Autobiography and History in Two Black Women's Cookbooks." *Food in the USA: A Reader.* Edited by Carole M. Counihan. New York: Routledge, 2002.

Zlotnick, Susan. "Domesticating Imperialism: Curry and Cookbooks in Victorian England." *Frontiers* 16.2–3 (1996): 51–69.

Index